D0371792

New Orleans

New Orleans

Behind the Masks of America's Most Exotic City

Carol Flake

GROVE PRESS
New York

Published simultaneously in Canada
Printed in the United States of America

FIRST EDITION

Library of Congress Cataloging-in-Publication Data

Flake, Carol.
New Orleans: Behind the Masks of America's Most Exotic City / by Carol Flake.—
1st ed.   ISBN 0-8021-1406-7
1. Carnival—Louisiana—New Orleans—History.   2. New Orleans
(La.)—Race relations.   3. New Orleans (La.)—Politics and
government.   4. New Orleans (La.)—Social life and customs.
I. Title.   GT4211.N4F53 1994   394.2'5—dc20   93-39966

DESIGN BY LAURA HOUGH

Grove Press
841 Broadway
New York, NY 10003

1 3 5 7 9 10 8 6 4 2

FOR GARY

Acknowledgments

I hope I have done justice to my cherished friends in New Orleans and to the city's "guardians of culture" who have lent their voices, opinions, and observations to this book. Some I have masked, at their request, and others appear as themselves.

I simply could not have written *New Orleans* without the support of Dalt Wonk and Josephine Sacabo, who were always there with an encouraging word, an intriguing idea, or a delicious meal. Their work, as well as their friendship, has been an inspiration. Nor could I have gotten very far into the mysteries of Carnival without the help of Henri Schindler, Sally Reeves, Jon Newlin, Eric Bookhardt, and Paul Poché, who bring wit and magic not only to their work but to the lives of those around them.

Bonnie Warren, Bob Tannen, and Jeannette Hardy offered friendship and insight. Maureen Detweiler was helpful in making a number of connections. Jim Amoss offered useful suggestions. Errol Laborde, Rosemary James, Lily Jackson, and Betty Guillaud were generous with their considerable knowledge of the city. Joe Falls and Roy Glapion of Zulu opened a number of doors. Ray Kern and Vivian Cahn let me tag along with the Krewe de Vieux. Michael P. Smith and Allison Miner Kaslow shared their knowledge of the city's music and culture. Temple Brown, Beau Bassich, and John Charbonnet were exemplary exponents of Carnival tradition.

Philip Frazier and ReBirth were a constant inspiration, and I will particularly treasure the time they sang "Happy Birthday," in their own inimitable style, to "Sister Carol."

I also want to thank Jim Moser, my editor, and Phil Pochoda, my agent, for their encouragement and guidance. Ande Zellman, too, offered advice and support.

Thanks, too, go to the folks at the Historic New Orleans Collection and to Judith Nies and my fellow compatriots of the Writers' Room of Boston, where I was able to find sanctuary during a turbulent time.

And most of all, my thanks go to Gary Chapman, who understands so well the allure and tragic flaws of New Orleans.

Finally, I owe a profound debt of gratitude to the city of New Orleans, where I recovered a sense of joy in my life that I thought was gone forever.

Who breaks a butterfly upon a wheel?

—Alexander Pope

They that carried us away captive required of us a song; and they that

wasted us required of us mirth . . .

—Psalm 137

Contents

Prologue: Revelry in the Ruins 1

I. Arrival 13

II. Transformations 71

III. Preparations 143

IV. Epiphany 207

V. Gotterdämmerung 237

VI. Parades and Pageants 277

Epilogue: Ash Wednesday and After 343

PROLOGUE

Revelry in the Ruins

Looming in the streets of New Orleans on Mardi Gras day is a giant white bull, the garlanded *boeuf gras*, heralding the arrival of the prestigious Rex parade as it rumbles downtown toward a round of toasts and tributes. The live steer that appeared in the first Rex parade in 1872 has been replaced by a hollow fiberglass replica, to which as many as a million Mardi Gras celebrants pay homage as it rolls down Canal Street.

A fancied link to ancient fertility rites, the colossal bull on wheels might evoke images of wild pagan frenzy, of bestial influence and wine-stained lips and togas in disarray. Carnival, the season of festivities that culminates on Fat Tuesday, or Mardi Gras, is both a celebration and a farewell to the flesh, and the sacrificial bull symbolizes the ancient hungers that must be sated before the subdued penance of Lent. The tractor-pulled floatloads of tipsy, masked men who follow the *boeuf gras* in the parade, however, appear more inclined to charades than orgies. The metamorphosis from men to myth goes only so far these days.

To television-sated bystanders, the fiberglass bull, like the disguised bankers, doctors, businessmen, and lawyers tossing gewgaws to the crowds from their rolling papier-mâché pinnacles, appears to owe as much fealty to Disney as to Dionysus.

Carnival in New Orleans is at once strange and familiar, decadent and tame. Its supposed Catholic and pagan roots have been completely subsumed by the peculiar Carnival culture that has evolved in New Orleans, where ordinary standards of behavior and taste simply don't hold. Mardi Gras has taken on the bizarre character of New Orleans itself, a mixture of the wondrous and the cheesy.

Mardi Gras, like New Orleans, has come to occupy a permanent place in the psyches of Americans, even those who have never attended, but mean to someday. For more than a century, travelers have been passing through New Orleans for a taste of forbidden pleasures. Even now, the Pavlovian response by a junketeer upon coming to New Orleans is to start lurching toward the dives of Bourbon Street. For otherwise practical strivers of middle America, Mardi Gras and New Orleans represent the possibility of waste and wantonness, the potential of escape from a relentless Puritan legacy of seriousness and self-improvement.

For the average American, the lure of Carnival is not so much the masks, the exotic spectacle, or the beads tossed from floats and balconies, but the chance to play the ultimate party animal for a day, completely blotto, in a place where nobody knows your name. Mardi Gras, for the traveling party hound, is the American version of the ancient Bacchanalia—a stumbling crowd of soused yahoos, masked only in their inebriation, yelling at any woman who comes along, "Show us your tits!"

To the inebriated outsider, whose expectations of Carnival may come from friends who have regaled them with tales of naked cavorting, or from brief snippets on the evening news, showing mob scenes on Canal Street, Carnival appears to be one big street party. To the casual observer, there is little distinction between the oldest Carnival parades, put on by the city's social elite, and the newer extravaganzas designed to beguile tourists. Behind the public spectacle of Carnival, and the seeming chaos of the streets on Mardi Gras day, however, are rigid traditions and an elaborate social structure, defined by kinship, money, and neighborhoods, that have been built up over nearly a century and a half.

Carnival, for all its masks and disguises, mirrors New Orleans society, with its peculiar social hierarchies, its pockets of strange traditions, its wild diversity, its partiality to drama and spectacle. The events of Carnival, extending over an entire winter season, range from debutante balls and luncheons for Carnival royalty to a costume contest for drag queens and the chants and displays of the Mardi Gras Indians, the plumed and beaded tribes drawn from poor black neighborhoods.

Although it sometimes appears a spectacle designed exclusively for misfits and sybarites, there is a place in New Orleans Carnival for anyone who cares to join in. Unlike other great American spectacles, such as the Rose Parade or the Indianapolis 500, Carnival usually inspires some sort of participation from those who attend. When in New Orleans, as in Rome, outsiders try to emulate or even outdo the natives.

If the official Carnival, a series of enigmatic public parades and private balls, sponsored by social clubs known as "krewes," seems rather formal and remote to the carousing outsider, the shadow Carnival, or the Carnival of the fringes—gay Carnival centered in the French Quarter and black Carnival that flourishes in pockets around the city—offers the kind of revelry that adventurous voyeurs long for. It is here on the streets and in the shadows that Carnival serves its more ancient functions of defying death, prudence, and poverty for a day.

Carnival has endured in New Orleans in its current form since 1857, an eternity in a country of disposable popular culture. In various guises, it goes back even further, at least to the days of French ascendancy in Louisiana, if not, as some scholars claim, to medieval and pagan sources.

Mardi Gras in America actually began first in Mobile, Alabama, where it continues today, and it took hold briefly in other cities— Memphis, Saint Louis, even Houston. But it was in New Orleans that the conditions proved ideal for incubating a permanent Carnival culture.

The damp tropical heat, the permissive colonial regimes, the pomp-loving expatriate royalty, the human flotsam and jetsam washing up from the Mississippi, the enclaves of practical nuns and worldly priests, the pirates and prison escapees, the influx of Caribbean planters and slaves, the gens de couleur libres, the floods, the fevers, the voodoo altars, the madams of Storyville, the ragtime professors, Louis Armstrong, the spasm bands, the shot glasses of absinthe, the spices in the market, the iron-lace balconies, the jazz funerals, the Mardi Gras Indians, Tennessee Williams, and all the revelers just passin' through, made New Orleans a place like no other in America. If Carnival had not existed, surely New Orleanians would have invented it. Even the broad avenues of the city, divided by tree-lined neutral grounds, seem to have been designed with parades in mind.

Sold up the river by the French, undefended by the Confederacy, New Orleans nevertheless never really gave in to its Yankee occupiers. Losses, retreats, disasters, plagues, decay, and pestilences did not bring more than passing clouds of gloom and pessimism to a city literally sinking, day by day, further below sea level. Even the newest pestilence, AIDS, and all the skulls at the feast, have not killed Carnival, but have fed its more morbid fantasies. The permanent plague of locusts, the tourists, who flock to New Orleans to feed on its oddities, are also its last source of sustenance.

In a city where everything seems perishable, and where everyone is constantly reinventing or improvising an identity, the papier-mâché and satin culture of Carnival has flourished, to be tossed away and recreated every year. A poet of Carnival could create cantos of mutability to rival those of Spenser.

How can a city so ostensibly Catholic celebrate with such pagan gusto? How can a city so poor concoct such extravagant displays, year after year? How can a city with a majority black population so proudly proclaim the reign of bewigged white pseudo-royalty, even for a day of official pandemonium? In New Orleans, where there is no such thing as cognitive dissonance, these were not paradoxes until recently.

Mardi Gras, or Fat Tuesday, the day before the beginning of Lent, is the culmination in New Orleans not merely of Carnival season, which begins on January 6, the day of Epiphany, but of an entire year of preparations. There are themes to be selected, proclamations to be read, balls to be planned, orchestras to be hired, stages and platforms to be built, parades to be routed, marching bands to be recruited, guests to be invited, costumes to be bespangled, floats to be decorated, beads and doubloons to be bought, cakes and ale to be ordered, royalty to be chosen, protocol to be practiced, rites to be rehearsed. New Orleans is driven not merely by Carnival culture but a Carnival economy.

If Carnival, however, were truly the topsy-turvy, social-leveling, order-breaking, neo-Dionysian rite of liberation some chroniclers have proclaimed it to be, then New Orleans, the city most permeated by Carnival culture, should be the most open, unfettered, unleashed, carefree place on earth. All that masking and unmasking, all that dressing up and striptease, all that gender confusion and sexual fantasy, offer a feast for deconstructionists and other theorists of disorder.

Yet for all the psychic steam that undoubtedly has been vented in revels over the years, all the demons loosed, all the bottles uncorked, all the doppelgängers embraced, all the sexual urges indulged, all the fantasies played out, all the private parts bared, all the skeletons freed from closets and armoires, New Orleans is still a stratified city, constrained by secrets and social codes and double lives. The most alluring and festive of cities, it is still a crushingly poor provincial outpost burdened by corruption and a petrified elite.

One might be tempted to believe the Puritans were right all along about living in the realm of the senses. Parades, parties, spices, and even music aren't enough to save the soul of a city, although those things may make a city worth saving.

The *boeuf gras*, with its gilded horns and pure white façade, could also serve as a symbol of an abiding ambivalence in New Orleans about its annual season of revelry. For some, Carnival is a sacred cow, a virtual religion, whose traditions cannot be tempered without stifling the city's festive, tourist-beguiling spirit. For others, however, Carnival is the altar of the golden calf, the glittering idol of the idle rich, blinding the city to its sins and shortcomings.

Even as krewes and revelers were girding up for Carnival 1992, that deep, sometimes bitter ambivalence erupted into open conflict when a black city councilwoman introduced a long, complicated ordinance that, in effect, prohibited discrimination on the basis of race, gender, or religion in Carnival organizations. The unheralded initiative gained surprising momentum within the black community and stirred increasing resentment and defensiveness among the city's white minority.

The squabble over the new ordinance quickly escalated into a social and political conflict that divided the city and threatened to destroy forever the blithe, giddy façade of Carnival that had endured

7

for more than a century. The battle over Carnival, however, was also a war over the heart and soul of the city, over the dwindling base of power and money that has left New Orleans, for all its celebrating, the poorest city of its size in the United States, plagued with a rising crime rate, deteriorating housing stock, and an epidemic of white flight.

It was the kind of conflict that was taking place, in less exotic form, in the rest of the nation. In New Orleans, the divisive language of decline and fear took the form of a full-blown, rhetoric-tossing morality play, with captains of private Carnival krewes going public, defending their rites, blustering about civic generosity, as though the Carnival spirit were something the krewes were tossing to the crowds like free beads and doubloons.

The winter of 1992 was a time when the masks finally came off, when the velvet gloves were removed, and New Orleanians for the first time openly faced the realities of race and class prejudice that had remained hidden behind the grand illusions of Carnival. Neither Carnival nor the city of New Orleans would ever be the same.

Better than a gilded bull as a symbol for Mardi Gras 1992 would have been a Trojan horse.

No one could have predicted the great Carnival war, which began less than a year after the Gulf War and less than a month after the ringing defeat of crypto-Klansman David Duke for the office of governor of Louisiana. I had arrived in New Orleans to write a book about Mardi Gras and found to my surprise that I had arrived on a rapidly developing battlefront. Wounds that had just begun to heal were ripped open again.

The brief, heady alliance between blacks and whites that defeated David Duke, allowing him less than 15 percent of the vote in the city of New Orleans, proved to be an illusory bond.

For the most bitter proponents on either side of the issue, it was as though the Civil War were about to be reenacted on a small, absurdist stage, some actors bedecked in period costumes, others in clown suits. Blacks began harking back angrily to the days of slavery, and whites began to talk indignantly about secession from Carnival rather than compliance.

If the suddenly escalating tensions took the city's leaders by surprise, there was something inevitable about this symbolic showdown, whose roots could be traced back as far as the Louisiana Purchase, the Napoleonic sellout that set Creoles against Yankee newcomers; to the slavery era that reinforced the multitiered caste system in New Orleans; to the Reconstruction years that fueled provincial paranoia and preceded the golden era of Carnival; to the Civil Rights movement that challenged the tenets of exclusion; and to the Reagan and Bush years that had left New Orleans, like other cities in America, so starved for resources that it was devouring its own young.

I had returned to New Orleans after more than a decade away to chronicle a season of Carnival, to write about the paradox of an enduring rite in a crumbling city. Instead, I found that I had become witness to a bitter conflict that threatened to destroy one of the oldest traditions in America. I had also become a bystander at the beginning of a chaotic new era in New Orleans.

The notion of fighting over a festive season of balls and parades might seem a mere ice-cream war. But the war over Carnival was a symptom of the larger forces of change that were reshaping the city as well as pulling it apart. David Duke and the divisive governor's race had reminded New Orleanians that despite their romantic sense of isolation, they were still living in the South, with all its bitter legacies. For better or for worse, some kind of strange, voodoo spell that had kept New Orleans preserved in a state of perpetual escapism had been broken. And like the muddy waters of the Mississippi rushing through a break in the levee, nothing could hold back the flood.

For some, the Carnival war came as an unforeseen tragedy, the final blow to a dying city; for others, it was an unplanned but inevitable revolution, the first step toward rebirth. And for still others, it was the ultimate in absurdity, a sort of Swiftian spectacle, as lawyers and politicians squabbled over bits of fluff and feathers, as though creating a politically correct Carnival—a contradiction in terms— would redress all the historic injustices and hurts inflicted on the city's less privileged citizens.

For some of those individuals and groups I had chosen to follow through the Carnival season—for the Mardi Gras Indian chief slowly drinking himself to death, for the young brass band trying to follow in the footsteps of Louis Armstrong, for the anarchistic yuppies and bons vivants of the Krewe de Vieux, for the oldest drag queen in the gay Krewe of Petronius—Carnival would go on as before. But for others—for the devoted float maker who had revived the fading élan of the Krewe of Comus, for the public-minded aristocrat trying to keep the old-line krewes from folding, for the grande dame heading an all-women krewe, for the newly crowned Rex, king of Carnival—it was as though the world had ended.

On all sides, there was great disillusionment, a canker at the heart of Carnival.

Trouble and care, the worst enemies of Carnival, had finally caught up to its slow, flimsy parades. And as long-repressed prejudices and resentments came pouring out, the city's tattered, dirty linen was hung up for all to behold. More than the fate of a few frivolous Carnival clubs hung in the balance. In jeopardy, too, was the very essence of the city, an aura of pleasure-seeking and tolerance that had set it apart from the rest of America.

New Orleans, the last bohemia, has been a haven for odd enclaves and subcultures. It has served as a last-resort Lourdes for the misbegotten, a fount of minor miracles and transformations for restive spirits longing to be freed from ill-fitting identities or from the shopping-mall blandness and meaningless fast-track motion of life in middle America.

Walker Percy often wrote about the redemptive quality he found in New Orleans. "If the American city does not go to hell in the next few years," he once predicted, "it will not be the likes of Dallas or Grosse Pointe which will work its deliverance, or Berkeley or New Haven, or Santa Fe or La Jolla. But New Orleans might. Just as New Orleans hit upon jazz, the only unique American contribution to art, and hit upon it almost by accident and despite itself, it could also hit upon a way out of the hell which has overtaken the American city."

Lost in all the bitterness and commotion of the Carnival war was a valuable clue that New Orleans holds for the rest of America—a clue to civic survival in a world of diversity, a hint of inclusive harmony that has glimmered so often in its streets, wafted on music and high spirits in a spirit of celebration.

I came to think of that vital essense peculiar to New Orleans as a sort of elixir or potion, something like the sassafras found in filé, the secret of good gumbo. New Orleans, with its capacity to stir up a joyful spirit in the midst of decay, diversity, and contradiction, may hold the cure to a disease that has not yet even been diagnosed in America.

It is not an essence that can be reproduced with the same spirit elsewhere, as anyone can testify who has witnessed the artificial mummery of Carnival in other American cities or who has listened to New Orleans music in upscale, all-white settings. You may get a taste of the real thing, but it's simply not the same. That elusive, soulful essence that has survived for so long in New Orleans, thriving amid all the strangeness and decadence, is as rare and fragile as an endangered tropical plant, deep in the swamp, that may die before its curative powers are recognized.

That festive spirit is so infectious that when I first began my journey through Carnival, I found that I could not always remain a bystander, standing still as the parades passed by, or sitting in the balcony as masked couples whirled below. Like many Carnival onlookers, I found that I could sometimes get the best view when I became a participant as well as an observer. And so at times, when the parade marched by, I joined in.

The route I followed on my journey through the Carnival season may seem to be patterned after the unpredictable path of the Zulu parade in the days before the club began to follow a standard, fixed route. The Zulus used to meander through the city, with frequent stops to socialize and reminisce and offer toasts at private homes and popular watering holes. I have taken even more liberties and ranged even further across the city in my own Carnival pilgrimage.

In my search for the secrets of Carnival, I have ranged from neighborhood to neighborhood, from uptown to downtown, from present to past to future, from white uptown parlors and enclaves to French Quarter retreats and bars and streets in black neighborhoods. I have removed many masks, and I have revealed some secrets, although one can never get down to bare truth in New Orleans. As Oscar Wilde once said, surfaces have their realities.

I have found that it is impossible to extricate Carnival from its complex social and historical context, and so in writing about Carnival, I am writing about a state of mind, a way of life—in short, the city of New Orleans.

I

Arrival

The Subtle Gradients of Decay

When you approach New Orleans from the east, driving along the Interstate from the sandy shores of Mississippi's Redneck Riviera across the marshy reaches of Lake Pontchartrain and the reclaimed swamps of New Orleans East, the skyline of the city appears to recede like a mirage until you are almost upon it. There is something unconvincing about the smattering of Texas-inspired skyscrapers and high-rise hotels poking up from downtown New Orleans, most of them built during the height of the oil boom during the 1970s or during the frenzy of speculation before the World's Fair in 1984. The mind's eye, anticipating the movie-set vista of old New Orleans, airbrushes them away.

On a bright, balmy December day, as I neared the end of my long journey from Boston, New Orleans appeared more than ever a provincial outpost that had been invaded, then deserted, by a succession of empire-builders who succumbed to the climate.

Shimmering in the distance was the silver arc of the Superdome, an appropriate symbol, perhaps, for a place where gamblers are given to chasing after bubbles. John Law's Mississippi Bubble was the first big one, luring shiploads of French criminals and café dreamers and earnest German colonists to Louisiana before word of fever and swampland got out.

According to legend, a band of Frenchmen, led by the explorer Pierre Le Moyne, Sieur d'Iberville, discovered the murky mouth of the Mississippi the day before Shrove Tuesday and began the ascent of the river on Mardi Gras day. The French revelers named a bayou in honor of the occasion, and on the following Friday, continuing up the Mississippi, they arrived at the present site of New Orleans, where they killed a buffalo and erected a cross. In 1718, Iberville's brother, the Sieur de Bienville, christened the outpost Nouvelle Orléans, as a sop to the Duc D'Orléans, the regent of France, and as a note of comforting familiarity for John Law's deluded recruits. Bienville had the streets laid out in a square, the Vieux Carré, which regularly flooded until levees were built. In the early days of the city, the din from the encroaching swamp, a cacophony of frogs and birds and insects, was said to be deafening.

From the beginning, visitors to Louisiana were wont to celebrate, all the while swatting mosquitoes and looking for higher ground.

Even now, New Orleans, which lies below sea level and well below the crest of the Mississippi River that winds through it, is a city barely afloat, and anything of weight tends to sink, including the Superdome, which came close to bankrupting the city, and which began to subside in the muck almost before it was completed.

The usual order of things has been inverted in New Orleans, which at times seems a lost kingdom of Oz. Even without the ritual disguises of Carnival, New Orleans would be a city of riddles and paradoxes. Eric Bookhardt, a photographer and cryptographer of New Orleans mysteries, once observed, "Euclid doesn't apply here. There's no down or up." Boats churning down the Mississippi appear to sail by on air, their flags flying high above the levees.

Even the living and dead occupy strata different in New Orleans from elsewhere. Since corpses buried in watery ground tend to rise to the surface, the dead are interred in New Orleans above ground, in conspicuous necropolises, and thus appear to be always with us as neighbors. New Orleanians, who spend All Saints' Day with the dead in crumbling cemeteries, need no memento mori whispered in their ears, no symbolic skull at the feast, to remind them of their mortality.

As I neared the last exit sign for the Vieux Carré, better known as the French Quarter, with the crowded whited sepulchres of Saint Louis Cemetery No. 1 lying off to my left, I contemplated the prospect of spending an entire Carnival season among the living and the dead and the ghosts of New Orleans.

Carnival season, linked by the church calendar to the arrival of Easter, was to be longer than usual this year. It would begin officially, as it did every year, on Twelfth Night, January 6, the evening of the

Epiphany, twelve days after Christmas, and end at midnight on Mardi Gras day, March 3, the day before Lent. The season would begin at a leisurely pace, with a smattering of masquerade balls, and gradually intensify as it approached Mardi Gras day. During the last week of the season, there would be balls every night and parades around the city and through the suburbs, night and day. During the season, there would be over a hundred balls and more than sixty parades.

For most New Orleanians, Carnival is as much a part of the calendar as Christmas, although the level of participation varies wildly, from fanaticism to indifference. Some blasé types even leave town to escape all the hullabaloo. For the average New Orleanian, Carnival is a casual but unavoidable affair, which involves a few parties scattered through the season with friends or neighbors and maybe a gala ball or two, watching a few parades, and costuming on Mardi Gras day.

For many of the Carnival artisans, insiders, and organizers who make it all happen, however, Carnival is never really over. For them, this Carnival season had actually begun last year, on Ash Wednesday, the day after Mardi Gras. Virtually before the hangovers wear off, before the smudge of ashes on their foreheads are even washed away, the artists and true devotees of Carnival begin thinking of next year's theme.

Like Christmas, Carnival has grown beyond its boundaries in the calendar, and it seems to come around so fast that it's tempting just to leave the decorations up all year, even if things begin to look tattered. For a number of New Orleanians, Carnival is not merely a way of life, but a state of mind. For them, the masks and the feathers never really come off.

This year, however, the idea of Carnival in New Orleans seemed more than ever like parading in the ruins. With the city's coffers empty after a decade of recession and draconian federal budget cutbacks, and voters regularly turning down property and income taxes, civic leaders had been resorting to more and more desperate attempts at official, revenue-producing gaiety. Street sweepers could hardly keep up with all the parades, fairs, and festivals jammed into the city's annual schedule of events. Behind its imported throngs and the thriving façade of its tourist attractions, however, New Orleans was in deep trouble. Like so many of its beautiful cypress Creole cottages, it was rotting away at the core.

New Orleanians, white and black, had turned out for the polls in November and helped prevent a surgically enhanced Klansman from becoming governor of Louisiana, but they had elected, instead, an avowed gambler and acquitted scoundrel. Always ready with a joke, the winner, Edwin Edwards, observed that one-armed people in New Orleans hadn't been able to vote for him, since it required one hand to hold your nose and another to pull the lever.

Whites, who had been trickling away from New Orleans for decades, had begun deserting the city in droves. New Orleans appeared to be a sinking ship. Census figures the previous year showed that whites now comprised only 34.9 percent of the population of Orleans Parish, as compared to 42.5 percent in 1980 and more than 50 percent the previous decade. By some counts, whites now made up only a quarter of the city's population. In the 1960s, when the city finally got around to desegregating its schools and lunch counters, the white population in New Orleans had been nearly 70 percent. New Orleans, which ranked a century ago as the nation's fifth-largest city, had fallen to twenty-second in 1980, and to twenty-fifth by 1990.

I had once felt a kind of exultation that I had managed to escape New Orleans, whose clutches have been compared so often with those of bewitching temptresses, beguiling whores, or watery bogs. I came to New Orleans as a graduate student in 1969, a Southern Baptist rube from Texas, an easy mark for the city's enticements, and I left reluctantly eight years later, during the boom years, when Texas oil money was still pumping in and inflating the city's fortunes.

I had come to feel that I had stayed too long at the fair, that I had frittered away too much of my life on a bizarre sideshow while real life was going on somewhere else in America. And for years afterward, I thought of myself as One of Those Who Got Away, one of the few lotus-eaters who had found the antidote to the city's sweet oblivion.

Now, it seemed, everyone was leaving, one way or another, even if just to move across Lake Pontchartrain to quieter—and whiter— parishes north of the city. Even the Mississippi River was trying to get away. Without the diversionary tactics of the U.S. Army Corps of Engineers, Old Man River would have headed for greener pastures, cutting south at the Atchafalaya Basin, in western Louisiana, leaving New Orleans high and dry—or rather, still low and damp, but without its muddy vital artery.

The secret of getting away, I once thought, was to leave quickly, before mildew claimed every book and idea, and to travel light. To look back, like Lot's wife, I imagined, was to turn into a pillar of mold, immobilized by regret. I had left New Orleans so fast when I turned thirty that I barely had time to give away my cheap proto-Madonna collection of Mardi Gras costumes and accessories—the assortment of glittered batons, scepters, veils, go-go boots, and bustiers that I had continued to accumulate even during the height of a feminist awakening.

It took me a dozen years after I left New Orleans to realize that on some murky, subconscious level, I had been living in exile ever since. The city had never really let go of me. Safely ensconced in Boston, I tried to dismiss reports from friends in New Orleans of the city's rapid decline, of a crime wave, of whole neighborhoods boarded up. During a particularly long and cold New England winter, I began waking up in my chilly apartment in the middle of the night and throwing off the down comforter, terrified that I had forgotten something. Like the victim of a delayed voodoo curse, I would sit up with a jolt, breathless, close to tears, trying to remember what I had lost. A gold earring. My purse. Or maybe my soul.

This feeling about New Orleans was something like homesickness, but more like a subliminal yearning, a midlife urge to search for something left behind. I knew, somehow, that it was time to return.

Watching the Wild Bamboula

Coming back to New Orleans always suggests a musical theme. I did know what it means to miss New Orleans, as the song goes. But coming back this time felt more like the Fats Domino rendition of "Walking to New Orleans," a kind of pilgrimage that was half pain, half relief:

> I'm gonna need two pairs of shoes
> When I get through walking these blues,
> When I get back to New Orleans.

Driving from the Interstate down the ramp that feeds into Basin Street, continuing past the badly frayed edges of Tremé, the black Creole stronghold that had been home to so many of the city's artisans and musicians, I engaged in a ritual that has become customary since I moved away from New Orleans: the decadence check, an assessment of the relative state of decline of familiar landmarks and neighborhoods.

For a number of years, the edge of decay had been creeping closer and closer to the Municipal Auditorium, the Depression-era civic fortress between Basin and Rampart streets that replaced the old French opera house as the scene for most of the major Carnival balls in New Orleans. For many years, the symphony had to move out during the height of Carnival season, when balls were scheduled every night. It was here, as Mardi Gras wound down to its last moments before midnight, that the courts of the krewes of Comus and Rex traditionally met for a toast, once televised around the city, with all the pomp and solemnity of crowned heads of state, signaling the end of Carnival season.

Like Southern schools prior to desegregation, Carnival balls once operated under a separate-but-equal rationale. Theoretically, any minority group, snubbed by the traditional krewes, could form its own krewe and stage its own ball. Over the years, however, the snubbed groups came to outnumber the white uptown cliques. Black and gay krewes, who held balls for years in hotels, labor or veterans' halls, or neighboring parishes, had finally been permitted to stage their celebrations in the Auditorium—according to cynics, because the decline of the traditional white krewes would have left the Auditorium empty for too many evenings.

It is either ironic or appropriate, depending on your point of view, that the Auditorium was built on land that historians have identified as the edge of Congo Square. Also known as the Place du Cirque, it was here, at the end of Orleans Street, that slaves in old New Orleans congregated to trade goods in a thriving marketplace.

The Code Noir, established by the French in 1724 to govern treatment of slaves, and still observed in antebellum New Orleans, required not only that slaves be instructed in the Catholic faith but that they be exempt on Sundays from forced labor. Slaves used their day of liberty not only to hunt and fish, to till their own small plots of land, to gamble and attend cockfights, but to revive dimly recalled rites from their homeland. These rites drew white spectators as well as black.

Novelist George Washington Cable described the variety of dances performed on Congo Square to a frenzied African beat: the babouille, the counjaille, the calinda, and the wild bamboula, the latter finding its way into a composition by the patrician New Orleans composer Louis Gottschalk. The calinda, accompanied by a "hideous din," according to Cable, was "a dance of multitude, a sort of vehement cotillion." The lyrics chanted to the calinda beat often satirized local politicians, and for generations, noted Cable, "The man of municipal politics was fortunate who escaped entirely a lampooning set to its air."

Congo Square lingers in New Orleans as no more than a name, much like Storyville, which once occupied several square blocks just up Basin Street. As states of mind, however, these two ghostly marketplaces, Congo Square, with its cutting calindas and its wild bamboulas, and Storyville, with its musical prodigies and its briefly legalized sin, can still be felt in New Orleans.

Before I turned toward Rampart Street and the French Quarter, I glanced up Basin, which, unlike Bourbon Street, retains nothing of its former tawdry allure. Once the shady main drag of Storyville, the legendary stretch of sex emporiums, it now borders the sprawling Iberville Housing Project, whose drab reddish-brick monotony is relieved by strips of green railing.

It is difficult now to imagine a trip down Basin Street when Lulu White, the "Octoroon Queen," was reigning over Mahogany Hall; when the Arlington, a four-story showplace topped by a neo-Byzantine cupola, was lauded in the Blue Book, a popular guide to Storyville attractions, as "the most decorative and costly fitted out sporting palace ever placed before the American public"; and Emma Johnson, known as "French Emma," was advertising her "sixty-second plan," which offered free services at her "studio" for any man who could restrain his orgasm with her for a full minute. One unsuspecting voyeur was startled one day to encounter a bevy of beauties who were miming their specialty in a picture window, using their thumbs to demonstrate their virtuosity.

Storyville, the city's experiment with legally sanctioned prostitution, was closed down in 1917 in a burst of postwar civic virtue. Most of the city's red-light-district relics decayed quickly and disappeared several decades before another wave of "progress" resulted in the brick housing projects, now sinister and seedy-looking, that have spawned more drug deals and murders than the Storyville demimonde managed to inflict on the genteel populace of New Orleans. Basin Street itself disappeared for nearly thirty years, disguised as North Saratoga, until the growing fame of such anthems as the "Basin Street Blues," written by Lulu White's nephew, drew tourists looking for the fabled thoroughfare, the cradle of jazz. The old street signs went back up, although not a single balcony or turret of Storyville remained.

People still come to New Orleans in search of the phantoms of Congo Square and Storyville—white people, mostly, looking for music and sin, for places where they can act decadent for a cover price, where they can watch the wild bamboula in relative safety. Sometimes they are satisfied with sipping too many fake absinthe cocktails on Bourbon Street, sweating out a set of Dixieland at Preservation Hall, or buying a T-shirt with an image of copulating alligators and an obscene slogan on the back.

Poverty, the Best Preservative

The problem with conducting a decadence check in New Orleans is defining a clear standard or benchmark, when such notions as decay and progress are as scrambled here as other concepts of order and disorder. For one thing, New Orleans has always been in a relative stage of decay, depending on the standards of the observer, and for another, "progress" in New Orleans has often meant disaster. A certain kind of architecture in New Orleans, for example, lends itself to picturesque decay, and things look better here with a bit of patina to them. Live oak trees look bare without a bit of Spanish moss drooping from the branches.

There has been an odd sort of rhythm to New Orleans history, with a kind of unexpected backbeat to it, like the rhythm known as the second line, which evolved from jazz and parade music.

Celebrating Carnival every winter for generation after generation has shaped life in New Orleans into a kind of timeless round, the kind of recurring pattern associated with preindustrial civilization. There is a sense of cyclical renewal in the rites of Carnival, simultaneously Catholic and pagan. The crowning of Rex, the king of Carnival, on Mardi Gras, the day before Ash Wednesday, ushers in the lamentation of Lent and prefigures, in its worldly travesty, Christ's sacred crown of thorns and the redemption of Easter. Rex is a sort of frivolous fisher-king, a mythic avatar peculiar to New Orleans.

Superimposed over that recurring ritual is the ongoing drama in New Orleans between the ancients and the moderns, the do-nothings and the progressives, the keepers of the flame and the movers and shakers. Long periods of fallow decay in the city are interrupted sporadically by brief, intense bursts of civic reform or instant-prosperity schemes that often cause more lasting damage to the city than carefree laissez-faire.

After the Civil War, for example, which left New Orleans demoralized and defeated, a kind of Vichy Paris, the city languished during the days of Reconstruction. In 1877, that myopic collector of exotic cultures, Lafcadio Hearn, the "distorted brownie," as one editor called him, arrived as a reporter from Cincinnati and sent home encomiums on the ravished beauty of the city, where, he said, "it is better to live in sackcloth and ashes" than "own the whole state of Ohio." He tempered his reverie with sadness, however, saying, "I must speak with pain of her decay. The city is fading, moldering, crumbling—slowly but certainly . . . in the midst of the ruined paradise of Louisiana." New Orleans brought tears to his eyes, he wrote, as though he were beholding "a dead bride decorated with orange flowers."

Less than a decade later, in order to restore its honor as "Queen City of the South," and to show up its rival Atlanta, New Orleans played host to an extravaganza known as the World's Industrial and Cotton Centennial Exposition. The Centennial of 1884–1885 was touted by its backers as the herald of the economic renaissance of New Orleans, signifying to the world that the city had roused itself from its dreams of the past and joined the New South, the South of industry and progress, the South of smart money and Yankee hustle. On the centennial's opening day, the Reverend T. Dewitt Talmadge delivered an invocation that combined blind faith with civic booster-ism: "Gracious God! Through this Exposition solve for us the agoniz-ing question of supply and demand."

The Centennial, however, like the World's Fair held in New Orleans a century later, was not the answer to the city's economic prayers. Visiting reporters mocked the slapdash exposition buildings and debunked the exhibits, which included a Statue of Liberty made of corn, a cathedral made of crackerboxes, and a large wreath woven from the hair of Confederate generals. They deplored the city's muddy streets and primitive sanitation system. Partly because of the bad press, fewer than a fourth of the expected six million visitors turned up. When the exposition was over, the city was left with losses of nearly half a million dollars, and the flamboyant, politically con-nected director of the fair, Major E. A. Burke, skipped the country. Shortly thereafter, the state treasury, of which he had been in charge, was found to be short $1.7 million.

Nowadays, the only tangible legacies of the great exposition in New Orleans are a large iron-ore boulder from the state of Alabama residing on a golf course and the water hyacinths from Japan that still clog local bayous.

Oddly enough, it may well be its decadence that has preserved New Orleans. For more than two hundred years, New Orleans has remained as timeless as Venice in its imperceptible descent, defended from floods by levees and from reality by levity, isolated from the frenzy of progress revising the culture and landscape of the rest of America. Even after the city, encased like a cocoon in its old-world Napoleonic code, became an outpost of the Yankee republic, New Orleans continued to observe its own peculiar rites, moving to its own syncopated beat. The Americans began to take over the city, bit by bit, but found themselves succumbing to its rhythms.

Carnival itself was founded by Americans who were attempting to upstage the Creoles. Ignoring for the moment the disputed origins of pre-Lenten Carnival back in prehistoric Bacchanalian mists or somewhere amid ribald Rabelaisian folk rites of late medieval Europe, the origin of Carnival as a bona fide men's-club tradition in New Orleans can be traced back to 1857 and a single parading organization, made up of uptown Anglo-Saxon swells, who called themselves the Mistick Krewe of Comus.

If the Centennial failed in its short-term mission of reviving the local economy, it did succeed in a more long-range goal: establishing New Orleans as a tourist destination. The city's reputation for lawlessness and yellow fever had kept casual travelers away from New Orleans. But its very isolation had produced a quality of great value as a lure for tourists: oddity. The city's architecture, its cuisine, and its customs had evolved in a voluptuous if fever-ridden isolation, and its civilization had become as exotic as that of some steamy tropical isle.

Ironically, it was a Boston abolitionist and author of the "Battle Hymn of the Republic" who helped preserve and promote the city's strange and valuable heritage. Julia Ward Howe, who was hired as director of a special women's exhibit at the Centennial, organized a collection of the city's historic memorabilia that served, according to novelist Grace King, as an "opening of the past history of the city, not only to strangers, but to the citizens themselves." Reporters who found the exposition disappointing and the streets dirty nevertheless came to realize that New Orleans was like no other city they had ever seen. As local historian Clive Hardy described it, "Americans would learn for the first time that New Orleans was unlike anything they knew, and their curiosity would be excited."

For their part, New Orleanians discovered that many of the oddities they took for granted were regarded by outsiders as wonders worth paying for. But that discovery brought with it a question even more agonizing for civic leaders than that of supply and demand, a question that would continue to divide the city for the next century. How could they capitalize on the quaintness of their culture without destroying it? How could they sell their cake and eat it, too?

That question would become more and more pressing as everything else in the city's economy failed—first, at the turn of the century, as the cotton market began to fall, next, as the port began to decline, and during the 1980s, as the oil and gas boom went bust. New

Orleanians were left at the beginning of the 1990s with their oddities as their primary assets, and with tourism as the last best hope of prosperity.

I used to think that some secret Mardi Gras moly kept New Orleans perfectly preserved in a perpetual state of slow decay. I imagined that the city, like a cache of uranium, with its slowly depleting radioactivity, would decay into eternity without dying. I had found it comforting, after I departed the city at the end of the seventies, to believe that New Orleans would remain under a spell of suspended animation—that I could always go back and pick up where I left off, finishing a conversation I had begun years ago at the Napoléon House, catching a Neville Brothers song I had missed last time around at Tipitina's, complaining again about the line at Galatoire's.

People in New Orleans have always lived with a central paradox: the notion of permanent impermanence. Given the perishable nature of the city's cultural artifacts—food, music, and festivals—a certain amount of transience is to be expected. People are always in the middle of changing costume. And in a city where mold and mildew thrive, it becomes difficult to keep up appearances. And yet despite that disturbing sense of entropy, there was once a comforting certainty that some things, like Carnival, remained constant, and that certain resources were renewable.

These were the verities: that New Orleans would remain poor but picturesque; that the supply of musical prodigies miraculously produced in the city's poor black neighborhoods would always be replenished; that the French Quarter would remain a balance between tourist trap and crumbling refuge from middle America; that fast talkers would convince city leaders to demolish something important or build something big; that the city would recover from its folly until the next temptation to go for broke came along; that Texans would continue to buy up the mansions on Saint Charles Avenue; that the dwindling uptown enclave of inbred bluebloods would always rule society; that the Boston Club and Mistick Krewe of Comus would remain at the top of the pyramid; that life would be full of pleasures, especially for the rich, but also for the poor; that there would be enough left over to satisfy the tourists without giving away the store.

Above all, there was the assurance that the show would go on. The recurrence of Carnival every winter lent a certain stability to a city perpetually out of synch with the rest of the country.

For all its airs of improvised frivolity, Mardi Gras had remained an astonishingly durable tradition in New Orleans, surviving French snobbery, Spanish prudery, Creole decline, Anglo-Saxon co-optation, the Civil War, the world wars, yellow fever, the Great Depression, Civil Rights boycotts, a police strike, and Texas boosterism. Traditions in the old-line krewes were as arbitrary and firm as holy writ and as difficult to change.

And yet there was always something flimsy and insubstantial about Carnival, something as fragile as the papier-mâché façades on its floats. It was a moving stage, an illusion, that could be blown away by a strong gust of wind.

Rock Hudson in Pompeii

As I drove down Rampart Street, once a fortified edge of the Vieux Carré, and now its least defended barrier, I was shocked at its deterioration. Once merely raffish, it now had a deserted, scary look. Across from the Auditorium, near the site of the old J & M Record Shop, where Fats Domino had recorded "Goin' Home" and other hits, was a block of disreputable-looking bars and boarded-up buildings. Further down, two restaurants that had anchored café society and the symphony-going crowd when I lived there, Marti's and Jonathan, were boarded up, the buildings so rundown they were hardly recognizable. The owners of both establishments had died of AIDS, and the symphony had died, too, although the musicians had revived it, temporarily, vowing to keep it going on their own.

I thought about the big clock that once stood on Canal Street, the other edge of the Quarter, marking the transition from downtown to uptown, where revelers used to rendezvous on Mardi Gras day or after a night on Bourbon Street. I could remember hot, muggy days and nights when time seemed to move so slowly that I thought the clock was broken. John Kennedy Toole had set one of the wildest scenes from *Confederacy of Dunces* there. It was while watching the

27

clock, in front of the now-defunct D. H. Holmes department store, that Toole's disaster-prone hero, Ignatius Reilly, with too much time on his hands, nearly started a riot.

Now I envisioned the hands on the clock spinning around like a speeded-up movie sequence. I imagined the city, already lying so low on the horizon, sinking faster and faster.

Things were so bad that Ingersoll Jordan, an enterprising scion of an old New Orleans family, had suggested turning New Orleans into a mecca for retirees. "We have all these empty houses and empty hospital beds and the worst education system in the nation," he explained to me one day. "So who would be perfect to fill the houses and hospital beds? Old people. Retirees. They can buy the houses cheaply, and they don't need schools. They don't need skilled labor—just someone to push the wheelchairs."

The decline had begun long before the recession that had followed the end of the oil boom in the 1980s, long before the virtual abandonment of the city during the last decade by federal agencies, long before the epidemic of drugs that was destroying the core of so many of the city's neighborhoods, before the epidemic of AIDS that decimated the gay community, and even before the invasion of Formosan termites in the 1950s that had begun to eat out the heart of the city's grand architectural heritage. But time was running out, I feared, for those things that had miraculously held the city together during its darkest times and had lent it the capacity for renewal and reinvention.

As I drove further downtown, my memories of Rampart Street and so many other places, now full of ghosts, had a quality of phantasmagoria, of glimpses of a vanished era. The memories were not so much of Edenic innocence as of a final fling before the flood.

I remembered one extraordinary banquet I attended at Jonathan not long before I left town. The over-the-top Art Deco decor at Jonathan, with etched glass designed by Erté and stylized flamingos and palm leaves everywhere, lent a kind of self-conscious Sunset Boulevard ambience to even the most casual events. The guest of honor at the banquet had been Rock Hudson, looking marvelous, who had brought along his lover at the time, a tall, robust-looking golf pro. Most of the guests were gay men, joined by a handful of women who appeared to be in double drag—as women impersonating drag queens.

The toasts to Rock Hudson and to one of the restaurant owners, who was said to be possessed of an enormous sexual asset, got more ribald as the evening wore on. As I left, I was crowded into the elevator with Rock Hudson and Becky Allen, a French Quarter "revue" actress and Mae West lookalike bombshell. Becky popped a breast from her lowcut bodice and asked Hudson to autograph it with her lipstick. He obliged with a flourish.

I continued down Rampart and turned east on another boundary of the Vieux Carré, Esplanade, the broad avenue with its spacious, tree-lined "neutral ground" in the center. Further down Esplanade was the Creole cottage where I lived for a time with a man I thought about marrying. My friend and I had bought the rambling cottage, which included three apartments and a tiny patio, for seventy-five thousand dollars in the early 1970s. The house had since changed hands a number of times and had been sold the previous year for seventy-five thousand dollars. Clearly, real estate had not been a growth market in New Orleans. The purchaser, I had learned, to my surprise, was a former wild woman of the French Quarter, a flamboyant costumier with long red hair named Robin. Robin had decided to settle down, although she had maintained her notoriety by entering the Mardi Gras costume contest on Burgundy Street last year, usually dominated by cross-dressing men, and won a prize in the category of "best tits."

Robin would have made a good neighbor for Germaine Cazenave Wells, the ancient "countess" who had lived in the stately mansion next door, on the corner of Esplanade and Chartres. Germaine was the legendary hostess of Arnaud's, the old French Quarter restaurant often mentioned in the same breath as Antoine's, and she played the role of grande dame to the hilt, descending the stairs at the restaurant every evening in a rustle of satin and lace. She was famous for her Easter parades, a procession of horse-drawn carriages that began in front of the mansion and ended in Jackson Square. Every year, her Easter hats became larger and more ornate, her black wigs more assertive.

Germaine also liked to dabble in what my gay friends called "rough trade." Living next to the Countess had been like watching scenes from a Tennessee Williams play, as Germaine, fighting age, entropy, and a weakness for young men, tried to maintain her trademark standards of wealth and style. Occasionally, taking a respite from my own domestic turmoil, I would catch a glimpse of her, decked out in her long, black lace dresses, returning home accompanied by men with tattooed arms. The thick walls of the mansion muffled any sounds of passion or struggle from within, and Germaine would emerge late in the mornings, looking a bit dazed, her wig slightly askew.

Germaine had inherited the mansion and the fabled restaurant, Arnaud's, from her father, Arnaud Cazenave, a dapper man whose friends had dubbed him Count Arnaud because of his courtly air. Although Germaine liked to hint that old baptismal records back in France would support a legitimate claim to royalty, it was more likely that he had earned the title of Count by a certain virtuosity of charm, in the way that the musicians who played masterful barrelhouse piano in Storyville merited the title of professor.

Germaine's mother, a deeply religious woman known as Lady Irma, had painstakingly crocheted the lacy lamp shades and curtains in the house on Esplanade. Lady Irma's father, Jules, had been the chef at the famous Lamothe Restaurant, owned by his brothers Leon and Frank, on Common Street, where Carnival floats were said to have stopped during parades to offer a toast.

Frank Lamothe, known for his excellent taste in wine, had also been well known in Storyville as a sponsor, along with famous saloon keeper Tom Anderson, of the "Two Well Known Gentlemen Ball," a famous Mardi Gras tradition for the demimonde. This family connection to Scarlet Carnival, as Mardi Gras in Storyville was known, was not included in the small Mardi Gras museum Germaine had maintained in a room above Arnaud's restaurant. She had placed her own most spectacular Mardi Gras gowns, scepters, and tiaras on display, and her personal maid, an ancient black woman named Mary

Helen Ball, would give tours of the shrine, recounting for visitors the story of each dress, including its original cost. "She live just like a queen," Mary Helen had told me once, "in the middle of those costumes. The clothes she wears, she's queen all the time."

After Germaine's death, the mansion had languished until Daniel Lanois, the mysterious French-Canadian music producer with a penchant for voodoo, transformed it into a recording studio.

The Last Bohemia

I turned up Royal Street and then left on Governor Nicholls, proceeding to the block where my friends Dalt Wonk, a playwright, and Josephine Sacabo, a photographer, live with their daughter Iris. Josephine had offered to let me stay the winter in her photography studio, an apartment on Saint Louis Street, where uptown society families came to pose for portraits with a romantic Quarter background. Dalt and Josephine's whitewashed brick apartment building on Governor Nicholls, with its big patio shaded with tropical plants, is one of the most beautiful in the French Quarter. Known as the Old Spanish Stables, it had once been a carriage house and stable, and it had been lovingly restored and transformed into apartments by Clay Shaw, the tall, courtly businessman and alleged CIA operative accused by district attorney Jim Garrison of plotting the assassination of John F. Kennedy.

The previous spring, when director Oliver Stone had begun filming in New Orleans for his controversial movie *JFK*, which resurrected the walleyed Garrison's mothballed theories, Stone requested permission to shoot a few scenes in the apartment building. The current owner, a retired hairdresser and stalwart Shaw defender, had angrily refused. Shaw, who had also been a neighbor of mine briefly, had been a great favorite of preservationists and of the beau monde in New Orleans. French Quarter residents knew that Shaw had a double life, perhaps even multiple identities, but then so did nearly everyone else in New Orleans.

When FBI agents, working at Garrison's behest, searched Shaw's apartment, they found what appeared to be an executioner's cape and hood, chains, and a rope. Shaw had insisted that these items were accessories for his Mardi Gras costume, a defense that was credible to most New Orleanians. At the time, Mrs. Laurence Fischer, a float designer for the Mistick Krewe of Comus, had retorted, "You could raid any house in New Orleans and come up with some pretty far-out ensembles." Mrs. Fischer had added, sensibly, "Why didn't they take his Chinese or Danish outfits?"

The parameters of respectable life in New Orleans, and particularly the French Quarter, were more flexible than most anywhere else, as Garrison and Shaw well knew, and changing costumes was a way of life. Garrison, too, had his kinky little secrets, and a search of his own closets would have yielded as many curiosities as Shaw's.

In the Quarter, except for an occasional police raid that sent prominent people running down the back stairs, you could keep your secrets or flaunt them, depending on your mood. Even now, while in the Quarter, you could turn your back on the new high-rise eyesores on Canal Street and the business district and pretend that all you knew on earth and all you needed to know was contained within the dense square mile whose boundaries Bienville had laid out more than 250 years ago.

Periodic encroachment by commercial interests, a growing influx of tourists, and a recent infestation of T-shirt shops had shrunk the livable portion of the Quarter to a few square blocks in the lower end, toward Esplanade. But those few blocks were a quiet paradise. I sometimes thought the lower end of the Quarter should be declared a sort of special conservation district, not just for its ancient balconied buildings, which were already protected by various codes, but for its few remaining bohemians, an endangered species in America. Already, the tourists who passed through the Quarter in mule-drawn carriages tended to gawk at the locals as though they were in a zoo.

Josephine and Dalt had arrived in New Orleans nearly twenty years ago on a freighter, after expatriate years in London and Paris, and they had felt immediately at home in the French Quarter. Even their names, adopted on a whim, had a sort of nom de Mardi Gras air. They began to assemble a kind of salon, which also became a kind of way station for artistic waifs, in whose number I sometimes included myself.

Dinner at Dalt and Josephine's was a guarantee of good company and entertaining conversation. Those who became part of their circle seemed to bloom in unexpected ways. People came to Dalt and Josephine's ready to fall apart and left, if not whole, then more fully themselves. In New Orleans, one's personality was as much a creation, a work in progress, as one's art.

The centripetal effect of the Wonk/Sacabo household on the lower Quarter was much like that I imagined of Lyle Saxon, an earlier Quarter fixture. A writer and raconteur, Saxon had been at the center of the bohemian circle in the Quarter during the decades between 1920 and 1940, when it gradually emerged from a seedy underworld into a picturesque artists' enclave.

Faulkner had been a frequent visitor, living for a time during the 1920s in a house on Pirate's Alley. Faulkner, however, had hung around New Orleans just long enough to soak up the atmosphere, muster some myths, and insult the hospitable artists and writers who had gotten mired in the comfortable languor of French Quarter life. In his early novel *Mosquitoes*, New Orleans appears a sweaty cultural outpost, where characters, tormented by murky sexual urges, strike poses and pontificate while swatting insects or thinking about escape.

Saxon, it was said, exerted as much of his energy on his friends as on his work. He had a talent for "creating" people. "No one knows how many people he did create," writer Robert Tallant later observed. "He could take the dullest persons and bring out whatever latent charm or talent they possessed, and if there was really something there—some real talent, for instance—somehow it came to life after they had known Saxon for a while, and they were never the same again."

The mood during dinner this time at Dalt and Josephine's was more somber than usual, as we discussed the city's chances for recovery from forces that seemed to be tearing it apart. Sadly, even the gubernatorial election that should have brought the city together in opposition to David Duke had left it still divided. David Duke had cloaked his covert racism in euphemistic anti-welfare slogans, and the white citizens of New Orleans who opposed him bolstered their position, too, in terms of economics. Consequently, although Duke won only 24 percent of the white vote in New Orleans, many blacks felt that whites had simply voted their pocketbooks rather than their consciences.

Nevertheless, despite all the bitterness, Dalt had been astonished at unexpected moments of euphoria during the campaign, when spontaneous demonstrations of solidarity against Duke had erupted at clubs or restaurants. A cluster of diners or dancers would start chanting, "No Duke," and the rest of the crowd, black and white, would join in, like an amen chorus. Frequently, a carload of blacks would pass a car of whites loaded with anti-Duke stickers and honk loudly, with a thumbs-up sign.

I remembered a few such moments during Dutch Morial's campaign in 1978 to be elected the first black mayor of New Orleans. I had stood proudly on a corner on election day, near the voting station on Saint Peter Street, in the Quarter, holding a Morial placard, demonstrating, I suppose, that young white women weren't afraid of a black mayor. Dutch, of course, a black Creole, actually looked whiter than many uptown white Creoles, and there were rumors that in his youth he had occasionally been a *passeblanc*—someone who passes for white.

I had gotten as many thumbs-up signs from white voters that day as from blacks. The euphoria had passed quickly, however, for Morial, who won a solid block of white support. Morial had proved an irascible, equal-opportunity martinet, who had gone after an entrenched system of black patronage with the same verve that accompanied his assault on the long established white dominance of the "independent" city agencies, such as the Sewerage and Water Board, that actually controlled the city's pocketbook and its business.

The euphoria after Edwin Edwards was elected had evaporated quickly, too, with a number of voters already clamoring for a recall. After all the bunting came down, New Orleanians began to recall that during his three previous terms, Edwards, a regular at the gaming tables of Las Vegas, had survived two corruption trials and fourteen grand-jury investigations.

After dinner, Dalt drove me over to Josephine's studio on Saint Louis Street and helped me carry some of my things upstairs. As we walked back down the winding stairway to the patio and toward the iron gate to the street, we could hear the telltale clank that French Quarter residents have learned to recognize from blocks away, the sound that they dread more than the awful tootling of the riverboat calliope, more than boom boxes at full blast at 3 A.M., even more than than the screeching of drag-queen hookers in a cat fight.

We rushed through the gate to find Dalt's ancient Toyota hitched to a bright red tow truck. The tow master, a strong-looking black man in a brown jumpsuit, had just opened the door to the cab of his truck. We begged for mercy, even though we knew from experience that New Orleans tow trucks, like snapping turtles, never let go of their prey. Towing cars from the French Quarter, where tourists are either too confused or too drunk to remember where they parked, and where residents tend to get absentminded, is a major source of income for the city.

The tow master paused and gazed at us with the deadpan expression of the neutral executioner. Then he noticed the sign Dalt had displayed prominently on his windshield. NO DUKE. The man nodded and gave us the hint of a smile. He walked over, detached the car, and drove away.

2

City Hall and the Guardians of Culture

As I rode my bike over to City Hall to pick up a schedule of Carnival parades and a list of balls to be held at the Municipal Auditorium, I pondered the connection in New Orleans between the private world of old-line Carnival krewes and the public world of the city.

The motto of the 120-year-old Rex krewe, known formally as the School of Design, is *pro bono publico,* making it ostensibly the most public-minded of the old-line Carnival clubs. Rex, the king of Carnival, is supposedly chosen each year for his civic-mindedness rather than his bloodlines, and he rules unmasked over his temporary domain, his face obscured only by a fake beard and wig.

The other monarchs of old-line Carnival, however, remain masked, a peculiar reversal of the national cult of celebrity. My friend Bookhardt claims this is because the mock kings are actually killed at the end of Carnival, like pagan sacrifices, for the sake of community fertility and the good of the crops. The followers of Comus, however, have never been known for their willingness to sacrifice their pleasures for the common good. The motto of Comus is *Sic volo, sic jubeo:* As I wish, thus I command.

On Mardi Gras night, as the Rex and Comus balls are winding down, the Rex krewe sends its unmasked king through the back halls of the Municipal Auditorium to the smaller ballroom occupied by Comus to pay tribute to the anonymous masked monarch chosen from the city's most elite group of old men. The gesture acknowledges not only the importance of pomp and secrecy in old-line Carnival, but the primacy of social whimsy over civic duty in the Mardi Gras hierarchy.

The revelers on the parade floats remain masked, too, a practice now codified by city ordinance. There is something surreal and even ominous about floatloads of costumed men capering anonymously behind the fixed smiles and hollow eye sockets of full-face masks.

Theoretically, you can watch Mardi Gras parades all your life, fighting the crowds for beads and doubloons as though they were made of pearls and gold, without knowing anything about the masked riders who are tossing them at your feet.

Although the krewes of Comus, Momus, and Proteus have been parading through the streets of New Orleans for over a hundred years, no one in the city, outside the small coterie of men's clubs who make up the charmed circle of traditional Carnival, is supposed to know who actually belongs to the clubs, much less who has been crowned as monarch each year.

Consequently, finding a way to the inner circles of Carnival and to its secrets is rather like one of those Nintendo quest games, where you first have to find the hidden doors and corridors before you can even begin the action.

There is no center to Carnival, no official headquarters, no public access except during parades, no published protocol. The old-line all-male, all-white Carnival krewes operate as private cults, guarding the rites and memberships of their clubs as zealously as the Masons, the Elks, or the CIA. They meet at the ancient clubhouses affiliated with their krewes; in dens, where the floats are built; or in private rooms in Antoine's restaurant on Saint Louis Street.

"Their dance cards were filled a hundred years ago," a frustrated Texan friend once told me. He had been courting a woman from a "good" family. You can't simply ask to be invited to an old-line ball, nor can you buy your way in. Membership in Comus is the social pearl without price. Like the yokel in the snobbish boutique, if you have to ask the price, you can't afford it.

The least direct route to Carnival, in fact, is through City Hall, which historically exercised little official control over Carnival or its krewes. Statutes governing the observance of Carnival cover twenty-seven pages in the city code, but most of those regulations concern the technicalities and safety requirements of parades, specifically of floats and "throws," the favors tossed to the crowds. Floats carrying mask-ers, for example, must be between twenty-three and sixty feet long, no less than nine feet wide, and no more than seventeen feet high, "exclusive of animation." Riders, who must be masked at all times, are prohibited from throwing "insects, marine life, rodents, fowls or other animals, dead or alive," from their floats.

The most stringent sections in the code deal with the prohibition of "sexually indecent dress or characterization" and of political or commercial advertisements in parades. The idea, as one city official told me, is to keep Carnival "pure." When the makers of Popeye's Fried Chicken, for example, wanted maskers to distribute doubloons touting their product, city attorneys and the Carnival establishment had united in their opposition, on the grounds that such blatant commercialism would taint the free spirit of Carnival. Even the giant Oscar Mayer weiner that appeared in parades had to be disguised as a generic hot dog.

Satire of public officials is specifically permitted, however. As the law reads, "Nothing contained in this provision shall be construed to prohibit the humorous caricature of current social events and issues." This provision, I was told, had been added specifically for the benefit of Momus, the krewe famous for its wicked satires of City Hall.

The only direct means of control exerted by City Hall over Carnival thus far has been through the issuing of parade permits and of alcohol licenses to the men's luncheon clubs, such as the Boston Club, the Louisiana Club, and the Pickwick Club, affiliated with the krewes. Groups who want to parade in the streets during Carnival season, either on foot, on floats, or on decorated trucks, are required to apply for a permit, which guarantees police protection and cordoned-off streets for a fee of $750. The slots for most of the parades, however, have been taken for generations, with old-line krewes claiming the prime days and nights just before and during Mardi Gras day. Comus has been parading on the night of Mardi Gras and Rex during the day for more than a century.

There had been a great deal of uneasy equivocating following the announcement in early December by black Councilwoman Dorothy Mae Taylor, known for her strong advocacy of civil rights, that she had asked the city attorneys to draw up an antidiscrimination ordinance that would apply to Carnival. The ordinance, an extremely long document written in confusing legalese, would in effect extend the powers of a newly created Human Relations Commission to the city's private clubs and Carnival krewes, thus transforming the tentative relationship between the krewes and City Hall into an ironclad bond and turning Carnival upside down.

Among other things, the bill called for fines and imprisonment of Carnival krewe captains whose organizations discriminated against prospective members on grounds of race, gender, or physical disability. No one gave the bill much chance of passing, however, since previous complaints about discrimination by Carnival krewes had not gotten very far.

At the time, no one in City Hall was very popular, and there was a widely perceived vacuum of power and leadership in New Orleans. The current mayor, Sidney Barthelemy, generally recognized by friend and foe alike as a nice man, was adrift in the middle of his second term of office, bedeviled by charges of wishy-washy leadership and by innuendos of corruption directed against some of his associates. Sidney, with his light skin and green eyes and gentle, unassuming manner, came from the privileged social class in New Orleans known as black Creole. Like Dutch Morial, he had won considerable white support in his first election campaign, but like so many black Creoles, he seemed torn between his white and black constituencies.

The eternally bickering City Council, too, comprised of three black men, one black woman, one white man, and two white women, had exasperated black and white voters alike, and a recent referendum limited their terms of office, making all but one of the seven current members lame ducks. There was speculation that Dorothy Mae Taylor's unexpected assault on Carnival was the first salvo in a bid for mayor.

Henri Schindler, the float designer for the Krewe of Comus, had expressed the frustration over the move that was typical in white Carnival circles. "New Orleans finally had something to bring it together—uptown society and SOUL and COUP," he said, referring to the two major black political alliances in the city. COUP was regarded as the stronghold of black Creoles, including Sidney Barthelemy. "Instead of just letting the city bask in that togetherness," said Henri, "here comes this banshee. She took everybody by surprise."

The Revenge of Funky Butt Hall

New Orleans City Hall, designed during an unfortunate period of
architectural aphasia in the 1950s, has a drab Third World look to it,
a theme carried through by worn carpets, missing doorknobs, and a
general feeling of neglect around the place. Conceived as the centerpiece of a sweeping plan of urban renewal, it was constructed on a
stretch of land, between Perdido and Poydras streets, that was once
the heart of black Storyville, a neighborhood crowded with shotgun
houses, narrow cribs, balconied tenements, and honky-tonks. Unlike
patrons of Storyville proper, the habitués of these emporiums were
not particularly interested in high-priced pseudo-French finesse.
Louis Armstrong grew up here among pimps and prostitutes and the
sporting life before he was picked up by the police for waving a pistol
in public and sent to the Colored Waifs Home, where he was re-
deemed by music.

Those who prefer music over politics in New Orleans can take
satisfaction in the notion that somewhere beneath City Hall are the
remains of Funky Butt Hall—officially known as Union Son's Hall—
where Buddy Bolden and other pioneers of jazz played. There is a
certain "geopsychic" coincidence here, as my friend Bookhardt might
say.

On my way to the second-floor offices of the Mayor's Mardi
Gras Coordinating Committee, I found another of those conver-
gences of civics and music. I passed a small room lined with shelves
and filing cabinets, where someone had affixed a small cardboard sign
to the wall: JAMES BOOKER MEMORIAL LIBRARY. Booker, I thought,
would have loved this small tribute, though he might have preferred
something grander, perhaps a bronze plaque with the legend: JAMES
CARROLL BOOKER III, THE PIANO PRINCE OF NEW ORLEANS. Sometimes
Booker had called himself the Black Liberace; at other times, he was
Little Chopin in Living Color.

Booker, who had lost an eye in a fight, wore a trademark black
patch adorned with a silver star. He also wore a variety of wigs,
ranging from Little Richard–style to Nat King Cole understatement.
On his best days, Booker was the greatest piano player in New Or-

leans since Tony Jackson and Jelly Roll Morton had played in Story-ville. He liked to claim sometimes, when he was not posing as Libe-race or Chopin, that he was Jelly Roll reincarnated. On bad days, he was a clinically paranoid junkie doing his best to die young.

When my friend Bill and I met Booker in the mid-1970s, he was playing to miniscule audiences at a small club on Rampart Street called Lu and Charlie's. Bill decided to try to "rescue" Booker, and for a few months, he became Booker's manager, which meant taking some wild rides and unexpected detours.

On the day of his first scheduled performance at the New Or-leans Jazz and Heritage Festival, Booker had spent most of his advance money on a big white limousine. We arrived at his aunt's house, somewhere in the Ninth Ward, where he was staying, and Booker was fretting because he couldn't find his favorite piano-prince wig. In desperation, he grabbed one of his aunt's Sunday-best wigs, which made him look like Flip Wilson as Geraldine, and shoved the band of his eyepatch over it to hold it down. We were late, and the limou-sine went blasting through the gates and lurching through the crowd, bumping across the muddy field to the stage. It was one of Booker's more memorable performances.

The last time I saw Booker, he had been commandeered to play for a talent night at the Euterpe Street Drug Rehabilitation Center, where he was required to go for counseling and a daily dose of methadone. Booker's performance that night was preceded by an impromptu fashion show by Truman's Tigress Revue, a group of black female impersonators, who lip-synched to various disco tunes. Booker started off his set, smiling wickedly, with a rousing perfor-mance of his theme song, "Junco Partner." He deliberately drew out the refrain, "Give me some heroin, some heroin, and a little cocaine, before I die," looking over the director of the center, who simply nodded and smiled tolerantly.

Booker, who kept running out of money and tolerant employers, had spent a few months before his untimely but not unexpected death typing forms at City Hall. He had relished his job there, telling ac-quaintances he was now politically connected, with friends in high places, and that he could fix their parking tickets for them. "He typed like a madman," a friend who worked in City Hall had told me. I loved the thought of his impossibly long fingers flying wildly over the typewriter keys, filling in blank forms with names and titles that he must have embellished as he did melodies and riffs.

Booker had once told me the key to his music was "metamorphosis." What he meant, I think, was the way he would take a song and let it percolate through memory and wild association and become something else. Chopin's "Minute Waltz" became the "Black Minute Waltz," which Booker could play so fast that your head whirled and then so slow you could sip a drink between beats. "When the music gets back to the place of origin," he told me one night, "it's a different product altogether. That's what keeps it flowing—bastardize it into something else."

I think Booker had given me not merely the secret of his music, but the key to Carnival and to all mythologies in New Orleans: metamorphosis. Rebirth in a different key, a different shape.

Taking on the Enemies of Tradition

As I pursued my way through the strange world of Carnival in New Orleans, I often felt like a shipwrecked mariner in a mythic saga, distracted by cryptic clues, lost in mazes, confused by hidden identities and secret passwords. And like anyone engaged in a mythic quest, I had to go to a number of sources to find my way through—to the sibyls, the griots, the dragons at the gate, and the other custodians of culture in New Orleans who hold its secrets.

I was amused to discover that the public relations people in City Hall had actually come up with an official label, "guardian of tradition," for certain Carnival aficionados. It sounded like an honorary title that might be accompanied by the awarding of a sash and a medal and a kiss on both cheeks.

Along with the parade schedule I picked up from the Mayor's Mardi Gras Coordinating Committee was a "Carnival Resource List" that included the names of a number of Carnival experts, along with a blurb describing their field of expertise. George Schmidt, for example, an eccentric painter, musician, and premature curmudgeon I had known from the old days, was listed as "Artist/Historian/Musician, art and music of Mardi Gras, guardian of tradition."

I could easily imagine George, who looks like an Edwardian aesthete, wearing a "Royal Order of Guardians" sash over his white linen suit, with a blunderbuss or sword at his side, ready to charge the enemies of tradition in New Orleans. George, whose formal style of painting was reminiscent of nineteenth-century French Academy painters, went beyond conservatism in his cultural politics: he was a reactionary. I envisioned George more as an avenging angel than guardian angel.

Another traditionalist on the list was Henri Schindler, the float designer for Comus. Henri had taken over the job just four years earlier, after a long apprenticeship, but already he seemed a permanent fixture of traditional Carnival. As floats for newer Carnival krewes grew bigger and more topical, with obvious references to the latest icons of pop culture, the Comus parade, under Henri's influence, grew more subtle and arcane. Henri turned to the Golden Age of Carnival, to fin de siècle glitter, to forgotten myths and mildewed tomes of flora and fauna, for his themes and designs. Henri, whose own modest origins precluded an invitation into the clubs he defended so ardently, knew more about traditional Mardi Gras than any blue-blooded krewe captain or king.

The only bona fide blue blood on the mayor's list, in fact, was Beau Bassich, a genial retired businessman who had become an important link between City Hall and uptown Carnival krewes. Beau had earned Carnival's highest public honor, reigning as Rex, king of Carnival, in 1989, and he was also captain of an old-line krewe, a fact that was supposed to be secret. Beau, who belied the notion of the uptown aristocrat as effete snob, had worked hard at a number of preservationist causes, including the restoration of City Park. He had been particularly active in restoring the park's carousel.

At the other end of the social spectrum was photographer Mike Smith, who was listed as an expert on the Mardi Gras Indians. These are the gangs, or tribes, of working-class blacks who dress in costumes of brilliantly hued beads and feathers on Mardi Gras day and parade through the streets, chanting their challenges to rival tribesmen. Mike, now in his fifties, had been photographing black cultural traditions in New Orleans since the late 1960s, and he still looked the part of the eternal radical, with his silver-streaked beard and jeans.

For Mike, who sometimes liked to call himself a "cultural environmentalist," the city's decaying black neighborhoods were cultural "wetlands," and he hoped to promote a different kind of tourism, based not on the dives of Bourbon Street or the mansions of the Garden District, but on the music and folklife of the streets and neighborhoods where ordinary tourists never ventured.

The mayor's list was remarkable in its eclecticism, reflecting the diversity of traditions, black and white, deemed worthy of preserving in the city. New Orleans, I realized, was full of guardians of culture— some of them members of the elite doggedly holding on to the past, but most of them, like Julia Ward Howe, outsiders, who recognized the unique but perishable quality of New Orleans artifacts and traditions. If you hang around in New Orleans long enough, you acquire the curatorial instinct.

A number of people I knew from the old days, who had been devotees of various aspects of New Orleans culture, particularly music and Carnival, had evolved into chroniclers or collectors and then into protectors and preservationists. They had made the transition, like Dian Fossey with her endangered gorillas, from academic appreciation to avid partisanship. They had found that there can be a middle ground between reveler and voyeur. Deciding that they couldn't leave, in spite of all the city's flaws, nor could they just parade and party while the city crumbled around them, they devoted their lives to saving the things they loved about New Orleans.

The Greening of Carnival

There was a certain irony in Mardi Gras now being recognized, almost universally, as one of the city's perishable assets. When I was living in New Orleans during the 1970s, the notion of Carnival as harmless diversion was already being questioned by a number of the city's residents. A schism had developed on the subject of Mardi Gras between the ancients and the moderns—that is, between the city's old-line social elite, composed of club-connected businessmen, professionals, and bons vivants, and a small "progressive" element, composed mainly of the new blood in town, a handful of academics, and civic-minded dissidents who were beginning to question the ancients' long-held traditions and prerogatives.

The overlap between traditional Carnival clubs, the city's elite white society, and many of its business fiefdoms, particularly its banks, law firms, and brokerage houses, was so obvious that it was difficult not to view traditional Carnival—the older parades and formal balls—as a pageant of the ruling class. To rule Carnival was tantamount to ruling New Orleans, according to some theorists.

In 1972, Phyllis Raabe, a graduate student at Penn State, wrote a doctoral dissertation called "Status and its Impact: New Orleans Carnival, the Social Upper Class and Upper Class Power," which documented the social stratification in New Orleans and stressed the importance of Carnival in reinforcing the power and conservative elitism of the upper class. Between 1920 and 1970, the total percentage of new blood brought into the Krewe of Comus was less than 1 percent.

An obscure study titled "Who Rules New Orleans," published in 1971 in the monthly *Louisiana Business Survey* by Charles Chai, an assistant professor of political science at Tulane University, asserted that even if the scions of Carnival and other elite clubs were not as powerful as they appeared to be, their importance in the city had become a self-fulfilling myth.

The two weekly newspapers in town, the radical *Vieux Carré Courier*, for which I had worked briefly, and the savvy, moderately provocative *Figaro*, regularly took on the Carnival establishment for discrimination against blacks and Jews. In an article titled "Is Mardi Gras Unconstitutional?" Bill Rushton, the *Courier*'s conspiracy-sniffing managing editor, asserted that Carnival was actually a mechanism of "social control," involving the "manipulation of the need to belong and to be social."

The ancients, countering the first assaults on Carnival during the 1970s, defended it as good fun, something like a family circus. It was the greatest free show on earth, they said, courtesy of private organizations devoted to a glorious tradition. For the moderns, however, the city's elite social and business leaders were latter-day Bourbons who had gotten stuck somewhere in the pre-democratic past, expecting to continue their extravagant reign over the city as their own private playground.

At that stage of the game, when the main challenge to Carnival was coming from a small phalanx of progressive politicians, academics, arrivistes, and counterculture critics, the ancients still held most of the cards—dance cards, at least. Doctors, lawyers, bankers, brokers, and heirs of family businesses, they controlled membership of the city's top men's clubs and Mardi Gras krewes, and they still controlled a stronghold of money and power.

For the moderns, Mardi Gras was the epitome of New Orleans decadence, a pageant of snobbery and racism, a drain on the city's cultural and financial resources. For some, Mardi Gras was not merely a symptom of the city's malaise, but a cause. For the moderns, Mardi Gras became a symbol for everything wrong in the city. New Orleans seemed to be caught in yet another epidemic, the disease milder in its symptoms than yellow fever but more permanent in its effects. The city was plagued, said social diagnosticians, by the Mardi Gras Syndrome: a general inclination toward backwardness, lethargy, or escapism.

By 1990, however, when the city's new chief administrative officer proposed to tax the riders of Carnival floats one hundred dollars each for the privilege of parading in the streets, using the old charge that Mardi Gras was a drain on the city, the krewe captains could muster a more practical defense for their rites. With the recession settled in for an indefinite stay, tourism had become the only economic game in town, and the glittering image of Mardi Gras had become so entwined with the city that for visitors to think of New Orleans without Carnival was to think of India without the Taj Mahal, of Pisa without its leaning tower. No tax was levied on the riders.

The next year, when the the first bombing raids of the Gulf War coincided with the beginning of Carnival season, it became clear that Mardi Gras was no longer a luxury for the city of New Orleans; it had become a necessity. In New Orleans, hedonism had become the primary industry.

During the days after the beginning of the war, the mayor's office was flooded with calls, half in favor of canceling the remainder of the season, half for letting the show go on. There was a precedent, in fact, for dealing with Carnival during wartime. It had been canceled during the Civil War, both world wars, and during the first year of the Korean War, but it had continued, unabated, during the Vietnam War.

Krewe captains discussed the possibility of calling off the celebration. "If the war had escalated rapidly, and produced a lot of local casualties, the mood would not be to celebrate," the captain of Rex told me. When Mayor Barthelemy announced, however, that Carnival would not be canceled, in spite of the Gulf War, his rationale was one of economics. He cited a study by University of New Orleans economist James McLain, initiated the previous year by a cadre of krewe captains, indicating that Carnival was an economic boon to the city.

According to the study, nearly five hundred million dollars altogether was spent each year on Carnival by local revelers and tourists. The hotels, restaurants, king-cake bakers, bead importers, musicians, liquor distributors, costume makers, and other suppliers of the accoutrements of good cheer who had come to depend on the extra boost of Carnival season would suffer if the show did not go on.

In typical New Orleans Janus-faced fashion, krewe captains decided that they could celebrate and be patriotic, too. Since the official Mardi Gras colors were purple, green, and gold, it was often a matter of just adding an extra yellow ribbon here and there. The captain of Rex announced, for example, that his krewe would tie yellow ribbons on the tractors pulling the floats in the Rex parade. "We want to show that our sentiment is with our troops and we're thinking about them," he said. Military bands, which had fallen out of fashion in favor of flashy high school marching bands, were suddenly in demand.

Endymion, the megakrewe that had begun as a small suburban club, and which now paraded into the Superdome, hired army, navy, air force, marine, and coast guard marching units to lead the parade. The krewe's flagship steamboat float was covered in red, white, and blue bunting, yellow ribbons, eagles, and American flags. Even Momus, the old-line krewe known for its satirical parades, managed some last-minute thrusts at Saddam Hussein. In keeping with the parade's theme of "Toxic Roux" or "Mean Cuisine," were floats featuring "Iraq of Lamb" and a "Bush Kabob," the latter featuring George Bush as a crusader impaling Saddam on a missile-barbed skewer. Only a few dissidents in the crowd wore buttons declaring MAKE MARDI GRAS NOT WAR.

Endymion krewe captain Ed Muniz surprised his membership by disinviting the krewe's celebrity guest star, Woody Harrelson, the actor who played the dimwitted bartender on the TV sitcom *Cheers.* Harrelson had been spotted in a crowd in Los Angeles during an antiwar rally led by disabled Vietnam vet Ron Kovic, and Muniz decided that absence would be the better part of valor for Harrelson. Harrelson, however, seemed bewildered by the controversy, telling a reporter that his only motivation in coming to New Orleans as king of Endymion had been to "hang out and party."

Carnival suppliers who were quick to capitalize on patriotic themes soon sold out of their hottest items—plastic cups adorned with flags and Desert Storm mottoes. A company called Hot-Stamped Cups sold 140,000 red, white, and blue Desert Storm cups to the Krewe of Endymion, which in turn sold them to its 1,550 members for five dollars for a sleeve of twenty-one. They boasted of their "twenty-one-cup salutes to our men and women in the Persian Gulf."

Float designer Blaine Kern, known as Mr. Mardi Gras, whose firm designed and built floats for some forty krewes, was asked by all of the krewe captains to add a patriotic touch to their parades. Kern's own club, the Krewe of Alla, of which he was captain, and whose members were known as SOBs (Sons of Baghdad), was presented with something of an image problem. Kern hastened to explain to anyone who would listen that the krewe had not been named for the Muslim god, but for the city of Algiers, Louisiana. Ordinarily, the krewe members riding on the title float, which featured a giant genie in a turban, would also wear turbans. Kern decided to add a giant flag for the genie to wave and to tie yellow ribbons around the headgear of the krewe members.

Only the Krewe of Comus, whose parade was the last of the

season, kept to its traditional timeless irrelevance. Its theme was insects, and the floats included fire ants immolating themselves in the sun, an enormous praying mantis swaying in deadly devotion, and a huge spider vibrating on a gossamer silver web.

3

The Carnival Economy

Wakened by the *clip-clop* of hooves on pavement, I peered out from my balcony onto Saint Louis Street, where a young black man seated on the driver's seat of a carriage was urging on a mule wearing a straw hat bedecked with plastic flowers. "Come on, girl, we've got to find some tourists," he coaxed. All day, the brightly painted surreys and mules in silly hats clattered by, jammed with sightseers in the usual tourist getups, adorned with strings of Mardi Gras beads or carrying drinks in plastic go-cups.

The drivers, most of them black, offered tidbits of New Orleans lore along with the mule-drawn tours of the French Quarter. They began at Jackson Square, where they anchored their buggies, near the equestrian statue of Andrew Jackson, the first and perhaps the last leader to unite the motley population of Louisiana in a winning battle.

Jackson, unversed in the byzantine ways of the swampy, newly annexed territory, had managed to pull together on the fields of Chalmette Plantation a most improbable army to defend the city of New Orleans in the last major battle of the War of 1812: rough Tennesseans and Kentuckians who had come down the river on barges; aristocratic Creoles, of French and Spanish descent; Mississippi planters; a Jewish philanthropist from Boston; Choctaw Indians; free men of color; slaves; sailors; pirates from nearby Barataria; and a handful of regular soldiers.

In Johnny Horton's rock 'n' roll ballad, the ragtag Americans even loaded up an alligator with cannonballs and fired, sending the British back through the briars and brambles to the Gulf of Mexico. Nowadays, however, I doubted that even Andrew Jackson could unite the city of New Orleans for the crucial battles that would decide its future. The city was still living on its past.

After drivers snagged their quarry in Jackson Square, the tourist-laden buggies proceeded up Decatur, parallel to the Mississippi River, and turned right on Saint Louis, passing beneath my balcony. On the corner of Saint Louis and Chartres, the drivers described the former site of slave auctions in the same informative tone they used to indicate the old Pharmacy Museum, where a former rhythm-and-blues star, Oliver Morgan, of "Who Shot the La-La" fame, gave tours. The slave block was now a historical curiosity, lending a touch of atmosphere.

The drivers also pointed out the Napoleon House, with its tiny cupola, home of a popular bar, where supporters of Napoleon were said to have plotted his escape from Saint Helena and awaited in vain his arrival in America. Far from despising Napoleon for bartering New Orleans to the Americans, French descendants in New Orleans continued to revere "The Man," or "the Greatest of Mortals," as they referred to him. Napoleon, after all, had revived pomp and Carnival in France, after the *citoyens* of the Revolution had banned such displays as ancien-régime folly.

If the drivers did not turn right on Chartres Street, they could have continued straight ahead down Saint Louis and pointed out the old Wildlife and Fisheries building, between Chartres and Royal streets, with the roots of its huge magnolia trees protruding like writhing snakes through the grass. It was here, during the early 1960s, that the Fifth Circuit Court of Appeals, led by patrician Judge John Minor Wisdom, gradually dismantled the tangled web of laws and regulations that had kept black citizens from voting in Louisiana. Judge Wisdom and his colleagues had frequently walked across the street to lunch at Antoine's or up to Canal Street and the all-white Boston Club.

These buggy-loads of tourists, which clog the French Quarter most of the year, even in August (when horses used to drop dead in harness, before they were replaced by heat-resistant mules), represent the economic future of New Orleans, a fact accepted with a sigh of resignation by some civic leaders, and with frustration by others.

51

Since 1975, when James Bobo, a professor of economics at the University of New Orleans, published a study on the city's economy, titled "Pro Bono Publico?", appropriating with a certain irony the motto of the Krewe of Rex and dismantling a number of New Orleans myths of progress, various civic leaders had attempted to prod the city out of its lethargy and fatalism. Bobo's report, which focused on the city's chronic unemployment, exuded an aura of doom, portraying the New Orleans economy as stagnant, with little chance of ever improving.

Expectations had certainly been lowered since Thomas Jefferson's prediction that New Orleans, by virtue of its location, would become not only the greatest commercial city in America, but in the world. Jefferson, in urging the purchase of the Louisiana Territory, noted that New Orleans, as the natural port of the Mississippi Valley, which he foresaw as the seat of a great and populous empire, was positioned at the very gateway of the continent, a conduit for goods passing between Europe, Latin America, and the Caribbean. Nowadays, among the major products following the current down the Mississippi River were chemical runoffs from fertilized and pesticided farms of Middle America and effluents from the chemical plants upriver known as Cancer Alley. Instead of a gateway, the city had become, as my friend Mike Smith noted, the "cloaca" of America.

Dutch Morial, like Bobo, had envisioned manufacturing, rather than tourism, as the only means to cure the city's chronically anemic economy, with public education as the key to revitalization. Morial's speech before the Metropolitan Area Committee, a coalition of influential business leaders, just prior to taking office in 1978, was a powerful piece of oratory, charged with the kind of plain-speaking and clarity of vision that the city had rarely witnessed from a politician.

Morial cited a letter he had recently received from a high school English class at Grace King High School, enclosing a copy of Cicero's essay on the duties of the individual to the state. Morial quoted a relevant line from Cicero's text: "For there are men who for fear of giving offense do not dare to express their honest opinion, no matter how excellent." Morial proceeded, accordingly, to "dispense with platitudes, half-truths and sophistry," and with "illusions which retard growth and leave hurt and disappointment in their wake."

Morial was just getting warmed up. "We have preferred to live in an ancient dream of economic magnificence just around the corner," he said, "while thousands and thousands of our citizens have never climbed out of soul-searing poverty and black unemployment reaches toward an incredible flood-tide mark."

New Orleans had become paralyzed, he said, by its byzantine power structure, "which comprises a multiplicity of enclaves, each powerful in negative influence, but limited in constructive input. Is this why so often we have become polarized, paralyzed and fractured?" Tourism, Morial declared, was being used as a palliative to "paper over" the defects in the economy.

Six years later, when plans for a New Orleans World's Fair began to be bandied about, with visions of hundreds of thousands of tourists pouring into the city during the height of the summer, Morial tried to pour cold water over the feverish boosters. A fair, he said, recalling the Cotton Exposition a century earlier, would bring "a considerable measure of confusion, costs, and congestion, frustration, foolishness, and fighting."

The fair's director, Petr Spurney, sounding remarkably like the Cotton Exposition's Major Burke, had been dubbed the "Music Man" by local businessmen for his upbeat, carnival-barker luncheon speeches. In one speech to local civic leaders, Spurney declared, "An awful lot of people feel that there is a Mardi Gras Syndrome here—let the bands play. Let everybody have a good time. Once that is all said and over, the streets still have potholes. There are still high crime rates. The school system still needs improvement. . . . This isn't my song."

Spurney's song, the song of the Music Man, was one of optimism, of bountiful tourist dollars. It was an attractive siren song to the handful of businessmen and developers who owned the riverfront property where the fair was located. It was particularly appealing to Blaine Kern, Mr. Mardi Gras, who encouraged the building of a "people-mover" monorail across the Mississippi from the fair site to the West Bank, near his float-building business, where he envisioned an ever-expanding Carnival-making empire, "Mardi Gras World."

When the fair opened, venerable eighty-one-year-old architect Nathaniel Owings, who had helped design the Chicago World's Fair fifty years earlier, called the New Orleans enterprise a mere "sideshow, a county fair." It was Owings's own firm of Skidmore, Owings and Merrill, in fact, that had attempted a decade earlier to lead New Orleans out of its wrought-iron-and-gingerbread provinciality by designing the city's first towering example of International-style architecture: One Shell Square. When it was constructed, in 1972, the white, boxlike building loomed forbiddingly over Poydras Street, as alien and impenetrable as a fortress. Dubbed "One Square Shell" by one critic, it seemed a lonely outpost of progress, a Texas embassy, until other tall buildings went up, creating what one local architect called "an eighth-rate Sixth Avenue."

Other world's fairs had celebrated the triumph of technology, offering a fanfare to progress; geodesic domes and space needles had given vertiginous views of the future. But the New Orleans World's Fair was a paean to the city's past and present—to its aura of celebration and license. You entered the fair through a gate guarded by scantily clad mermaids lounging amid a gaggle of alligators. The principal architectural curiosity was the Wonder Wall, which resembled a frozen Mardi Gras parade. With its scaffolded jumble of turrets, towers, plaster peacocks, and gilded cherubs, the Wonder Wall, designed by California architect Charles Moore, was a playful parody of Carnival, of the cheap theatrical effects and mock-up antiquities so beloved by captains of Mardi Gras parades.

Not surprisingly, the fair became mired in financial trouble even before it opened, and then-Governor Edwin Edwards was prevailed upon to bail out the city with a ten-million-dollar state loan, even as he recommended one hundred million dollars' worth of cuts in state services to the legislature. The fair went bankrupt, along with its chief architect. The fading neighborhood surrounding the fair, the Warehouse District, had been revived and restored, inspiring an influx of hip young urban professionals, but the cost had been high. The city itself, already about to sink into recession, went so deep into the hole financially that it never really recovered. Eventually such emergency measures had to be taken as shortening City Hall work weeks to four days.

The World's Fair had not been a remedy for the Mardi Gras Syndrome that plagued New Orleans, but a symptom. Concocting yet another tourist attraction or putting on yet another show seemed to be the only solution local leaders could come up with for the city's problems.

The credibility of the ruling class had been called into question not merely for its atavistic social practices, but for its lack of political and economic leadership. New Orleans was suffering an identity crisis. Accused of dozing at the helm as the city sank further into the doldrums, the self-absorbed social elite of New Orleans turned further inward and left the majority of the population of the city to fend for themselves.

The Banana Republic

"I think there's no question but that we have been demoralized," said George Denegre, a prominent attorney and uptown aristocrat of Creole heritage who was perhaps the least fossilized member of his dwindling social class that I knew.

I had gone to visit Denegre one day at his office in Saint Charles Place, one of the downtown high-rises that had been built during the brief speculative boom of the mid-1980s. Denegre, a small, cherubic-looking man who resembled the actor who played Santa Claus in *Miracle on 34th Street*, had been involved in a number of business-oriented civic groups, including the recent MetroVision Partnership, which had issued yet another chastening study of the area's economy.

Under a section titled "Image," the study's authors suggested that while the "Big Easy" image of New Orleans might be helping tourism, it was hurting efforts at economic diversification. In a recent study, which inquired of a group of CEOs which city they favored for doing business, New Orleans came in dead last.

For Denegre, the problem had to do with one of those old uptown New Orleans paradoxes: a feeling of social superiority coupled with an economic inferiority complex. New Orleans society had a habit of snubbing the brash Texans who came into town throwing money around and buying up mansions on Saint Charles Avenue, then watching helplessly as the Texans and other outsiders displaced local gentry on the boards of banks and businesses. Three leading local banks—the Whitney, the NBC, and the Hibernia, long bastions of local gentry—were now run by CEOs from out of town.

The most successful businesspeople in New Orleans in recent years, Denegre admitted, tended to come from out of state, particularly from Texas. Pat Taylor, a soft-spoken independent oil baron, and Jim Bob Moffett, the flamboyant head of Freeport-McMoRan, the biggest company in town, had made everyone else look like they were standing still. Taylor had won national recognition for his personally funded education incentive program, and Moffett had founded the Business Council, modeled on business leadership groups in other cities: the Citizens Council in Dallas and the Vault in Boston.

Moffett had arrived in town in 1985, after taking over Freeport Minerals in New York, and moved the headquarters of his new company to a building across from the Superdome on Poydras Street. At the time, there were only four other companies listed on the Fortune 500 actually based in New Orleans, so that Moffett was joining a very small club of important CEOs.

The corporate elite in New Orleans had always been minuscule, compared to other cities, and it had never managed enough cumulative clout to knock loudly on the door of the social clubs in New Orleans. Since money had never spoken loudly in New Orleans either, the occasional would-be party crasher tended to be snubbed, not only by elite Carnival clubs, but by the other social clubs affiliated with them. Recently, a brash CEO of a big local bank was blackballed by the New Orleans Country Club.

Nevertheless, a few foolhardy climbers continued to poke their heads above the walls, daring to be shot down. Even Texans, however, could succumb to Mardi Gras Syndrome. Moffett had bought the Saint Charles mansion that had previously been occupied by another flashy oilman, Norman Johnson, who had come to town with big plans and wound up committing suicide after a stint in jail. Johnson's last wife, Gayfryd, known in New Orleans for the gaudiest jewelry in town, had better luck social climbing in New York, after marrying takeover mogul Saul Steinberg.

Moffett himself ran into trouble when the state of Louisiana, in a belated spasm of environmental concern, took away his company's permit to dump gypsum into the Mississippi, and a crusading television reporter went after Freeport-McMoRan tenaciously until Moffett hired him away from the station as a PR man. Moffett, who had tried to play things the Louisiana way, including hiring Governor Edwin Edwards's brother as a lobbyist, held a press conference in which he denounced the state as a "banana republic."

The problem, as Moffett saw it, was that New Orleans just wasn't an American city, with American values and American institutions. Perhaps if New Orleans were to pull itself away from its long tropical vacation and become more like Houston or Atlanta, a vision its boosters were always harkening to, things could get back on track. In other words, New Orleanians should get over their smugness and decadence and acknowledge the fact that the invaders had won—that the city had finally been conquered by the Americans, whose ancestors had bought it nearly two centuries earlier. The old families might control Carnival, but they no longer controlled the destiny of New Orleans.

Now, of course, that Houston and Atlanta, and nearly every other American city, for that matter, were looking the worse for wear, it was difficult to find a model of civic progress for New Orleans to emulate.

Denegre handed me a copy of a speech he had given in 1990 to the Chamber of Commerce, which articulated the paralyzing contradiction that made New Orleans a sitting duck for Sunbelt competitors: "We have always had a love for our homeland, but our love is coupled with a strange lack of pride, a tendency to apologize and a strange ambivalence, in that whereas we think our lifestyles and customs are superior, we, nevertheless, feel that we cannot compete in the commercial arena." Denegre had attempted a little Texas-style boosting, based on the strong survival instincts that underlay the city's apparent lassitude: "This inferiority complex is unfair and unjustified. We have carved our region out of an impenetrable swamp. We have survived floods, fever, defeat and our own brand of self destructive politics."

The worst sting of all was that even those with the deepest roots in New Orleans were discouraged or fatalistic about the future of the city: "The recession has destroyed our morale to the point where those who should be the staunchest say that they wish they were somewhere else."

Although New Orleanians had not been known for their heroism since the War of 1812, the times now called for courage. Addressing those who might have lost their nerve, Denegre had concluded his speech to the Chamber of Commerce with a quote from the *Aeneid*:

> Call the nerve back; dismiss the fear, the sadness.
> Some day, perhaps, remembering even this
> Will be a pleasure.

Many men of Denegre's age and class, who constituted the upper crust of private clubs and Mardi Gras krewes, were simply carrying on the only way they knew how, living on the remains of the day, as their fathers and grandfathers had, caretaking inheritances or family businesses, going to lunch at the Boston Club or Galatoire's, riding in Carnival parades, orchestrating their daughters' debuts at the Municipal Auditorium, and watching as political power and eminent domain passed to blacks and economic power to Texans and other invaders.

With most of the middle- and lower-middle-class residents of the city departed, the demographics of the city now resembled an hourglass—all top and bottom and only a sliver of a middle.

If the men of Denegre's age and class did leave, which was rare, for all their talk of wanting to be "somewhere else," they tended not to go farther away than Old Metairie, the old-money suburb, or perhaps across the lake. "They don't want to get too far from their clubs and restaurants," observed Denegre. If Carnival and its attendant social life had come to be perceived by outsiders as an atavistic charade, the clubs and krewes were also the ties that bound the elite to New Orleans.

Still, the children and grandchildren of the ancien régime of New Orleans were leaving, and soon there would be no one to inherit the crowns and tiaras of Carnival. The old-line clubs and Carnival krewes, said Denegre, had become largely "irrelevant" in the life of the city.

For those who remained, apprehension was the order of the day. Sporadic rashes of robberies and murders uptown had left residents frightened, and a number of men had begun carrying guns in their cars or briefcases. They bought car phones for their wives, who notified guards from a security service when they would be arriving home, so that they could be protected while bringing in groceries or shopping bags into the house. The patchwork settlement pattern of the city had left poor black neighborhoods and housing developments in close proximity to prosperous white blocks, leaving no means of retreat behind walls or gates. Most uptown mansions, with their generous verandas, French doors, and tall windows, were not built for security.

When I suggested that New Orleanians who chose to leave might be demonstrating a certain disloyalty to the city, Denegre retorted, "I'm loyal, but not loyal enough to get shot in bed."

New Orleans, said Denegre, needed a round of morale boosting from its leaders. "You picture Roosevelt with his fireside chats," he said. "Sidney won't come out and do it," he said, referring to the mayor. It was rather odd to think of Sidney Barthelemy, with his elegant Creole diffidence, donning a sweater, pulling a chair up to the fireplace, and reassuring white New Orleanians, who were quaking in their boots, that they were welcome in the city that they had once ruled.

In the absence of that kind of inclusive leadership, Denegre had joined yet another kind of civic group, this one a group of men who met for breakfast on a regular basis. Unlike the men's luncheon clubs in the CBD, the Central Business District, this group was composed of leaders of varying skin tones, many of them black Creoles. In the group were the founder of the first black-owned bank in New Orleans, a college president, a city official. While other forms of ties and networks between black and white leaders in the city were failing, this breakfast group had increased in importance and influence. Although the group was known unofficially as the Inter-Business Council, they might have named it the Realists' Club.

The Plastic People

For most blacks in New Orleans, the disheartening sense of decline was just as palpable as it was for whites, if not more so. Political victories did not compensate for the breakdown in community. "People are looking for leadership," said Edgar Chase III, another member of the Inter-Business Council, and a grandson of the founder of Dooky Chase's, the landmark black restaurant. I had gone to visit him one day at his office at Dillard University. Chase, known as Dooky, the nickname he inherited from his grandfather, is chairman of the business department at Dillard, a black school located on a pastoral campus near City Park.

"People in New Orleans are not looking for a savior," said Chase. "Just someone to bring the city back to where it was—the city in their memory. In the Inter-Business Council, we talk a lot about keeping the essence of the city alive."

The talk at the council went across racial lines, said Chase, and despite frequent disagreements, members spoke with openness and trust. This was just the opposite of what he had witnessed in the City Council, where a breakdown of trust and respect had occurred. "The City Council no longer represents New Orleans," he said.

Chase reminded me that there are black guardians of culture, too, and that black citizens are just as nostalgic as whites for the kind of life in New Orleans that is passing away, eroded not only by violence, but by intrusions of mass culture.

"The architecture of our buildings, the beauty of the people, our way of celebrating is inborn," said Chase. "When I was a child," he recalled, "people would sit on the stoops every evening. You'd take a bath and come out on the porch until mosquitoes made you come inside. You'd turn on the fan and cool things off. Life centered around your neighborhood. We've lost that idea of being safe and free in the neighborhood, talking with your neighbor until it gets dark or until you're tired.

"We've lost the days of the snowball man, the watermelon man." Chase sang out, imitating a street vendor, "I got black-eyed peas."

He continued, "We want to be a world-class city, but we have to be careful not to change our culture. We're different. We're not as plastic as other places. We want to be hospitable—and a little wholesome. We like to sin, but we don't want to be known as sinners. Sticking to our roots is how we should grow and evolve—not trying to be like someone else. In some ways, we've already sold out to outsiders and become like plastic people—putting on a show for somebody else."

As for Dorothy Mae Taylor's proposed antidiscrimination ordinance, Chase responded, "David Duke is dead in the water. I don't think civil rights are our major concern right now. I know the idea is noble, but that's not the purpose of Mardi Gras. Mardi Gras was never a civil rights thing for black people. Maybe the other 364 days. But on Mardi Gras, we really didn't care. Mardi Gras is the one day when people accept one another and put down all disputes."

Reforming Mardi Gras was not the way to save the city, observed Chase, and the attempt to reform it might destroy Mardi Gras in the process. Mardi Gras was already becoming too structured, in any event. "You can't regulate Mardi Gras," he said. "When you put too much structure on it you kill it." He referred to a movie in which Chevy Chase is trying to sell his house, and he wants to cue the deer to run across the lawn. "Cue Rex now. Cue the truck parades. That's okay for television, but not for Mardi Gras," said Chase.

The idea of reforming Mardi Gras was something like trying to ice a cake that was crumbling away.

4

The Dragon Lady of the Archives

One of the first Carnival organizations to respond to Dorothy Mae Taylor's proposed ordinance was a small club called Les Amis des Arts de Mardi Gras, whose members included Henri Schindler and Peggy Wilson, the white city councilwoman from the uptown district near Tulane University and Audubon Park.

Les Amis were known as Mardi Gras connoisseurs, discerning collectors of Mardi Gras mementoes and keepsakes and lore. They were Carnival purists, which meant that they treasured the relics of Carnival's golden years—the elaborate art nouveau invitations that unfolded like origami, the delicate, swirling pins and tiny jewel boxes and pendants that were given as favors by krewe members to members of the court and to women lucky enough to be called out for a dance. Les Amis had little use for "bourgeois" Carnival—the Carnival of the suburbs and the parvenu megakrewes who were always trying to commercialize their activities.

Ordinarily, the club met twice a year, once over a gourmet dinner, a sort of show-and-tell, then again shortly before Mardi Gras at the Comus den, where floats were built and stored, for champagne and a viewing of the floats. Upon hearing about Dorothy Mae's proposed ordinance, Les Amis had called an emergency meeting at Galatoire's restaurant on Bourbon Street to discuss the impending crisis.

"We can't have George Denegre deciding these things," said Sally Evans Reeves, one of the members.

Sally, who came from a "good" family herself, and who had been in the court of Rex in her day, agreed, however, with Denegre that the glory days of Comus et al. were over. "I've been trying to tell them

62

the handwriting is on the wall. My solution, if the ordinance is passed, and it becomes a matter of survival for the old krewes, is to relax and see who applies. What are the chances of someone paying all that money to associate with these hidebound old men?"

Sally held up the example of Texas millionaire John Mecom, who, it was rumored, had delivered an ultimatum that if he were not allowed to join the Boston Club, he would move the Saints football team, which he owned at the time. Finally, he was invited, as the rumor went. "He went one time," said Sally, "and said he was never going back. The stuffing was coming out of the chairs, and all they wanted to do was play bridge for a dollar a point and tell corny jokes." Said Sally, "It's not Bacchus," referring to the glitzy krewe of Carnival newcomers founded by float maker Blaine Kern and restaurateur Pip Brennan, among others, for the benefit of wealthy businessmen.

As guardians of culture go, Sally Reeves was something of a dragon lady, fiercely guarding her lair in the basement of the Civil District Court building, just across the way from City Hall. A sylph-like blonde of formidable charm, Sally might have chosen to join her uptown society friends in their daily rounds of lunch and shopping, but chose instead to toil in the Dickensian bowels of District Court, in a corner of the basement known as the Notarial Archives. In the archives were thirty-seven thousand notarial volumes, of one thousand pages each, from the year 1731 to the present.

Sally, in conventional Southern euphemism, would be described as "vivacious." In fact, she was sharp-tongued and brilliant, particularly in defense of traditional Carnival and of her treasure trove of early New Orleans history, a collection of five thousand early, folio-sized watercolor drawings of houses, lots, and tracts of land in fifteen Louisiana parishes made by civil engineers.

The buildings themselves might be crumbling, but Sally was there to ensure that the drawings of the buildings, on which their history had been written in scrawled notations, would survive, like Platonic ideals of buildings, in some timeless realm, safe from decay—an archetypal memory of New Orleans.

"I call this the briar patch," she said of her basement lair. "I've been doing this for twenty years. I finally got an M.A. in archival management. I always make a point of coming here on my birthday. There is no finer place to be on that day. I live in this world, isolated from rain and crime and urban stress. It's an ivory tower. No, an ivory dungeon.''

She mused, "Some krewe captains live in that world, too. They plan their balls year-round. They never stop working on their court, their tableau, their theme.''

Conversations with Sally always tended to get sidetracked to the subject of the civil code, an obsession, with Sally making sibylline pronouncements as she carefully inspected documents she removed from the protective Mylar pouches and file drawers she had acquired for the archives by means of a grant. She would carefully steam off old tape and glue, the result of clumsy repairs made of the documents during the WPA in the 1930s. Here in the basement, she felt, was a source for the unique history and character of New Orleans.

"These Notarial Archives," she said, "are the only ones in the United States because Louisiana is the only state in the nation that was governed by civil rather than common law. People in the other forty-nine states live in a common-law regime, but Louisiana and the rest of the world is civil law.

"The civil-law notary is a documentarist, and these documents are part of his plan. In civil law, the original document and attachments and plans and wills must be kept in a central place. You can trace a title of a piece of property here within an inch of its life. Wills, slave auctions, emancipation—you can flesh out the bare bones of history by running a title search. These are things you can count on. It's beautiful to think of civil law going back to Justinian.''

Civil law, from the very beginning, set New Orleans off from the rest of America, and it has been a factor in keeping the city from being completely absorbed into American culture. Civil law had also been a source of divisiveness within the city itself, between the Creole population and the Anglos who moved in after the Louisiana Purchase.

For more than three-quarters of a century, before the Louisiana Purchase, New Orleans had abided under laws rooted in Roman tradition, first under French, then under Spanish rule. The Gallic population liked to refer to themselves as the *ancienne* population, although when that epithet became too wieldy they acceded to the term *creole*, which technically applied to native-born population— white or black, free or slave. The white Creoles, for the most part, were refugees from the convulsions of the revolutionary and Napoleonic eras, from the continent or from Caribbean homes such as Saint Domingue, from whence they fled slave insurrection or economic ruination.

Some were said to have shed tears as the tricolor came down for the last time at the Place d'Armes (now Jackson Square) in 1803, before the American flag was raised. As one Creole had said of his Gallic inheritance, "A country is like a beloved first mistress: you can abandon her, you may love another, but you can never forget her." And so it was that the Napoleonic code, which encapsulated the old ways of life, became a cause célèbre.

The Creole population was determined to preserve their heritage, while the new American population was just as eager to live under Anglo-American common law, thought to be the foundation of American liberty and political independence. This enforced marriage of disparate cultures quickly broke up amid a sea of disputes. As one historian put it, "Nothing in their past histories had prepared the people of either Louisiana or the United States for the besetting complexities of the new relationship to which they were introduced by the treaty of 1803." Even Thomas Jefferson and James Madison, carrying their own cultural baggage, tended to identify "democracy" with peculiarly Anglo-Saxon forms. They perceived English common law, language, religious tradition, and social mores as the more "natural" vehicles of political freedom.

Historian Joseph Tregle has demonstrated that the old stereotypes of the sophisticated Creoles clashing with Yankee yokels were simply not true. The Americans, many of whom actually came from the East Coast, were better equipped than the Creoles to engage in a contest for supremacy, armed by superior education, wider experience in economic and political competition, and by "that dynamism and energy common to those daring enough to venture far from home to build a new life." In the old society ensconced in the Vieux Carré, they did not see a Creole aristocracy, but a backward, stagnant community.

The Creoles resented the Americans, calling them "Yankee buzzards." They fumed when Americans made English the legal language of the state, attempted to replace civil with common law, and tried to convert historic French street names in New Orleans to others more reflective of the new order.

Governor William C. Claiborne was a pivotal figure in the clash between Creoles and Americans. An ambitious Tennessee lawyer and congressman, he was appointed as governor of lower Louisiana late in 1803 to preside over the cession of Louisiana from France. Almost immediately, he became embroiled in ethnic conflicts between the two cultures.

The most visible—and violent—clashes occurred, absurdly enough, over dancing, which played a prominent role, then as now, in the life of the city. "I fear you will suppose that I am wanting in respect in calling your attention to the Balls of New Orleans," Claiborne wrote James Madison, then secretary of state, apologetically, "but I do assure you Sir, that they occupy much of the local mind, and from them have proceeded the greatest embarrassments which have heretofore attended my administration." In January, for example, a riot had erupted over the playing of an English country dance after the French had called for a waltz.

Claiborne wrote also about the resistance of the French to common law, particularly to the notion of trial by jury: "Men who have long appealed for justice to great Personages, whom they looked up to as wise and learned, cannot at first, without reluctance, submit to the decrees of Men, no better than themselves."

Finally, a civil-law digest adopted by the territorial legislature in 1808 set the terms for Louisiana's entry into the union. As legal scholars have noted, the establishment of a civil-law system in Louisiana forced the new American nation to accept an alien culture and a truly foreign legal code. As for Claiborne, he eventually married into an aristocratic family and became a pillar of Creole society.

The pressure to assimilate reinforced the clannishness of the Creoles, who clung to the importance of family, even as they eventually intermarried with "good" American families. "In my view," said Sally, "the story of the old prominent families in New Orleans can be boiled down to whether they have continued to produce heirs who can restore or repair the family fortune, whether they continue to be aware of their name or identity, whether they stay around. That is the test of an old solid society, whether they hang in there and introduce their children to the continuity of culture."

The social rites of Carnival, tied up with the tradition of debutantes, said Sally, were a means of instilling that continuity: "The younger generation gets to know the older generation, and the older generation finds out who the young are as individuals. The younger generation begins to buy into the older generation. The honors of Carnival are the carrots that make them want to do it.

"The children are scions, by heritage or environment, carrying the momentum on into the next generation. In an earlier era, they were merchants—cotton brokers or food brokers. In this age, they might be doctors or lawyers." George Denegre, she said, for example, was a true "scion." Said Sally, "He's carrying the name forward, and certainly rising to the level his forebears did."

I wondered about the next generation, however, the men of my age and a little older, who were now coming into power in the clubs and krewes. I knew a great number of wastrels, dilettantes, and nutty eccentrics of impeccable bloodlines who hardly seemed likely to carry on the traditions—or guard the family fortune—with the same verve their fathers had. One prominent scion, who had helped to elect former Mayor Moon Landrieu, the city's last white mayor, with a coalition of blacks and upper-class whites, and who had appeared the most likely candidate in the city to merge political and social leadership, had left town after being caught by a TV news team on videotape soliciting a hustler.

"The old society," she observed, "carries on in its vestiges. In my view, the economic hegemony of the old families was broken for good in the 1970s, first by the prosperity of the newcomers and second by the prostrate poverty in the 1980s. There was new money and then everybody was going bust. The old cultural practices are carrying on, but fewer and fewer can afford country-club living.

"The royalty at the most elaborate balls has to be wealthy people, and fewer and fewer can afford to be queen of Carnival or Comus. You have to pay not only for outfits, which run into five figures—you have to pay for the queen's supper after the ball at the Fairmont Hotel on Mardi Gras night for hundreds of people. At Christmas, there is another five-figure party to introduce the girl at her coming-out party.

"You wonder why Rex is dipping into newcomers now to be crowned Rex—or someone too young to have accomplished a lot. Qualifications are of less concern if you can write a check."

The bulk of the money that was being spent on Carnival, she said, was largely going into the "bourgeois" part of Mardi Gras—the newer krewes. "The only part that is really declining is the stylized, decadent, old-guard part." As "parvenu" krewes like Bacchus, she said, "get bigger and gaudier, Comus gets smaller and more refined."

One factor in the inevitable decline of the old-line krewes, theorized Sally, was the "emancipation of women." Her daughter, for example, made her debut. "But is she going to keep going to balls when she gets older and sit there like a sheep waiting to be danced with by a member of a krewe that excludes women? My generation tolerates that, but without enthusiasm. The old decadent stuff is going to carry on, but as women become more educated, with less enthusiasm."

Sally herself had been the classic reluctant debutante. She was loud and wild, she said, but obeyed her parents. She had been queen of a "mid-tier" ball, as she described the Athenians, and she had her choice as maid in the court of one of the top balls, which included Comus, Rex, and Proteus. She chose Rex.

She recalled the giddiness of being swept up in it all, of the "wonderful Cinderella moment, from blue-jeaned student to having this faraway fantasy swoop down on you"—beginning with "the call by the krewe captain upon the young queen, on a cold day in January, who delivers a gaily painted scroll with her name on it, expecting to be served champagne. When the day comes, you spend the whole day getting your hair done and makeup. I remember being amazed that when the powder was applied and dried, it wore like iron until three in the morning.

"You have a reception at your home. You're all dolled up with your scepter and your train. You arrive at the Auditorium, and white-tied and black-tailed gentlemen make sure the space around you is clear. Your picture is taken. Champagne is passed around. Your maids, your peers, are standing around, attending you. You're whisked away like Cinderella in a limousine."

Nearly twenty years later, Sally had a second belle-hood, an experience denied to most society matrons. "When I was thirty-six, and the mother of five children, my husband died. But I had a beautiful house on Saint Charles Avenue and money, so I had a lot of dates. It was one of the phenomena of my widowhood. One of my suitors was active in Mardi Gras, so I went from matronly wife sitting in the audience, half the time pregnant, waiting for her husband to call her out, to belle of the ball. I had to bring a sack to carry home the favors. And the gentlemen who called me out to dance wouldn't tell me who they were. It felt like the early nineteenth century.

"In the world of today, the mysterious identity of maskers is so rare. Every woman knows her husband's shoes or his eyebrows. But I had this incredible opportunity. I experienced what it was supposed to be all about—these enigmatic men who would call me out for a magic moment on the floor. I had a rare insight into what masking is all about."

Perhaps it was simply the headiness of being king or queen for a day that would make Carnival last, Sally mused. "There is still great prestige attached to Mardi Gras. Everybody wants to be famous for fifteen minutes. It's a stylized and beautiful way to provide that fifteen minutes of fame. You get caught in the vortex. People spend their savings for a moment of prominence on the same old broken-down dance floor.

"People will do anything to be somebody. In the history of the world, from biblical times forward, there has been a group of suzerainty, having their courts and ladies in waiting. We have transformed that into a pageant.

"We have a bourgeois society with democratically elected officials, so we transform that need for prestige into a make-believe system that does fulfill people's need to have prestige. The captain of the ball walks around in an ermine-tipped velvet cape. All the colorful dukes around him are partaking in his glory.

"Given that people from all walks of society are willing to do that, this whole system of prestige we call royalty must have a hold on the community.

"The magic of Carnival is still there, inside the Auditorium and outside on the streets. There is nothing that can match the feeling of turning a corner from Saint Charles onto Canal Street and seeing a sea of humanity reaching out to you, a sea of hands lit by flickering flambeaux, the floats lurching and rocking in their silver and gilt highlights.

"Everyone can still suspend disbelief about Carnival. When people pierce the veil of make-believe, it will collapse."

Perhaps, however, for some, it was egalitarianism that was make-believe, and the longing for royalty that was the reality.

Sally finally paused, took a breath, looked down at a drawing, and exclaimed, "Oh, no, another ant. I've got to get back to work."

II

Transformations

5

Rules of the Game

If uptown Carnival seemed at times no more than an exclusive game of make-believe, the rules of the game appeared very real to those who felt excluded.

In the middle of Carnival season 1972, City Councilman Peter Beer delivered a famous Mardi Gras speech, in which he questioned the expense of the celebration to the city. "Should we consider a limitation on the use of city facilities," he had asked, "where there is in conjunction with that use, systematic exclusion of certain percentages of the city's taxpaying population?"

Beer, who was Jewish, said that although his religion had made him "think long and hard" about Mardi Gras, his questioning came as a member of city government, and not primarily as a Jew. "Every guy in here has been through what I've been through," he said. "You sort of experience a change in the air about a week before Mardi Gras, when a good many of your friends seem preoccupied with something they don't want to discuss. Some of us can only stand a certain amount of hurt—for lack of a better word—before we begin compromising what we're willing to give to our town."

Beer's speech caused a few ripples around the city, but did not appear to disturb a single hair on the wig of Comus. Even now, twenty years later, if oddsmakers in Las Vegas had been taking action on Dorothy Mae Taylor's antidiscrimination ordinance, even Edwin Edwards would probably not have bet on it.

Hardly anyone showed up on time for the City Council meeting on December 5 at which Dorothy Mae Taylor was to call for a vote on her proposed ordinance. When I arrived at the City Council chambers, across from City Hall, a young man was playing Christmas carols on an upright piano, and a few people were wandering about the large, high-ceilinged room. Peggy Wilson and Jackie Clarkson, the two white women on the council, were still absent when the clerk called roll.

Dorothy Mae Taylor, as head of the council, sat near the center of the dais, with Joe Giarrusso, the former police superintendent, and Lambert Boissiere, a black Creole regarded as a moderate, to her right. Giarrusso practiced a sort of New Orleans-style realpolitik. He once said, "There are more mullets than redfish, and I'm for the mullets." To Taylor's left was Johnny Jackson, her ally on many issues, and Jim Singleton, whose uptown district encompassed black and white constituencies. Singleton was a tall, distinguished-looking black man who spoke in a soft voice with a trace of a lisp. Singleton's votes were often unpredictable.

Dorothy Mae Taylor had a severe, schoolmarmish look about her, with her big glasses and her hair pulled back tightly into a bun. Taylor had generated considerable white support during her first campaign for the council, including an enthusiastic endorsement by grocery magnate John Schwegman, who had printed her face on grocery bags as a campaign booster. Her support in the white community had largely faded away, however, even before her introduction of the antidiscrimination ordinance.

When Peggy Wilson and Jackie Clarkson arrived, it was clear that there was little love lost among the three women. Taylor and Wilson, in fact, were famous for their verbal tussles. One particularly heated argument over a telephone had ended with the item in question being yanked in a tug-of-war.

Jackie Clarkson, like Taylor a young-looking grandmother, represented a district that included the French Quarter and Algiers, the old town across the river. Like Taylor, too, she looked a bit prim, with her conservative suits, reading glasses, and well-controlled bouffant coiffure. The newcomer to the council, she had proved a diligent worker, fearless on issues of neighborhood preservation, although her gay constituency in the French Quarter had found her to be disappointingly conservative on social issues.

After all the council members were seated, there seemed to be no rush to get to the business of Carnival discrimination. Heading the docket were a number of issues involving contracts for water mains, zoning variances, and the awarding of liquor licenses. Discussions on various matters of city patronage dragged on toward the lunch hour. When her fellow council members asked to postpone the vote on her antidiscrimination ordinance, claiming that they had not yet had time to fully peruse the document, Dorothy Mae Taylor agreed to a two-week delay, until December 19, for a public discussion and vote. At this stage of the game, no one but Taylor seemed eager to start yanking off the mask of frivolity that had protected Carnival from serious scrutiny.

Discrimination in Disguise

This was hardly the first time that Carnival had become something of a political hot potato. There is something inherently subversive, perhaps, or at least suggestive of covert intentions, in the act of masking. Carnival has always been a sensitive issue for governing authorities, since to forbid it risks not only the charge of authoritarianism, but of Puritanism.

After Don Antonio de Ulloa took over New Orleans for Spain during the late eighteenth century, setting up headquarters in the Cabildo on the Place d'Armes, the city's Spanish governors periodically outlawed masking. Regulation of masquerades during the Spanish period of rule in the city became somewhat arbitrary, if only sporadically enforced. There were fears at the time of social unrest and of rebellions, by slaves against their owners, or by French or American malcontents against Spanish authority. For the dons of the Cabildo, there were enough difficulties in discerning the enemies of public order without the further confusion of masking.

In 1781, for example, the syndic, a Spanish police official, reported to the Cabildo that people of color, both free and slaves, were taking advantage of their disguises, using the custom of masking as a means for committing robberies, and even worse, gaining entrance to society balls.

Following the Louisiana Purchase, the Americans permitted masking to continue for three years, until 1806, when masquerade balls and the custom of masking in the streets were suppressed. As a pretext for the crackdown, authorities cited the rumors that Aaron Burr was on his way down the Mississippi to New Orleans in a Napoleonic quest to conquer the city and use it as the base of an empire. Although Burr was intercepted at Memphis, the ban remained.

Carnival was canceled during the Civil War, and following a brief resumption during Reconstruction, it was again canceled in 1875, following another war, of sorts—this one a clash between the Crescent City White League, a paramilitary and political coalition that included most of the members of the elite Boston Club, and the metropolitan police, a largely black force then under the control of Republican carpetbaggers. Although the White League won the battle, federal troops, under the command of Lieutenant General Philip Sheridan, arrived to restore order. According to one source, "It is safe to say that every member of the Pickwick, Boston, Chalmette, and Louisiana clubs, capable of bearing arms, participated." The clubs, of course, were closely affiliated with Carnival krewes.

In 1891, an obelisk was raised on Canal Street to commemorate the "Battle of Liberty Place," as the main skirmish in New Orleans was dubbed. Liberty Monument, as the obelisk came to be known, became a sort of lightning rod for civil rights tensions in New Orleans. For blacks, the monument symbolized the era of repressive Jim Crow laws. David Duke had once marched around it, shouting, "white power," and white supremacy groups had continued to use it as a rallying point. The uprising, according to one historian, had been romanticized by many white New Orleanians as part of a "white mythology of redemption."

Dutch Morial had tried to have the monument removed when he was mayor, and in 1989, prior to Sidney Barthelemy's reelection campaign, the obelisk was removed from Canal Street, ostensibly in order to facilitate the flow of traffic.

Except for a boycott of Mardi Gras in 1961 by the black community, following a harrowing period of school integration, the Civil Rights era in New Orleans largely bypassed Carnival. Blacks had developed their own Carnival hierarchy and their own distinctive Carnival traditions, including Zulu, the parade over which Louis

Armstrong had reigned, and the Mardi Gras Indians. Before the Interstate cut a swath through Tremé, taking with it the trees and the open grassy space of the neutral ground, blacks celebrated Mardi Gras along Claiborne Avenue, seldom venturing across the few blocks separating them from the festivities in the French Quarter or Canal Street near the Boston Club, where they were in danger of being harassed. For the most part, they had chosen to pitch their battles against discrimination elsewhere, although there were periodic rumors in uptown circles that protestors along the parade routes had armed themselves with knives and rocks.

Often, in fact, it was not local critics, but out-of-town reporters who pointed out the obvious discrimination practiced in the city under the guise of Mardi Gras, and it was more often the krewes' policy of excluding Jews than that of excluding blacks that came under fire.

In 1967, a Catholic newspaper was the first to publish the scoop that the navy had advised sailors who were participating in Mardi Gras that they should not protest the policy of discrimination against blacks, Jews, and Italians followed by many of the Carnival krewes. A memorandum to that effect had been sent to officers of five ships designated to represent the navy at Mardi Gras, including the fleet's flagship, the USS *Yosemite*, and the USS *Guadalcanal*, an amphibious assault ship. The memo stated, "Whether or not this meets with your personal or official approval, it is the way things are, and we have to go along with it."

The following year, Calvin Trillin wrote a brief, stinging article for *The New Yorker* reporting on the provincialism and hypocrisy that passed as Carnival tradition in New Orleans. Trillin noted that some prominent Jews left town during Carnival, and he linked the policy of discrimination by Carnival krewes with that of the city's elite men's clubs—a policy that yoked New Orleans and Carnival not with Paris and Rome but with small-town middle America.

Observed Trillin, "It is impossible to separate the fact that no New Orleans Jew is permitted to attend the Comus ball on Mardi Gras Night from the fact that no New Orleans Jew is permitted to enter the Boston Club for a business lunch at any time—one of the peculiarly American features of Mardi Gras lending weight to the theory that underneath that gay Carnival costume beats the heart of Zenith, Ohio."

The religious argument for excluding Jews from a rite sanctioned by the Catholic Church didn't hold water, since, as Mark Twain observed of Carnival before the turn of the century, "The religious element has pretty well been knocked out of it." And as for the Boston Club, the only rites followed there were playing cards, drinking, and passing around copies of the *Times-Picayune*.

Carnival captains could have pointed to their policy of equal-opportunity discrimination, since it was not only local Jews, blacks, and Italians who were excluded, but out-of-town bigwigs as well. Collecting apocryphal stories of bigshots from New York or Hollywood who were said to have been snubbed by Comus has been one of the favorite pastimes of Carnival observers.

In 1966, Lynda Bird Johnson, the eldest daughter of President Lyndon Johnson, was invited to attend the Comus ball, to the dismay of some krewe members, although her invitation was not for the coveted call-out section, which would have entitled her to sit on the main floor, but for the spectators' balcony. The trouble came when the Secret Service asked for a list of the krewe's members in order to conduct a security check. The captain of Comus refused, demanding in turn the names of the Secret Service agents who would be accompanying Lynda Bird so they could be put through the same scrutiny as other potential guests.

Dr. Seuss has also been mentioned as a Carnival *refusé*, although there is some evidence that his failure to attend a certain ball resulted from his own fatigue rather than last-minute prejudice.

According to Monroe Edmundson, an anthropologist at Tulane University, this upholding of standards not recognized anywhere else in the country was a means for old-line society in New Orleans to maintain its status as a "stable provincial society," thriving as an island of exclusivity well outside the aegis of New York, Washington, D.C., or California.

There were times, of course, when the exception proved the rule. In 1969, the first year that the new Krewe of Bacchus, whose founding members were Irish, Italian, and Jewish, rolled down the streets on the Sunday night before Mardi Gras, the Boston Club on Canal Street, where the Rex parade stopped to toast its queen, remained dark, its viewing stands empty. A few years later, however, when club members learned that the king of Bacchus was to be Bob Hope, the club invited Bacchus to stop at the club for a toast on its way down Canal Street.

There were a number of historical ironies involved in the exclusion of Jews from many Carnival krewes, beginning with the fact that the first ruler of Rex, the krewe begun in 1872, was a Jewish accountant named Louis Solomon, who had been active in raising funds for the parade that year, and another prominent Jewish citizen, Harry Isaacson, served as captain of Rex from 1889 to 1904. Rex, in fact, still includes Jewish members, although customarily not in the "inner circle" of captain and lieutenants.

Over the years, the city's small Jewish population has exerted a considerable impact on the city. Jewish names appear on the mastheads of top law firms and businesses, on streets, hospitals, schools, and other landmarks. Judah P. Benjamin, who immigrated to New Orleans in 1826, was elected to the Senate and later became secretary of war in the cabinet of the Confederacy.

The tradition of Jewish philanthropy and civic involvement in New Orleans began with the city's first prominent Jewish merchant, Judah Touro, a former Bostonian who settled in New Orleans in 1802 and who served valiantly under Andrew Jackson in the War of 1812. For a number of years, Touro was known as the only Jew in New Orleans. As late as 1826, the Jewish population of the entire state was estimated at only about one hundred.

At the turn of the century, when Carnival krewes were using the Atheneum, the hall built by the Young Men's Hebrew Association, as the locale for their masquerade balls, civic leaders were boasting of the city's prominent Jewish population. Jews play a prominent role, for example, in a book published in 1903 by the *Picayune* newspaper, touting New Orleans as a pleasant place to live and do business. In a section of the book listing the city's social attractions, the writer notes that the "principal social clubs proper are the Boston, the Pickwick, the Chess and Checkers and the Harmony of the Jewish residents, this last named sumptuously housed in the fashionable region of upper St.

Charles Avenue." The writer continued, "In the Young Men's Christian Association and Young Men's Hebrew Association, the city has exponents of its philanthropic spirit."

By 1939, however, Perry Young, the Texas-born chronicler of Comus, was articulating the tortuous reasoning behind the exclusion of Jews from top Carnival organizations. In his odd little book, *Carnival and Mardi Gras in New Orleans*, Young observed, "Prominent Jews, gentlemen of prestige and position, enjoying the esteem of the community, make strong issue, persistent and increasing, of the point, as they see it, that their race, or religion, is excluded from Carnival." Young countered, "Of carnival business the Jews get their full share—they control Canal Street, where carnival merchandise is bought." He noted, too, that Jews were admitted to two Carnival organizations, Rex and Hermes. The Mystic Club, he noted, which was in fact organized to remedy the "supposed injustice to the Jews," could not recruit enough Jews, and the less liberal minded Christians who were recruited soon voted to eliminate the small number of Jews who signed up. (The club currently includes Jewish members.)

In a final twist of snobbish casuistry, Young noted that it was, after all, not the finer Jewish families who made an issue of their exclusion: "Those few whose importunities have fortified the intolerance of carnival societies are never of the old-established and long-esteemed Jewish families of Louisiana."

A few leading uptown families, who were entwined in the Carnival hierarchy, were rumored, in fact, to be of Jewish heritage, although they had long since become Episcopalians or Christian Scientists. During the Civil Rights era of the 1960s, when Judge John Minor Wisdom, of the Fifth Circuit Court of Appeals, became extremely unpopular in certain circles, rumors began to swirl of his Jewish heritage. Judge Wisdom, however, a member of the Boston Club and of the krewes of Comus and Momus, diffused the rumors by acknowledging publicly that he could indeed claim a Jewish ancestor.

The arbitrary nature of Carnival snobbery cut across family boundaries. My friend Tina Freeman had reigned as queen of Carnival, and both her father and grandfather had ruled as Rex. Tina's mother, Montine, was one of the pillars of uptown society. But Tina's aunt, Rosa Freeman Keller, a strong-minded woman active in civil rights causes, who had married a Jew, found certain doors shut. Her husband had never been invited to join a Carnival krewe.

Another of my friends, who was half Jewish and half Catholic, married a scion of a leading uptown family, and although she herself was welcome at various Carnival balls, her sister, whose last name aroused suspicion in a krewe invitation committee, was not. "Is this a Jewish girl?" a committee member had inquired. My friend's husband resigned from the krewe in protest.

Most Jews, in fact, chose not to leave town during Carnival, nor did they make an issue of their exclusion. Trillin's article and others like it had inspired more embarrassment than indignation. The noted philanthropists Edgar and Edith Stern, for example, who had funded a new wing of the New Orleans Museum of Art, and whose home in Metairie, Longue Vue, was one of the great estates in the city, were known to have resented the off-limits nature of uptown Mardi Gras, as Edith Stern's biographer later noted, but would have regarded an active protest as unseemly.

The frustration of cultured New Orleanians who were fed up with the archaic snobbishness and general silliness of uptown Carnival was articulated by Ben C. Toledano, the bookish, unsuccessful Republican candidate for mayor, whose family had been in the city since 1719. Before leaving town, he gave an embittered interview, in which he observed, "Men plan the social season, which takes up six months of the year in New Orleans. They sit around and drink and play gin rummy and discuss for hours why some girl should or should not be allowed to debut. They could better spend their time and energy solving some dirty problems." It was not just the matter of priorities that disturbed Toledano, but the oddly joyless nature of the Carnival balls. "They plan the balls and then do not enjoy them," he said.

Hippie Orgies and Al Hirt's Lip

Prior to Dorothy Mae Taylor's ordinance, the greatest threat to Carnival, at least according to certain civic leaders, was not local dissent, but the invasion of the city by hippies. It seemed that every counterculture type in the country had seen the movie *Easy Rider* and decided to come to New Orleans during Carnival to trip out in the cemeteries, just like Peter Fonda. During the late sixties, would-be merry pranksters descended on New Orleans for an endless party. Hippies were everywhere, camped out in parks, thronging at Pontchartrain Beach, crowding the stoops of the French Quarter, swilling LSD-laced rotgut from vinyl wineskins.

In theory, Mardi Gras was the perfect venue for the playing out of the festive principle professed by counterculture gurus. Most New Orleanians, however, were less than enthusiastic about the blissed-out, panhandling hordes who arrived with their own notions of how to indulge the senses. In retrospect, New Orleans and its characters were surreal enough without taking mind-altering drugs.

Carnival, as it had evolved in New Orleans, was the province of subcultures rather than countercultures. It was the showing forth of cliques and clubs, of certain circles within circles: the uptown white community, the black Creole community, the working-class black community, the gay community. What's more, for all its vaunted wildness, it depended on a certain order. Even in the French Quarter, pageants and parades, with their predestined routes and familiar rites, created a structure of sorts to the madness. On Mardi Gras day, Saint Charles Avenue, the parade route that linked uptown and downtown, was far closer to a family outing than an orgy. There was a certain wholesomeness to the custom of entire families, down to toddlers and infants, dressing up in matching costumes—devils, turtles, insects, gorillas.

For most New Orleanians, Carnival was more the illusion of chaos and license than the real thing. And that fragile illusion appeared to be threatened by the invading hordes, who weren't even contributing to the city's coffers.

Police and politicians promised a crackdown, and in 1970, the Grateful Dead were busted, an experience the band later immortalized in their song "Truckin'," with its rueful recounting of being "set up like a bowling pin" and "busted on Bourbon Street." That year, Mayor Vic Schiro, who had defeated uptown candidate Adrian Duplantier, the last blueblood politician in New Orleans, threatened to close down Carnival to prevent out-of-town riffraff from inundating the city.

On the Saturday before Mardi Gras, police arrested more than a hundred hippies at the riverfront near Jackson Square, charging them with vagrancy, and followed up on the day before Mardi Gras by arresting another hundred or so at the lakefront. Joe Giarrusso, who was then serving as police superintendent, and who referred to street people as "the element," complained that they were there to "really have an orgy," in contrast, presumably, with the more decorous observances of Carnival by local citizenry.

As though in fulfillment of Vic Schiro's dire prophecies, trumpet player Al Hirt, who was riding on a float in the Bacchus parade, suffered an injury to his lip, which he claimed was caused by a brick hurled at him by a spectator. Since that time, Al Hirt's lip has become a symbol for the potential violence lurking in the Carnival crowds. Hirt's lip took on yet another dimension as he began to complain about the decline of the city in ensuing years. Business at his Bourbon Street club did not thrive as before, and eventually he left town. He returned in 1991 to make a comeback on Bourbon Street and was welcomed like the prodigal son.

As for the hippie invasion, it had been a trumped-up fear, as had so many previous threats to Carnival. A Mardi Gras Coalition was formed, composed of city officials, liberals, and local hippies, in order to provide health care, legal advice, and places to stay for street people. What's more, the hippie phenomenon was considerably more short-lived than the indigenous culture of Carnival, and the counterculture became yet another phase that Carnival had survived and absorbed.

Except for a police strike that canceled official Mardi Gras in 1979, Carnival did not become a political issue again until 1988, when a New York City ordinance forbidding discrimination in the city's luncheon and athletic clubs on the basis of race or gender was upheld by the Supreme Court. At the behest of Dorothy Mae Taylor, Assistant City Attorney Bruce Nacchari drew up a similar ordinance for New Orleans. Taylor had been spurred on by an influential group of civic-minded women called the Committee of 21, whose well-connected membership included the formidable Rosa Keller. The City Council sponsored hearings to discuss the ordinance, but they were sparsely attended, and the matter was dropped.

Now, four years later, Bruce Nacchari, at Taylor's bidding, had dusted off that obscure ordinance, added more teeth to it, and mustered a new assault on old-line Carnival.

6

Royal Predictions

It would be a mistake to base the legal assault against Carnival discrimination on the theory of unfair economic exclusion, according to a friend, whom I'll call Judy, whose opinion in these matters I respected. "Those most involved in Carnival are the ones who don't have anything else going," she declared, pooh-poohing the notion of the Carnival elite as the movers and shakers in the city. Judy had married into New Orleans society, and she worked at a job that involved close contact with debutantes, but she regarded the social whirl with a rather cynical eye.

I had driven uptown after the City Council meeting to meet Judy for lunch at the Café Atchafalaya, a watering hole for uptown society women. I intended to pump her about Carnival secrets—in particular, the likely candidates to reign as queen of Comus and queen of Rex, the latter more properly referred to as queen of Carnival.

One of the principal functions of the uptown Carnival clubs is to allow members to present their debutante daughters in grand style at a Carnival ball, where the young women may serve as maids in the royal court, or if their fathers wield enough clout in the krewe, as queen. In the old-line Carnival hierarchy, Comus and Rex reign supreme, while Proteus and Momus, the other old-line parading organizations, rank near the top of the pyramid. Also in the top tier are a handful of elite nonparading krewes, who present their courts and tableaux at balls, including the Twelfth Night Revelers, whose ball opens the season, and the Atlanteans, the smallest of the krewes.

The courtly side of Carnival is fueled by secrecy, particularly by the convention of shielding the identities of the kings and queens of the top Carnival krewes every year until the last possible moment. In some cases, even the queen herself is kept in the dark until the time comes for a dress fitting or a lesson in scepter-waving protocol.

"You can make book on my predictions," Judy once told me, and I was going to call her bluff. Judy had recently moved uptown after finally giving up on life in the Quarter. The termites and the thieves finally got to her, she said. One evening, her ceiling had caved in, and that night, a cat burglar had broken into her apartment from the back balcony, after hopping from rooftop to rooftop.

As we sat down in the café, Judy greeted a group of well-dressed women at a nearby table. I recognized a slender, elegant woman as the wife of the captain of Rex and former president of the Junior League. Learning that I had just come from the City Council meeting, she inquired what had happened and seemed relieved that the vote on the ordinance had been postponed.

These were the kind of women, with their perfectly coiffed hair and gleaming manicures, their bright silk print dresses, and their perfectly matched shoes and purses, who always made me feel as though I had a run in my stocking, and that I had left the price tag on my hat, like Minnie Pearl. I thought of them as iron butterflies, particularly those who aged regally into grandes dames.

Women from these circles tend to follow certain preordained patterns, proceeding from the right private schools—McGehee's if they were Protestant, Sacred Heart if they were Catholic—to Sophie Newcomb College in New Orleans or one of those small, atmospheric Southern colleges, like the University of the South in Sewanee, Tennessee, that no one in the North has heard of. In the old days, they abandoned their studies during their sophomore year in order to make their debuts. As Judy put it, "You went to McGehee's and Newcomb and piddled around, made your debut, and rarely did you go back to finish. A lot of women who are divorced or widowed now are finding out what a stupid thing this was."

Although New Orleans had experienced something of a revival of the debutante tradition after a hiatus during the sixties, when feminism and protests against the "Establishment" had made the tradition of coming out unfashionable, young women were much less likely now, Judy observed, to let their debut interfere with their education. Some of the debs, she said, were going into nursing or teaching. "Of course," she said, "a lot of them are still airheads." Recently, she said, a leading debutante had listed shopping as her primary hobby.

The number of debutantes from old-line families had begun to dwindle, not from disillusionment, but from attrition. One demographic study had revealed that out of a total of two hundred thousand households surveyed in Orleans Parish, the number that included a family with one or more white daughters, age fifteen or under, was twenty-five thousand.

Although some uptown doyennes claimed that standards for choosing debutantes had not declined, one dowager from an old-line family had picked up a recent copy of the debutante section of the *Times-Picayune* and asked, in a puzzled tone, "Who *are* these girls?"

It was just three years earlier that the *Times-Picayune* had begun including black debutantes in its annual debutante sections. Of the eighty debs included, thirty were black. A group of white matrons, said to be shocked by the inclusion of black faces in the section, had begun publishing their own society bulletin, in which they could be as selective as they pleased. It had made no difference to the matrons that the black debutantes who appeared in the *Picayune* had as much claim to being rare birds as their own daughters and granddaughters. Most of the black debs were being presented by elite black Creole Carnival organizations that were at least as selective—and protective of their gene pool—as those of the whites.

Yet another challenge to the old debutante system was developing in an unexpected place—in an uptown family, where love had prevailed over tradition. A childless couple from fine uptown stock had adopted two little girls, whose light skin as infants had gradually darkened, until it had become apparent that the girls were of African-American heritage. The adoptive parents, however, who adored the girls, simply ignored the changing skin tones. As one uptown observer described the situation, "Ten or fifteen years from now, when the time comes for them to make their debuts, the current generation of elders will be gone, and for the next generation, it will be a close call."

*   *   *

On the surface, the elite Carnival balls, with their elaborate coronation ceremonies, appeared to be for the benefit of the young women who were honored in the court. Perry Young had proclaimed, "Consider, reader, that when she has finished her season in New Orleans that young lady knows more of courts and regal ways than princesses of the purple."

Carnival, wrote Young, is "Elysium for debutantes, and deliverance of their progenitors. . . . Carnival does everything that needs doing for every debutante, and with such delicacy, such splendor, such acclamation as no other mediary could approach . . . A few hundred men, generously, known only under aggregates and fanciful aliases, and for their own joy in seeing others happy, build thirty to forty fairyland palaces a year."

The reality, of course, is that the debutante system, unlike that of other cities, is determined by the patriarchs rather than the matriarchs of uptown society. "The social system of New Orleans is run by men," observed Young. "Women have their place, dowagers their say, but when there's justice to be done, carnival defies the female fiats. It is generous and adamant and male."

The selection process for Carnival courts as well as for membership in old-line krewes is about as far from the democratic process as you can get in America. It involves cronyism, secrecy, nepotism, blackballing, and subjective judgments. One never asks to become a member, much less dares to lobby on behalf of one's daughter to be selected queen. These things are supposed to happen as though by divine right. The notion of actually campaigning for honorary posts, as do members of Zulu, the leading black club, would be considered unseemly by the aristocrats of Comus.

Historically, there have been waiting lists for membership in the top old-line krewes, whose membership rosters vary from about 180, for the Atlanteans, a nonparading krewe, to between 400 and 500 for Rex. When openings come up, the most important consideration for membership is kinship. If your father is a member, you are a virtual shoo-in. Your name is posted as a prospective member, and the membership at large is free to make comments, positive and negative, which are submitted to the membership committee. Final judgments, however, in this as in all matters, are up to the krewe captain.

I once asked a former captain of the Krewe of Comus about the importance of personality in choosing members, and he replied that "conviviality" was important, since no one wanted a "sourpuss" hanging around the club.

As for the choice of queens, again, bloodlines are far more important than looks or personality. There are few teenaged girls who can't be made to look comely in a white gown.

Although Sally Reeves and a number of other women I interviewed believe that the male domination of Carnival will eventually cause the withering away of old-line Carnival, it is that domination, according to Judy, that has allowed the debutante system and Carnival itself to last so many generations. "It's survived all these years," she said, "because men control it. It's an honor to the man—that's what perpetuates it—not the girls. It's strictly payback. They use the word 'honor' when they talk about choosing a queen or the court—but it's honoring the father's servitude or longevity in the club."

Her own daughter, Judy said, "didn't want any part" of making a debut. But Judy had told her, "You do this for your grandfather; he has earned this honor. It's not up to you to decide.

"I think it's frivolous, but who am I to say this is wrong?"

Carnival had also managed to survive all these years, she theorized, because "no one wants to be known as the one who closed the show. Nobody wants to be the ones to close down Comus. There's always somebody next year to be honored." She shook her head ruefully, adding, "That's why we reluctantly go on."

Before she left, I asked Judy to reveal her winter-book favorites for queen of Carnival and of Comus. To reign over Rex, she chose Elizabeth Kelleher, whose grandfather, Harry Kelleher, had ruled as Rex in 1965, at a time when Carnival captains and kings also tended to preside over the city's civic and economic affairs. Elizabeth's mother had reigned as queen of Comus. Judy described Kelleher, who was currently enrolled at Sewanee, as a rather "proper, dignified girl." For queen of Comus, Judy selected Julie Learned Phelps, from the publishing family that owned the *Times-Picayune*. Julie, she said, was a "free spirit" with a fun-loving nature.

Notions of Cross-Dressing at the Napoleon House

After lunch with Judy, I met an old friend, whom I'll call the Duenna, in deference to his Mardi Gras alter ego, for drinks at the Napoleon House and a conversation about another group of iron butterflies who live in New Orleans. An extravagantly gifted artist and writer with a savage wit, the Duenna had chosen to remain in New Orleans and lavish his talents on a small gay-oriented weekly, a newsy, gossipy paper full of barbed satire and startling personal ads. If Judy was the diviner of uptown secrets, the Duenna was the unraveler of downtown mysteries.

The Duenna, who was built like a linebacker gone to seed, chose as his everyday look the male equivalent of the frumpy wallflower, the girl who defiantly emphasizes her most unattractive qualities. With his long, unkempt hair, softly rounded face, and intimidating body, he could look cuddly or forbidding, depending on his mood. On Mardi Gras day, he turned into the Duenna, the terrifying chaperon, in tattered black lace and veil, covered with cobwebs. Josephine had taken an extraordinary photograph of the Duenna, with his dog, Lady Ottoline, that resembled a Velásquez portrait.

He said that this year, however, would be the last for the Duenna disguise unless he could find a seamstress to let the seams of the dress out or locate a better corset.

Today he was wearing an oversized sweatshirt from Miss Porter's Girls School, and he looked endearing in spite of himself.

We were discussing the theatrical nature of life in New Orleans. "You never know what people are," said the Duenna. "People are acting out all the time. I've always thought of New Orleans as an artificial-looking place. It looks phony, like a Hollywood house on the studio lot. I can't think of a place more given to self-love and self-dramatization than New Orleans. It's like being buried alive in Sarah Bernhardt's dressing room. There is an element of flourish to almost everything. It's not the same acting out as in New York or Los

Angeles. Here, you can almost see the footlights and the baffles on the side of the proscenium arch."

Gay culture in New Orleans, in particular, might be described as a sort of permanent Carnival culture—or what writer Frank Browning has called the "culture of desire": a never-ending round of parties, parades, and pageants. The theatrical quality of New Orleans, said the Duenna, had been a magnet for drag queens. "All these street queens you see—we seem to have more drag queens than anywhere. It's a tremendous magnet. They come from the country, small towns, big cities to recreate themselves. Most of them don't have illusions of the Folies-Bergère—they're content to wear a blouse and lipstick and hang out all day. They think of themselves as the cast of *Steel Magnolias.*"

Edmund White, in his book of travel, *States of Desire*, had offered a plausible explanation for the popularity of drag in the South. Not only did drag "serve as a means of expressing a distinct identity within the straight world," he suggested, it also offered a certain glamour. "Oppressed people," wrote White, "often dream of another world, one kinder, more tolerant, more soignée . . . Moreover, Southern women, if I may be forgiven a bias, have always seemed to me more interesting than their husbands. The women are the readers, the dreamers, the church workers, the guardians of 'culture.' Gays, as outsiders, are drawn toward these feminine embodiments of warmth, fantasy and civilization. Drags, by adding yet another layer of artifice, boost both sides of the message: the make-believe of the form; and the hurt and anger of the content."

Chromosomes alone couldn't have accounted for the bizarre varieties of life, gay and straight, that flourished in New Orleans. The city was a perpetual stage, for which you were always rehearsing and working on your costume or your persona.

"People in New Orleans are always in the process of creating a new persona or honing and adding facets to what they have," said the Duenna. "People I know really well—I'm always being surprised by something that seems completely off the wall. I have elaborate theories or fantasies about people I know, but I'm still surprised."

Although the Duenna's newspaper did not engage in "outing," it was widely known that a number of socially prominent men in New Orleans were still in the closet or living double lives.

The "uptown marriage" was another of the poorly kept secrets of New Orleans society and may have been one of the reasons so many of the iron butterflies of the Garden District had been secret alcoholics. In the "uptown marriage," a gay or bisexual man came up through the customary social whirl, got married, and raised a family, but lived a shadow life in the French Quarter. Just as Creoles in the nineteenth century had maintained black concubines in apartments in the Quarter, in a system known as *plaçage*, gay uptown men were known to keep male lovers in apartments in the Quarter or in Faubourg Marigny, just across Esplanade Avenue. I knew of two men prominent in Carnival whose downtown lovers had committed suicide.

Category Crisis

When I lived in the French Quarter, I had been surrounded by sexual ambiguity and every shade of gender identity. If the presence of cross-dressing in a culture indicates cultural anxiety and a "category crisis," as literary critic Marjorie Gerber has suggested in her book, *Vested Interests*, then New Orleans, with its permeable boundaries and tireless masking, was a case study in permanent cultural panic. Things were hardly ever as they seemed, as the Duenna pointed out, nor were there any absolutes—of black or white, yes or no, male or female.

In retrospect, New Orleans during the 1970s was an extraordinarily confusing time and place to be a woman, particularly a feminist, in the early days of the women's liberation movement. The feminists I knew were talking about getting rid of the stereotyped notions of femininity, while many of the drag queens and transsexuals I met had taken on the personae of bimbos or femmes fatales. It was though they were grabbing up all the fuss and frippery we were so eager to cast off, like hand-me-downs that would have to make do until they could create personae of their own.

My friend Wilma, who ran a Haitian art gallery, had been one of the first transsexuals ever to undergo a sex-change operation. Born a stocky man, Wilma was now a stocky woman who clumped around in low pumps and frumpy housewife dresses. Although Wilma had been a successful engineer in her previous life, she said she had begun to feel helpless around the house almost as soon as she came out of the anesthesia, and now had trouble even hammering a nail into the wall.

Wilma told me once that she didn't think psychiatrists had been able to come up with an adequate explanation for her need to transform herself. "I don't think of my scene as an illusion," she said. "I don't think of feminine clothes as a prop. I think of them as a necessity." She said she felt that her femininity was a "spiritual thing, from the inner soul, not the flesh-and-blood image." She had made a deliberate choice not to get silicone implants or hormones. "After all, I'm not on stage," she said. "But then all the world's my stage."

Things had gotten particularly confusing for Wilma when she later fell in love with a woman.

Wilma introduced me to the French Quarter demimonde, including the two flashiest strippers on Bourbon Street. One was Sandra Sexton, a Latin-American bombshell who headlined her own club, the 500 Club, with huge posters advertising the wonders of her silicone-inflated body, and the other, Bobbe Sinclair, a veteran who specialized in a devil-and-virgin act. As it happened, Sandra Sexton was a transsexual, and Bobbe was a drag queen who had been posing as a woman for twenty-six years. After so many years of taking female hormones, which caused her manhood to atrophy, Bobbe was able to strip down to a G-string with no one the wiser. Bobbe lived with a straight taxi driver and his young son in a tract house in New Orleans East.

Bobbe, who ran away to the carnival—the kind with a midway— at age fourteen, had worked the "exotic" club circuit from Chicago to San Antonio, where she had often been busted, before arriving in New Orleans and Carnival with a capital C. She loved to reminisce about the "golden days" of burlesque, when the Opera House on Bourbon Street had three different shows every night, Louis Prima owned the 500 Club, and the Monkey Club and French Casino were still on Canal Street. This was the Bourbon Street of Blaze Starr, the headliner at the Sho-Bar who had so enthralled Earl Long, sometime governor of Louisiana and periodically institutionalized nutcase.

93

Strippers earned names for themselves in those days with an assortment of gimmicks. One night, over a glass of cold duck, her favorite drink, Bobbe tried to list all the legends for me. "There was Von Ray, the Texas Tornado, who used to sit on flagpoles and ride a pony down Bourbon Street in her cowgirl outfit. Yvette Dare used to have macaws remove her clothes. The secret was the pieces of tomato stuck on the snaps. Evelyn West called herself the $50,000 Treasure Chest and insured her boobs with Lloyd's of London. Of course, she only paid the first premium. Linda Brigette was a big success, but physically, she was just a midget with big boobs. And that champagne glass she used in her act wasn't original. She bought it from a queen who designed it to wear when he went to a Mardi Gras ball dressed as a shrimp cocktail.

"There was Velvet Night, known as the Heavenly Body; Patti White, the schoolteacher; Lonnie Young, the Venus in Furs; Lana Richards, who did the Girl and the Swan act; Lili Christine, the Cat Girl; Baby Doll, who weighed three hundred pounds; Zorita the Snake Dancer; Shalomar, with the face of Liz Taylor and the body of Frankenstein; and TNT Red, who could heat up anybody's blood."

Bobbe, in retrospect, had been perhaps the greatest illusionist of them all, keeping everyone fooled about her gender for so many years. She looked down on mere female impersonators, and would have cackled at the current politically correct term, "gender illusionists."

Impersonators, in fact, had not even been allowed into the French Quarter until 1970. For all the passion in New Orleans for masking, there was actually a law on the books forbidding masks and disguises, except on Mardi Gras day, that was originally used to control the Ku Klux Klan, but which the police used as grounds to arrest any man wearing feminine attire. Men were arrested under this ordinance for offenses ranging from sporting conspicuously arched eyebrows to wearing pants that zipped on the side. One transsexual was arrested so often she had to carry a letter from her doctor attesting to her medical and legal sex change. (In Louisiana a transsexual can apply through district court for a change of sex status on the birth certificate.)

The producer of the first drag show in the Quarter told me that his attempt to introduce an impersonator show at the Powder Puff on Decatur Street was closed down by the police despite people lined up on the sidewalk waiting to get in. The show, which became known as the My-O-My, moved outside Orleans Parish to three different locations. The My-O-My club burned down twice and was washed away once by a hurricane. The performers were continually harassed by the police.

During the late 1960s, veteran Bourbon Street club owner Larry LaMarca consulted his lawyer, who determined there was no actual law against female impersonators, and turned his show at the Gunga Den on Bourbon Street from a typical strip show into an "all-boy impersonator revue." Since then, drag shows have become a commonplace in New Orleans, onstage and off.

There hadn't been many happy endings in those pioneering days, though, for the transsexuals and strippers I knew, even before the advent of AIDS. Bobbe Sinclair had developed breast cancer, a result, she was convinced, of all the silicone implants and hormone injections she had endured in her quest to look feminine.

One of the saddest stories involved Perry Desmond, a transsexual and former impersonator who had repented not only of the sex-change operation but of all his former sins and had become a preacher on Bourbon Street. He would stand on a street corner and pass out little cartoon books titled "Living in Drag is Really a Drag: The True Story of Perry Desmond, once Billed as the South's Most Beautiful Boy."

Perry had told me that as a woman, he had wanted "what the average woman wants—love, affection, nice clothes, money and property, a swimming pool outside the door." But he had also been "chock full of vanity, pride and ego." He described his life as an impersonator as a "merry-go-round you can never get off." He became a silicone addict, he said. "You're never satisfied; you always want more." But he began to suffer in his female identity the same slow crisis any woman dependent on her looks suffers: aging and the loss of beauty. The silicone began to slip. When Perry would take a warm bath, he could feel it turning to jelly and sliding around like a lava flow under his skin.

Nevertheless, Perry would wind up his sad story with scrapbooks open on his lap, pointing wistfully to pictures of himself as Jayne Meadows, as Ann Sothern, as Rosalind Russell, and I always felt that he had been happiest in those guises.

The odd thing about stripping and cross-dressing was the way they reversed the usual notions of being clothed and being naked. It seemed that the more the Bourbon Street strippers took off, the less they actually revealed of themselves, while the cross-dressers bared their souls by dressing up. The clothes they donned revealed their deepest selves—the hidden selves that could not be revealed when they were naked. Perhaps they felt, as Baudelaire did, that one must be adorned to be adored.

The Duenna said that on the fringes, sexual behavior in the New Orleans gay community, which had become more cautious and conservative with the AIDS scare, was getting destructive again, that there were more hard drugs involved, and shooting galleries down near Frenchman Street. "I guess it has to do with self-hatred," he said. "Of course, that's not true of me. I love myself."

The Duenna sighed. "Still, there are times when some of us would just like to be drag queens and sink into the subculture."

7

Enchantments at the Comus Den

It was another one of those geopsychic coincidences peculiar to New Orleans that the theme for this year's Comus parade was to be "Enchantments and Metamorphoses." Changes and transformations seemed to be in the air.

There was always something eerie and phantomlike about the spectacle of Comus, the floats rumbling down Saint Charles to Canal Street at twilight on Mardi Gras day, the faces of the masked riders lit by the fires of the flambeaux, the naphtha-powered torches, carried by strong black men who danced in the streets with their flaming burdens like circus performers. To bystanders on the sidewalk, the parade seemed to materialize out of nowhere in the glow of the flambeaux and then to disappear without a trace.

The parade appears as a recurring demonic motif in novelist Anne Rice's *The Witching Hour*, hinting at a terrifying memory from the hero's childhood. The novel concludes on Mardi Gras night with the Comus parade, "ghastly, ghastly as it had been in childhood, these mammoth quivering papier-mâché structures rolling slowly down the avenue beyond the heads of the jubilant crowds."

Sally Reeves once described the parade as "a lovely after-dinner drink at the end of the day." As Comus had gotten smaller and more refined over the years, it had gotten quieter, too. The krewe had had difficulty recruiting marching bands from the city's mostly black public schools. "Comus is vestigial now," observed Sally. "You'd better not wink while you're standing on the neutral ground, or you'll miss it. You'd better not go back inside the house to get a drink at dusk, or you'll be too late."

Last year, Dalt and I had rushed over to Rampart Street to watch

97

the parade as it wound up near the Auditorium, and all we'd been able to make out through the crowds was the glimmer of a huge spiderweb on the last float, as it seemed to vanish into the twilight.

The Demon Actors

From the beginning, the Krewe of Comus seemed particularly fond of demonic or esoteric themes. The first Comus parade in 1857 had been titled "The Demon Actors in Milton's Paradise Lost." There had been only two floats that year, accompanied by street mummers in devilish guise. As Perry Young had described it, "They came! Led by the festive Comus, high on his royal seat, and Satan, high on a hill, far blazing as a mount, with pyramids and towers from diamond quarries hewn, and rocks of gold: the palace of great Lucifer, followed by devils large and devils small, devils with horns and devils with tails, and devils without."

New Orleanians had never seen anything quite like it, and the procession set the tone and pattern for succeeding Carnival parades, bringing the notion of formal theatrical pageantry to the celebration of Carnival in the streets and ballrooms of New Orleans. Comus had created, as Perry Young proclaimed, "The first torchlight scenic procession of New Orleans, a revolution in street pageantry, a revelation in artistic effects."

Before the advent of Comus, the celebration of Carnival had declined in New Orleans. Shrove Tuesday, or Mardi Gras, had been observed off and on since the French arrived in Louisiana, mostly in the form of masquerade balls and processions of carriages. During the 1850s, these balls, which took place during a yellow-fever epidemic, had a quality of frantic gaiety that must have resembled Poe's "Masque of the Red Death."

One year, the conservative newspaper, the *Bee*, lamented the decline of Carnival with a brief description of the events of Mardi Gras day: "The detail is very short. Boys with bags of flour paraded the streets, and painted Jezabels exhibited themselves in public carriages, and that is about all. We are not sorry that this miserable annual exhibition is rapidly becoming extinct. It originated in a barbarous age, and is worthy of only such."

Another paper, the Creole-influenced *Daily Delta*, blamed the decline on the invasion of New Orleans by non-Catholic Anglo-Saxons: "The march of AngloSaxon innovation has made sad havoc with the time-honored customs of our ancient population." Similarly, the *Crescent News* lamented the decline of the ancien régime and the growing dominance of irreverent invaders: "In the early days of our city, when it was peopled by a Catholic community who understood and could appreciate the observance of the day, Mardi Gras was a season of striking and memorable peculiarities. Then people of elevated rank took part in the processions, long lines of carriages, representing every nationality and filing through the streets in glittering throngs, gave to the thoroughfares a gala day brilliancy . . . But now the aspect of things has changed. Our population is not what it was. The old regime is no more. It has fallen into the list of forgotten things, and the sway over manners has passed to the swine-eating Saxon."

The great irony was that it was Anglo-Saxons who staged a Carnival coup with their infernal parade, ruled by Comus and Satan, in 1857, sweeping all before them. They took Carnival as their own in that one extraordinary night and shaped it into its current form: the parade, the masked tableau, the ball, and the banquet, all united by a whimsical theme. According to a centennial brochure issued by Comus in 1957, the krewe "brought to the Carnival of New Orleans the refinement which it lacked before, lending tone and dignity to the festivities."

The leading lights of the new Carnival club were a group of young men from Mobile, Alabama, who had initiated a Carnival group there known as the Cowbellions, in reference to the cowbells rung by the group and its spirit of rebellion. None of the original six who issued the first call for an organizational meeting of the new Carnival society were Creoles, nor were the earliest recruits.

The revelers called themselves the Mistick Krewe of Comus, in a parody of archaic literary allusion, choosing as their patron deity the obscure figure of Comus, who appears in myth as a rather jolly and benign figure, the patron of festive mirth. He was also the offspring of Circe and Bacchus, and according to John Milton, a sorcerer who "Excels his mother at her mighty art, / Offering to every weary traveler, / His orient liquor in a crystal glass."

Appropriately, in the Comus parade, the masked Comus, touting the transformative powers of strong drink, waves a big golden cup from his throne instead of a scepter.

Comus in Stately Passage

If anyone in New Orleans was responsible for keeping the traditions of Comus alive, it was Harry McCall, Jr., a former krewe captain and a recently retired partner in a law firm that bore his name. McCall resided in one of the more elegant mansions in the Garden District, the fabled uptown neighborhood lying between Saint Charles Avenue and Magazine Street. The style of McCall's house was reminiscent of Charleston, South Carolina, with balconies on the side. It was more compact and symmetrical than most New Orleans mansions, which tend to ramble.

I had gone to interview him one afternoon, and McCall had put me in my place right away by leading me into his study rather than the parlor used for entertaining regular guests. He seated himself across from me as if preparing for a cross-examination.

McCall's family history, which involved plantations and the intertwining of Irish and Creole blood, typified the lineage of many fine old-line New Orleans families. "On my mother's side, we have been here," he said, "since the late eighteenth century, and on my father's side we've been on the river since 1800 and Philadelphia before that." His mother's grandfather was a banker who married into an old French family. George Denegre's grandfather, he said, was his great-uncle, on his mother's side.

The McCalls had had two plantations upriver near Donaldsonville in the early nineteenth century. There was a portrait, he said, of the first McCall who came South and sagely married the daughter of a wealthy plantation owner. There was a sugar co-op up there now where the houses had stood. One burned, and the other was displaced by the levee. The plantation itself went under in 1913. His father, a lawyer, was the first scion not to raise sugarcane, he said. "Emotionally, you feel nostalgic," he said.

He felt a bit nostalgic, too, about the old days of Comus. Comus, he said, was still the "most imaginative and truly literary and artistic of all the parades. But today, the popular appreciation of myth, history, and art is not what it was."

In the old days, he said, "You might have had a hundred flambeaux to light a night parade. Today, there are only about twenty. It was more magical—the floats were pulled by mules."

What's more, there hadn't been the distraction of marching bands. "The marching bands have popularized the parades," said McCall. "Now they play jazz, and the majorettes pirouette around. I think that detracts from the parade."

He recalled fondly the days when Comus had not yet accepted the tradition of throwing beads. "Time was when Comus didn't throw at all. Momus, Proteus, and Rex all threw, and Comus came out in stately passage without throwing."

Comus, for a number of years, said McCall, "has been perceived as the preeminent social ball. I think Comus has become more sedate. Momus is more lively and fun-loving. But if you were really dignified, you wouldn't put on a mask and cavort on a float.

"That's the issue today that should be considered by people who want to open up Mardi Gras. You wouldn't do all this unless you were with friends. You wouldn't make a spectacle of yourself with anybody and everybody."

He felt that the traditional Carnival organizations had worked well over a long period of time. "Experience has taught me that this is an effective way to organize a ball and a parade. In the old-line krewes, no one is paid. Most of the members are fully occupied with something else, so it should not be a democracy, and it isn't. It's a democracy in the sense that the desires of the men are considered, but it functions through the captain and his aides. It's a very harmonious arrangement. No one is forced to do anything. The captain's power to coerce the members is dependent on their consent."

Choosing members, too, depended on the consent of krewe members. "New members of the krewe are subject to approval by the krewe members," said McCall. "If there is the perception on the part of enough of the members that you'd be a wet blanket or a drag, you'd be blackballed. It's not different from any club. You don't want people who aren't congenial. If someone is a sourpuss, you can live without him. It's no disgrace if you don't make a krewe—there are lots of people who live quite happily without it."

Said McCall, "Certainly there is life after Mardi Gras."

We returned to the subject of the old days, and as I was leaving, McCall said, "Some people here think things haven't been the same since the Emancipation Proclamation. But someone from Boston wouldn't understand that." I rode back downtown in something near the state of shock.

A Butterfly of Winter

I had learned the theme of this year's Comus parade from Henri Schindler. Henri, who pronounced his name the French way, was not merely a guardian of Carnival culture, but a sort of Don Quixote of Carnival, charged with a fierce chivalric loyalty to the liege-lords of uptown society. He believed in upholding Carnival traditions, partic-ularly in keeping Carnival secrets—the identities of royalty, little bits of gossip he heard while working at the den or talking to krewe members.

"I'm reluctant to spill the beans," he once told me. "One of the keys to Carnival is the aura of secrecy and mystery. In some ways, it's still quite unfathomable. It's important to hold on to this aura. With-out it, Carnival doesn't exist."

Nevertheless, Henri had agreed to drop the veil of secrecy long enough to let me view the Comus parade floats he and his crew were finishing up, on the condition that I would not reveal the theme until after Mardi Gras. He stopped by Josephine's studio on his way up-town to the den, from his home in Bywater, below the Faubourg Marigny, and we headed up Tchoupitoulas Street in his pickup truck.

During the day, Henri joined the artists at the den, and at night, he worked the late shift at the marine desk of the Lykes Brothers Steamship Company, one of the oldest and most prestigious firms in New Orleans. Henri alternated the shift along with his friend Paul Poché, the descendant of an old French family, and another colleague whose son had appeared in the Madonna documentary *Truth or Dare* as the only "straight" dancer on Madonna's concert tour. I liked to imagine that when everyone else in New Orleans was asleep, Henri and Paul were answering calls from navigators lost on the Indian Ocean or the Pacific and guiding freighters laden with exotic cargoes through dangerous shoals and heavy seas.

The first time I saw Henri, he had been dancing giddily in a white satin Pulcinella costume, an apparition from the commedia dell'arte, with a wild look in his eye, the impossibly high peak of his clown hat visible across the room. Today, however, he was dressed for business, and at first glance, Henri, gray-haired and bespectacled, garbed in a conservative, dark blue pinstripe suit, button-down shirt, and loafers, could be a successful accountant or, say, a middle manager with an Ivy League degree. Only the odd gleam in his eye would give Henri away as a mad Carnival visionary.

We drove along the river, through the dockside neighborhood known as the Irish Channel, once a stronghold of working-class Irish, and now predominantly black. Until quite recently, many of the white-owned bars and beer joints we passed had maintained service windows for blacks, reminiscent of segregated water fountains.

We arrived at the den, a large beige warehouse of corrugated tin, on the corner of Bordeaux and Tchoupitoulas, which Comus shared with the Knights of Momus. Across the street, an elderly black man in a wheelchair was sunning himself in his front yard. Parked on the street was a 1972 Ford Mercury Marquis painted silver, with black zigzags, and encrusted with metallic objects. This was the "Badmobile" that belonged to artist Russell Elliott, who was inside painting floats.

Inside the den, the floats were packed so tightly that the entire structure seemed to be a giant toy box, spilling over with magical papier-mâché creatures. The first thing I noticed was the startled face of a pig atop a float, flanked by two other pigs with equally alarmed expressions. These were not the nineteenth-century Anglo-Saxon "swine" who had become the heroes of Carnival, but the henchmen of Odysseus who had been transformed by Circe. The worst thing about Circe, according to Homer, was that men kept their reason even as they were turned into animals; they knew what had happened to them.

"I tried to get them right at the point of metamorphosis," said

Henri. "They still have human hair." They did have just a touch of Miss Piggy in them. The look on their faces lay somewhere between surprise and consternation, edging into horror.

The beasts were an allusion, too, to the mythic and theatrical origins of Comus. In Milton's *Comus*, written in the stylized form of private theatrical known as the "masque," the sorcerer, who combines his mother's power to enchant with his father's penchant for strong drink, enthralls his victims by means of a potion. Although they are turned into wolves, bears, hogs, or goats, they revel in the transformations and "boast themselves more comely than before."

Comus's seductive speeches prefigure the charismatic eloquence of Milton's Satan. Comus bids his beastly companions, who follow him noisily, bearing torches: "Welcome joy and feast,/Midnight shout and revelry,/Tipsy dance and jollity . . . Come, let us our rites begin;/'Tis only daylight that makes sin . . ."

Inside the den, just beyond the startled swine, was another victim of Circe, the hapless Glaucus, the demigod of the deep, whose float was a gorgeous indigo blue, in keeping with Ovid's description of "Blue Glaucus, swimmer of swollen waves." Circe had transformed Glaucus's love, the nymph Scylla, from the waist down, into a pack of hungry dogs, and thence into the rocky promontory that shipwrecked so many sailors.

"This is our first underwater float," said Henri. "We'll have Glaucus's hair trailing, like seaweed, and lots of scallops." Henri had worked his own kind of metamorphosis, since this float, the previous year, when the theme was insects, had been the fire ants of the sun.

Last year's eerie spider and diaphanous web had become this year's Arachne, the weaver, whose story, as Henri observed, was "an object lesson in how not to behave to a goddess." Arachne had woven the stories of the scandals of the gods into her tapestries, engaging in a contest with Minerva. Minerva, said Henri, had retaliated in usual divine overkill. "You like to spin, sister? Then spin, forever." Poor Arachne had become a spider, destined to spin webs into eternity.

Henri's vision of divine enchantments, I thought, combined the whimsy and humor of Ovid's *Metamorphoses* with the wistful beauty and grotesque undercurrent of fairy tales. In Ovid's retelling of Greek and Roman myths, the overriding theme is the irrational force of desire, which possesses, overwhelms, and transforms. Though things change in Ovid, they are not utterly destroyed. Better, perhaps, for some, to be a tree, a rock, a star, than to be ravished. Better, for others, to be a flower, even a pig, than to wither away, unloved.

Although Henri's victims of enchantment had been taken by surprise, trapped in their new identities, suddenly rooted to the ground or flung into the sea or sky, these unnatural additions to the natural world were also remarkably beautiful in their new shapes. I couldn't help but think of accidents of birth, of the transsexuals who felt trapped in the wrong body and who worked their own willful metamorphoses, and of a kind of metamorphosis in reverse, the way we all become trapped in bodies that betray us by getting old or infirm.

Across the den, Henri pointed out Merlin, imprisoned in a thornbush by the enchantress Vivien; Argus, whose thousand eyes had been transformed by Juno into the tail of a peacock; the goat-god Pan, who had just captured the nymph Syrinx as she turned into a stand of reeds, which he cut and played as pipes; the abode of Morpheus; and the altar of Lotis, the blossoming tree, "another nymph fleeing a horny god."

The bases of the floats, Henri pointed out, were the same wagons that had been in use for more than a century. It was a sort of Cinderella story, of old garbage wagons once pulled by mules being transformed into the moving palaces of fantasy ridden by the elite scions of New Orleans society. While most krewes used new wagons with rubber wheels, the metal-rimmed wheels of the Comus wagons caused the entire float to shake and shimmy, a motion that Henri had incorporated into free-floating leaves, tendrils, and flower petals that were gold-leafed and suspended from the float by flexible pipe, so that they would shimmer in the glow of the flambeaux.

Henri's aesthetic, he said, had been described best by Sir Francis Bacon in his little treatise, "Of Masques and Triumphs": "The colours that shew best by candlelight are white, carnation, and a kind of sea-water green, and oes, or spangs, as they are of no great cost, so they are of the most glory."

105

In the opinion of many Comus krewe members, Henri had re-turned the Comus parade, gleaming with its oes and spangs, to the glory of the golden age of Carnival.

Henri had never recovered, he said, from the first Comus parade he saw in 1946 at the age of five. "It was this marvelous hieratic vision that appeared out of nowhere and then disappeared. I was hooked." In those days, he said, Carnival was more likely to have that magical effect on children. "You weren't bombarded all day with color TV. All you had was picture books."

Henri had apprenticed with Mrs. Laurence Fischer, known as Louis, a flamboyant graduate of Newcomb art school who had been part of the bohemian scene in the French Quarter in the 1930s, when Sherwood Anderson and other literary lights were putting out *The Double Dealer*, the now-legendary literary journal. She lived in an apartment in the Pontalba on Jackson Square and worked in a studio on Conti Street. Henri had thought at first that Louis was his mentor's married name, that she was "Mrs. Louis Fischer." But Louis, in fact, was her given name, and she had a deep, cigarette-husky voice to go with it.

Louis Fischer had been the last of the legendary float artists, many of whom had been women. There had been Jenny Wilde, whose designs resembled the ethereal froth of fairy-tale illustrator Edward Lang, and the mysterious Carlotta Bonnecaze, for whom Henri had named his pet Pekinese, and who had been a proponent of themes evoking theology and whimsy. Henri was particularly fond of a Bon-necaze float titled "The Elves of Malaria," a bizarre swamp scene, and another titled "Salamanders holding high Carnival on the surface of the sun."

Henri's dream float, he said, would be a depiction of "Cemele's request." Cemele was the foolish nymph tricked into making a re-quest, as Henri put it, that "got her burned on the spot." She had asked to see her divine lover, Zeus, without his human disguise, and as Edith Hamilton put it, "Before that awful glory of burning light she died." Told as a Mardi Gras fable, Cemele had violated a rule of Carnival by looking behind the mask.

The most important Comus parade, Henri felt, had been the "Missing Links" parade of 1873, which was described as "a magnificent double satire tracing the evolution of life from the lowly zoo-phyte to the king of all creation, the gorilla." The floats had made fun not only of Darwin's *Origin of the Species,* but of Republican carpet-baggers of the Reconstruction era. Ulysses Grant was a tobacco grub; General Butler, the military governor of New Orleans, was a hyena.

The further impact of this particular parade, said Henri, was that it was the first to be actually built in New Orleans. The first floats had been imported from Europe. The "missing links" had been con-structed by a young French-born sculptor named Georges Soulie, trained in plaster, who had worked on a side altar of the Saint Louis Cathedral on Jackson Square.

Georges Soulie continued to build floats until World War I, when he was succeeded by his son until 1950. The designer of the parade was Charles Briton, a soldier of fortune who had fought in the army in Mexico for Emperor Maximilian and Empress Carlotta. He then came to New Orleans and worked as a lithographer in the Cen-tral Business District. He had been succeeded by a Swede named Wikstrom, regarded as the dean of Carnival artists, who had designed Rex from early 1880s until 1910.

Blaine Kern, the son of an Algiers sign painter, had taken the float-building business by storm during the 1950s, importing huge papier-mâché puppets from Italy, and, later, fiberglass figures from Spain, and turning it into a more commercialized and homogeneous operation. Nowadays, fewer than a dozen clubs built their own floats, while the other krewes, almost fifty of them, rented their floats from Kern and a handful of other float makers. The rental floats tended toward the generic in nature, resulting in parades that were rather bland and predictable in their themes. The focus changed, as Henri observed, from "the fantastic to the familiar."

Carnival should have a certain aesthetic, according to Henri, a sense of passing along the torch—or the flambeau. "I still have a romantic vision of holding on to the mystique," he said. "Carnival maskers should not be just businessmen who happen to stray into it."

Carnival, it seemed, had become more fragile than ever. Henri liked to quote Perry Young on the perishable quality of Carnival and its artifacts: "Carnival is a butterfly of winter, whose last mad flight of Mardi Gras forever ends his glory."

Carnival was as fragile as the papier-mâché floats that came back to the den every year in tatters—as fragile as the "oes" and "spangs" of "no great cost" with which it was adorned. It was as fragile, too, as the unwritten code of civility that had allowed it to flourish for so long. For more than a century, a kind of pact of festive immunity had allowed masked men and women to ride through vast crowds of drunken spectators without being harmed.

"I don't know how long the streets are going to be civil," said Henri. "You don't want a Carnival where you drive armored floats down hostile streets."

Even if Carnival managed to fend off the most recent assaults, Henri felt, it was headed nevertheless for a kind of theme-park aura. "The head of commercialism has reared itself," said Henri, indignantly. As evidence, he pointed to the 1990 Neiman Marcus Christmas catalogue, which had offered, as their annual big-splurge item, the opportunity to ride on a Mardi Gras float. For the price of $5898, which included four nights at the Windsor Court hotel, the lucky purchaser could ride on a float in the Endymion parade, the parade known for its double-decker megafloats, and attend the Endymion ball in the Superdome.

Later that afternoon, we drove back downtown and parked on Decatur Street, near the Café du Monde. We sat down at the café to order coffee and beignets. Henri placed some float designs on the table, and the waiter asked him, "Hey, do you work for Blaine Kern?"

8

Mr. Mardi Gras

It was a tribute to the homegrown peculiarities of New Orleans culture that Mardi Gras had resisted commercialization and co-optation by mass culture for so long. Since New Orleanians generally scorned most other cities' idols, the makers of Carnival had been free to create their own dream factories, to fabricate their own hybrid myths.

It occurred to me that some of the arguments being made in favor of Comus and the other old-line krewes were the same as those that were being made about the British monarchy, as it began to fall apart in scandal—statements about the importance of tradition and the economic benefits of tourist attractions. But perhaps one of the most important benefits of old-line Carnival, as Anthony Haden-Guest once argued about the British monarchy, is that it preempted the adulation of lesser celebrities. As Haden-Guest observed, "The monarch and the nobility still fill Britons with an old-fangled snobbery that shelters the nation from the celebrity worship that becomes more and more devout in the United States."

In that context, the notion of an anonymous monarch reigning over a parade was refreshing. Better a masked Comus than Madonna or Michael Jackson.

In recent years, however, Carnival parades seemed to be toting more odds and ends of pop culture, along with more fallout and debris from national trends. The newer parades, according to Henri, simply recycled the latest images from pop culture. "There's no thematic pizzazz—it's just hollow," he said. "The source matter is movies and TV and things on the Disney Channel—there's no real imagination. This is supposed to be the age of information, but one of the great casualties has been Carnival. Everything in the parades is so easily recognizable—there's never any mystery or challenge or surprise. It's all recycled second- and third-generation kitsch. You never see an original visual image—it's something from *Robocop*. You have celebrities from sitcoms or the latest quarterback star as grand marshals. A lot has been lost."

If Carnival was looking less and less indigenous, and more generic, it was in large part due to the efforts of Blaine Kern, who appeared to operate like an indiscriminate cultural vacuum cleaner. Kern, who sometimes played the part of a Mardi Gras buffoon, had exerted a profound influence over the evolution of Carnival. And now that the old-line krewes were under siege by the City Council, Kern stood to increase his hold over what Sally Reeves called "bourgeois" Carnival.

Kern was such a hustler, when it came to Mardi Gras, he put you in mind of carnival, without the capital letter, the world of midways and sideshows and barkers. His realm, Mardi Gras World, lay across the river, in the old town of Algiers, almost directly across from the former World's Fair site.

I managed to get an appointment with Kern late one afternoon, and I took my bicycle on the ferry across the Mississippi, to the West Bank, which actually lay southeast of the ferry terminal at the foot of Canal Street. Until the Greater New Orleans bridge was built in 1958, the ferry had been the only connection between Algiers, which had been part of New Orleans since 1870, and the rest of the city. According to legend, Algiers had been named by one of Spanish commander O'Reilly's soldiers, who had returned to New Orleans from an expedition undertaken by the Spanish against Algeria. Algiers, to old New Orleanians, was a faraway province.

Crossing the river by ferry was almost always romantic. You could see the riverboats anchored along the docks near Jackson Square, and the steeple of Saint Louis Cathedral on the horizon, as the ferry threaded its way past barges and tugboats. I watched a string of barges go by that appeared to be half a mile long.

Algiers still had a sleepy, small-town look. Its small old Creole cottages and shotgun houses resembled those of the lower-middle-class neighborhood of Mid-City across the river. Blaine Kern regularly sent a van to meet the ferry for potential visitors to Mardi Gras World, but it was late in the day, and I didn't see any tourists waiting around. I rode along the batture, heading toward the monorail tower, which marked the far edge of Kern's Carnival kingdom on the West Bank.

Kern had been buying up land on the West Bank for years, with the notion that it would someday become a New Orleans version of Paris's Left Bank. Mardi Gras World and the warehouses and workshops of Kern Enterprises comprised some twenty-seven buildings scattered near the batture.

Mardi Gras World had been conceived as a tourist enticement that fell somewhere between Disneyland and Madame Tussaud's, although it currently had the feel of a hastily concocted roadside attraction. A visit to Mardi Gras World included a tour of the warehouses where artists were working on floats, a multimedia film about Mardi Gras, focusing on Kern's contributions, and a gift shop, where one could buy trinkets, doubloons, and tiny replicas of some of his creations. At the entrance were various figures from old floats, including Marilyn Monroe, with her skirt swirling up, in the famous pose from *The Seven Year Itch*; Rhett Butler and Scarlett O'Hara; Jiminy Cricket; Tinker Bell; and Carmen Miranda.

I entered the side door of a huge warehouse where his offices were located, adjacent to the entrance for Mardi Gras World. Kern's navy blue Mercedes convertible was parked out front. Hanging on the wall in the reception room were photos and posters and testimonials from past Carnivals, including a shot of Blaine Kern dancing on a float, wearing a white satin suit and a mantle emblazoned with images of Mickey Mouse and Donald Duck. In another photo, he was standing in the hand of a huge King Kong he had built for the Bacchus parade.

Kern notified his secretary that he was free, and I found my way upstairs to his office, where he was seated behind a huge desk. A small, stocky man wearing what appeared to be a stage toupee, he looked to be in his early fifties, although I knew him to be considerably older. Said Kern, introducing himself, "If you address a letter to Mr. Mardi Gras, it'll come to me, just like Santa Claus." He had even copyrighted the name, he said, and he had also copyrighted the expression, "Throw me something, Mister." Said Kern, "I know it's audacious, but I'm a good businessman."

Kern bounded up from his chair and showed me around the room, pointing out a testimonial from the School of Design, as the Krewe of Rex was formally known, citing his contributions to thirty-seven consecutive Rex parades, including such permanent fixtures of the parade as the *boeuf gras*, the streetcar, and the Royal Barge.

Kern suggested a tour of the facilities, where his staff built floats for forty-one parades, including Bacchus and Alla, his krewe from Algiers. Most of the floats were actually rental floats, which would be slightly reworked—or at least renamed—between parades. A city ordinance forbid a float maker from using the same float more than twice in the same year. The work on the Rex parade was done at the Rex den across the river. Around Mardi Gras, his staff of half a dozen artists and thirty other employees grew to almost two hundred, he said.

We walked out of Kern's office onto a landing overlooking an enormous warehouse, jammed with floats. Papier-mâché heads with jester caps had been stuck on newel posts like guillotined heads on pikes. To the right of the stairs was a slightly reduced copy of Michelangelo's *David*. Two wilted watches from the Salvador Dali float in last year's Bacchus parade hung on the wall.

Most of the floats for this year's Bacchus parade were already completed, said Kern. The theme this year would be "What a Way to Go," celebrating various means of transportation, ranging from a chariot, a gondola, and a streetcar to a spaceship and a submarine. "We're right on schedule," he said. "We used to get a lot more of our fiberglass figures from Spain. We make 90 percent of them here now."

One huge room, lined with floats and assorted papier-mâché and fiberglass figures, was used for parties, said Kern. "You should see it when it's all lit up." He pointed out some of the characters crowded on shelves and on the floor. "Here's Cleopatra's barge from Alla. There's Freddie Krueger. Little Red Riding Hood. Fred Flintstone. There's the Bacchusaurus." The latter was an enormous dinosaur float built for the Bacchus parade.

"This will last forever," he said, slapping the fiberglass thigh of

Queen Kong, another standard Bacchus float. He had the air of a used-car salesman kicking a tire. "There's Dumbo and Wonder Woman and Louis Armstrong," he added.

We walked into a prop room crowded with more figures and accessories. "Name a creature," he demanded. "Kangaroo," I replied. "We've got lots of those," he said. "Try again. Think of something we don't have." "Armadillo?" I asked. He shook his head. "Come on, think of something harder," he said. "Giraffe," I retorted. He looked exasperated. "I have maybe four or five," he said. I was beginning to feel like Aladdin and the genie. "There's nothing you can name that we don't have," insisted Kern. "Even famous people. We have Michael Jackson or Mahatma Gandhi."

"How about writers?" I asked.

"We have Samuel Clemens, Jack London, Edgar Allan Poe," he began.

"What about Salman Rushdie?" I interrupted, triumphantly.

"No, I don't have Rushdie," he said, "but I have some of those who are trying to kill him—some Iranians."

He spun around, naming props, characters, and figures in a tongue-twisting litany. "Turtles, Buddhas, crazy whatchacallits, girls, pirates, the Spirit of '76, beer steins, swans, devils, panthers, mushrooms, a crooked man, cows, pineapples, prostitutes, Whistler's mother, Mary Poppins, mermaids, Lyndon Johnson, a hydra, scrolls, cakes in flames, the Leaning Tower of Pisa, a dragon, oysters, dwarves, elves, a fairy godmother, the *boeuf gras*, palm trees, a harlequin, rockets, a beer bottle." He paused for a moment to look closer at a headless figure. "This looks like trash, but I can make it look like new."

He kicked a tattered figure of a matador. Boom! "This toreador," he said, "would take one man a week to fix it up and make it nice. We can patch and repair anything."

There were more rows of heads: Crocodile Dundee, John Wayne, the Sieur de Bienville, Bob Hope, Louis XIV, JFK. In Kern's Mardi Gras World, there was no rhyme nor reason to the images, no discernible order, no distinction between real and fantasy, between cartoon and history. It was like wandering around a random repository of America's collective memory, with most of the images drawn from popular culture and short-term memory.

"This building represents my whole life," said Kern, wheeling around, with his arms outstretched, creator of all he surveyed.

Characters were never really lost or destroyed in Kern's Mardi Gras World, but simply retouched or recycled. "That's Martha Washington," he said, pointing out the head of the first First Lady. "If you look closely, it's really Mamie Eisenhower." He pointed to another figure. "See that Indian? It's Charlton Heston." He pointed to a large figure with pointed ears. That's the devil for the Devil's Triangle float for Endymion this year. That used to be the joker."

"There's Ronbo," said Kern, indicating a bare-chested Ronald Reagan as Rambo. "That used to be Rocky," he said.

He pointed out a gift he just made for Edwin Edwards. It was the papier-mâché head of a Klansman, with blue eyes glaring out from beneath the hood. It was labeled DUKKKE.

Kern had grown up in a rambling frame house just a few streets away from his Carnival kingdom. "This building used to be an ice factory," said Kern. As a kid, he would bring a little cart to pick up ice for six cents and sell it for sixteen cents. Kern's father Roy was a painter who did signs and notices and flagpoles. "He started out doing the vaudeville houses," said Kern. "He painted W. C. Fields, and Judy Garland. He couldn't make a living, so he went into business painting signs. He called it 'Roy Kern and Son Signs.' He was the fastest sign painter in New Orleans. He did the French Quarter from one end to the other, from the ferry to Rampart, from Esplanade to Canal. I was painting with him as a little boy. I carried his sign box around on a bicycle. Then he bought a secondhand truck, a '28 Ford. He put pipes on it, a ladder and scaffold. He'd have a pirogue on top to go fishing."

Roy Kern had worked briefly as a float maker, too. In 1931, when Blaine was nine years old, his father took an old trash wagon and turned it into a float for the Krewe of Choctaw. The next year, he made a float for the Krewe of Alla. Most of the krewe walked behind the float.

After being discharged from the army, Blaine Kern enrolled in the New Orleans Academy of Art as part of the "52/20 club"—for fifty-two weeks, he received twenty dollars a week for an apprenticeship. In 1946, his mother was ill and needed an operation. In order to pay for it, he painted a mural on the history of medicine for Dr. Henry LaRocca, who also happened to be captain of the Krewe of Alla in Algiers.

The next thing he knew he was working on the 1947 Alla parade. Meanwhile, he had been hanging out at the workshop of Soulie and Sons, who built floats for the major parades, including Rex. An old artist there had asked if he wanted to try his hand at painting the side of a float. The captain of Rex, Reuben H. Brown, a "big, tough guy," had reminded him of Douglas MacArthur, he said. "I have his picture down in Mardi Gras World." The next captain of Rex, Darwin Fenner, who would later become a key figure in defusing the school desegregation crisis, became a mentor.

Darwin Fenner, whose family cotton brokerage merged with Merrill Lynch in 1941, paid Kern's way to Europe, where he traveled around to visit the artisans of Carnival in France, Germany, Italy, and Spain. "I went to Viareggio, Italy," he recalled, "to meet the master float builders there, whose floats were politically oriented. I went to Valencia in Spain and met Regino Mas, the master builder in Spain, and the *falleros*, who burn what they do—the masks and figures. I went to Carnival in Nice, and I saw the beautiful masks, one hundred miles out of Paris, made by the César Masque company, the biggest mask company in the world. I came back with the idea of improving Mardi Gras in New Orleans."

In addition to expanding his float-building business, he started a mask and Carnival accessory business. "I brought masks from France, colors from Italy. Each country has given something. I went to Germany to find out about heraldry, to find out about medals in Mainz, Frankfurt, and Cologne. I found out about crowns from Paris, about rhinestones invented by an Austrian. Czechoslovakia was the center of the glass business, and I brought beads from there. It grew like Topsy, and one day I had the largest company of its kind in the world. This is a one-stop shopping center for Mardi Gras."

Kern said he had thought at one time of leaving New Orleans and going to Hollywood. He had gotten a nibble from Disney back in the 1950s, he said, after he had built a King Kong float for a movie. Darwin Fenner had encouraged him to remain here, he said. "He told me that Mardi Gras was going to grow. It was democratizing, and it was going to open up to everyone."

Fenner's prediction proved to be accurate. The demand for Carnival krewes was growing in the suburbs around New Orleans, and Kern was there to guide the new krewes from conception to parade. "I started more than half the krewes in existence," he said. He would sit down with prospective krewes, he said, and give them a set of bylaws, a list of parade themes, and sometimes even a name for the krewe. The names just seemed to pop out of his head: Cleopatra, Pandora, Shangri-la, Hercules, Aphrodite, Sinbad, Minerva, Nefertari, Ulysses, Mercury, Poseidon, Argus.

There was considerable evidence that the new krewes took themselves every bit as seriously as Comus and Rex, perhaps even more so. "There have been blood feuds in Shangri-la," I was told by one source, "and in Saint Bernard Parish, there have been champagne glasses tossed at the jugular."

Kern made Endymion, a small suburban krewe named for a popular local racehorse, a deal they couldn't refuse. He offered them a discount and told them he would turn them into a megakrewe, with megafloat parades that would wind up triumphantly in the Superdome. The krewe and its captain, Ed Muniz, would make money, predicted Kern. And it all came to pass.

As floats got bigger, Kern bought Russian tractors from the Belarus factory in Minsk. The tractors were the powerful Vladimirets model, named for Vladimir Lenin. "We used to have International Harvester," said Kern, "but they were too small. I went behind the Iron Curtain thirty years ago, and they had me in the headlines." Actually, it was 1976, the Bicentennial year, and Kern was called a Communist by a few ultra-patriotic types.

Kern had worked a similar metamorphosis on his own small neighborhood krewe, Alla, whose membership was now known as the Society of the Golden Griffin. Kern ruled over his krewe as firmly as the captains of Rex or Comus, and as a typical krewe captain, he objected to Dorothy Mae Taylor's proposed antidiscrimination ordinance because it appeared to interfere with his powers to rule with arbitrary whimsy.

"The captain is the benevolent despot, the power behind the throne," said Kern. "It's a mystic secret that's unique to Mardi Gras. If somebody tells me, 'Your queen has to be red or yellow,' they're not going to have a Carnival captain around. I already have the names of the queen for Alla up to the year 2008. You don't tell me who I've got to take into my club."

He picked up a copy of the ordinance. "Finally, it's unconstitutional. But if you're the one to take it to court, you're a racist."

Kern thumped the ordinance down on the desk, declaring, "I see a beautiful era coming to an end. There's a mean-spiritedness about this. People of all races have second-lined, fought over doubloons, stood on each other's shoulders. Nobody cared if you were black or white. The only thing I see when I go down the street in my Alla parade is big smiles and 'Hey, Blaine.' "

Nevertheless, Kern was already thinking about those streets that might be left vacant by the departure of old-line krewes. "A year from now, I expect we'd apply for one of those nights for my group, Alla—we'd roll into the Superdome—we'd put on a show for the tourists. I'd throw the best party for tourists and make money for my krewe."

Kern was something of a pioneer in tourist-oriented Carnival. In 1969, he was in on the founding of Bacchus, the krewe that shook the foundations of old-line Carnival. Bacchus was big, it was glitzy, it was multi-ethnic, and it was designed for tourists.

Owen Brennan, the famed restaurateur, of Brennan's Restaurant on Royal Street, and Dr. LaRocca, of Alla, had founded an earlier krewe of Bacchus more than forty years ago, but it languished after their deaths. Twenty years later, Kern met with Owen Brennan's son Pip and designer Larry Youngblood, who had revolutionized costume design as Kern had parade floats. As Kern described it, Larry Youngblood had decided that he would be captain of the new krewe, and they would call themselves "The Merry Men of Sherwood." Said Kern, "Pip is shanty Irish, and he said he wanted to drink beer and have fun—he wasn't going to wear all that froufrou. Then they got Pete Moss, from the antique shop next to Brennan's, to join. Pip said that he was Jewish, and there had never been a Jewish captain. I said, 'Let's have this open to everybody. Pete will be perfect.'"

They quickly dispensed with the old-line tradition of debutantes, which had allowed a token participation of women in the krewe. Recalled Kern, "I said, 'Let's just have a ball. No maids or queens or debutantes.'" What's more, they decided to import their kings from the outside world—primarily from Hollywood. Their first king was Danny Kaye, and the list grew to include Jackie Gleason, Perry Como, and Richard Dreyfuss. They didn't pay their kings to participate, but they could offer them something even better than money for those who craved fame. "They get treated like a god," said Kern. Bob Hope had reigned at age seventy-five, and he had told Kern, "This isn't just a movie star being welcomed. This is adoration, for God's sake." Kern had told him, "You have become the God Bacchus for a night."

The annual budget for Bacchus was now $1.5 million, he said, which didn't count the throws, for which members paid extra. "Last year, they threw $117,000 worth of beads from the Bacca-woppa," he said, referring to the giant whale float, the largest in the parade. Last year's Endymion party in the Superdome, he said, had cost $1.5 million.

Kern had always been prone to whopper-sized visions. He used to read Jules Verne, he said, and concoct all sorts of dreams. "I've got dreams of things so outlandish," said Kern. "I've dreamed all my life. I dreamed of floats that would open up and unfold and change color like a peacock's tail.

"Years ago, I told Dave Dixon, the guy who thought up the Superdome, about my dream of the Tiki Room in Disney World, those pagan idols, with lips going, eyes rolling, and parrots flapping their wings. I wanted to make figures like that, but of NFL football players—giant figures that would come out and walk around in the Superdome."

Said Kern, "I dreamed of a king and queen nine stories tall. Their legs would work like this." He demonstrated, walking like an automaton. "The king would come out one way, the queen from the other, and there would be a meeting of the court in the Superdome. Two gigantic figures, nine stories tall—I could build something like that."

Kern had big dreams, too, for his hometown of Algiers. "Thirty years ago I came up with the prototype of a people-mover across the Mississippi." Prior to the World's Fair, he sold the concept of a gondola over the Mississippi to August Perez, the architect of the World's Fair, who later went bankrupt. "Algiers was going to be my city within a city," said Kern. "There were going to be Flash Gordon elevators and twin towers on either side of the gondola. There would be the Hanging Gardens of Babylon. All these crazy things. That was my dream to rejuvenate Algiers."

Now the West Bank tower of the people-mover stood rusting in a vacant lot, surrounded by weeds. But that had not stopped Kern's visions of further glory for Algiers. With the land he had been buying up along the batture, he hoped to expand Mardi Gras World. He envisioned a huge riverside theme park with giant figures, such as Louis Armstrong, looking out over the Mississippi.

That park, he said, would serve as a kind of memorial for his work on Carnival all these years. "You know, at one time, I wanted to be a portrait artist. Many years ago, I felt I was prostituting my art. Nobody would ever remember what I did here on this earth or see anything of mine hanging in a museum. Then I realized, I'm bringing joy, which is no mean thing these days. I may never have anything hanging in a museum, but if I can bring happiness, that's enough."

As I was leaving, Kern observed, "In any other town, I'd be just a float builder. Here, I'm Mr. Mardi Gras."

9

The Shadow Carnival

Tonight there was an opening at Mario Villa's gallery on Magazine Street to celebrate Josephine's new book of photographs, titled *Une Femme Habitée*, which had been published in Paris, and from which she had made a series of large prints for the gallery. The book was an intimate study in chiaroscuro, with the image of a woman emerging from the shadows in fragments. The face and figure of the woman seemed to materialize, bit by bit, and then to dissolve, leaving only a crumpled shawl by a mirror, as though the effort to hold the fragments together into a whole image had been exhausted.

The photographs had been taken in Josephine's studio, where the light, filtered through the tall French shutters into the high-ceilinged room, can be so tricky and elusive that everything has a look of trompe l'oeil. Some of the prints had been hanging in the studio, keeping me company, like alter egos.

I wondered how the drag queens who immigrated to New Orleans felt the first time they shed their old identities, taking off the suffocating coat and tie, stepping into the peignoir and mules, walking out onto the balcony and pirouetting in the sun. I wondered how long the lightness of being would last, whether the feeling would ever be the same again after that first molting of identities.

I found Henri and the Duenna talking together in a corner, Henri in his conservative pinstriped mode, the Duenna in a long cardigan. I mentioned that I was worried that I still hadn't come up with a costume for Mardi Gras day, although I had settled on an antique black lace dress I was planning to wear to various Mardi Gras balls. The Duenna was discussing the virtues of okra, noting that the okra plant is a relative of the hibiscus, with beautiful blooms, and pondering why Northerners can't abide its stringy texture. Henri was suddenly inspired with an idea for my Mardi Gras costume. I could go as Okra Winfrey, the vegetable talk-show host, my face painted green.

I was reluctant to leave such good company, but it was time to move on. Café society in New Orleans is peripatetic, perhaps as a legacy of the city's long history of parades. On Saturday nights, the "hipoisie" circulates in a perpetual current, flowing through the art galleries, which are scattered in clusters from uptown Magazine Street and the Warehouse District to the Quarter, down to the small cafés and music clubs in Faubourg Marigny. Marigny was once the private estate of Bernard de Marigny, a curmudgeon who had owned most of the city below Esplanade Avenue, and who had conducted a Gallic campaign against American intrusions into Creole culture, threatening to "annihilate" the "very name American" in Louisiana.

I joined the flow and wound up at a fundraising party for the Krewe de Vieux, a kind of free-form, low-budget Mardi Gras club, at the Café Istanbul. The Krewe de Vieux had grown out of group of artists, calling themselves the Krewe of Clones, who created strange Carnival parades for the Contemporary Arts Center. The Krewe de Vieux put on a satirical, fairly lewd parade every year, and sponsored a ball, which was open to the public. The club, which attracted offbeat young professionals and creative café-society types, now included eight or nine "subkrewes" and a total of three hundred or so members.

The captain of the Krewe de Vieux was Ray "Plain" Kern, a systems engineer and former geophysicist, who was always careful to explain that he was not related to Blaine Kern. Ray had once described the club's membership as "a bunch of lunatics—a really deranged group who like to interpret creatively things that are going on in the world. We have university professors, doctors, dentists, teachers, artists, convenience-store clerks." Said Ray, "Carnival is celebrated at many different levels. You have the bluebloods, and at the opposite end of the spectrum is us." It was not a well-kept secret, however, that a handful of younger members of Proteus and Momus also belonged to the Krewe de Vieux.

Last year, the club had turned its satirical propensities to Saddam Hussein and the Gulf War. They were the first Carnival group to

121

parade, and their version of patriotism had been considerably different from the flag-wavers of Endymion. One of the subkrewes, the Krewe of Space Age Love, had dressed as proctologists and transformed the cart that bore the krewe's beer keg into an operating table, upon which a Saddam Hussein dummy had been tied down. The tipsy proctologists appeared to be probing the dummy with Patriot missiles. Another subkrewe, the Seeds of Decline, had already been planning to march as the Genitalia of the Rich and Famous, and they turned their giant foam-rubber, penis-shaped headpieces into Scud missiles, carrying signs: THIS SCUD'S FOR YOU.

The Krewe de Vieux represented a class of young-to-middle-aged New Orleanians who might have been squeezed into a typical yuppie existence elsewhere, but who in New Orleans had allowed every little quirk to blossom. For one thing, quiet, hardworking conformity wasn't going to get you that far in New Orleans. Making money just didn't have the same cachet as elsewhere. You couldn't buy your way into the upper class, and being nouveau riche was definitely outré. But on the upside, you could live quite well on a salary that would have put you close to the poverty line elsewhere.

"You can live well in New Orleans on twenty thousand dollars a year," the Duenna had declared. He had bought his house in Marigny for only thirty-five thousand dollars, and had made improvements using money from an insurance settlement following a fall from a float he had been working on at the Comus den.

There had been a brief phase of yuppie preservationist zeal in New Orleans during the boom years, involving a snobby connoisseurship of cypress shutters and marble fireplaces. But with the economic decline, and the inevitable sense of entropy, things had returned to a level of hanging-on-by-the-fingernails comfort. Those who had chosen to stay in New Orleans were a certain breed—on the whole, they either loved New Orleans passionately or were convinced they couldn't live as well anywhere else.

Although tonight marked the fiftieth anniversary of the Japanese attack on Pearl Harbor, I hadn't considered that the theme for the club fundraiser, "The Krewe de Vieux gets bombed," might have a double meaning. Getting bombed in New Orleans was not an uncommon activity. But I realized the theme also referred to Pearl Harbor and Hiroshima after I looked up at the ceiling of the café, where someone had hung a crudely constructed bomber, presumably a Zero, or perhaps the *Enola Gay*. There was a blinking mushroom cloud suspended on the back wall. Walking around the café was a young man dressed as a sailor, with fake blood all over his uniform, and a surgeon wearing a mask, carrying a severed leg. One woman appeared to be pierced by a papier-mâché torpedo. A group of young men had adorned themselves with kamikaze headbands, some with the symbol of the rising sun, others with logos of Japanese products.

I decided on the spot that I would join the Krewe de Vieux and march with them in their parade on February 15. I found my friends, Frank and Betty Cole, who belonged to the subkrewe of Mama Roux and told them I wanted to sign up. They pointed out Richard and Vivian Cahn, who headed the krewe. Richard, whose father Jules was something of a legend in the French Quarter as a landlord and patron of jazz, worked in real estate, and his wife Vivian was an interior designer. Vivian said that the dues were fifty dollars, which included costume materials and a ticket to the ball.

When I called Vivian the next day, she explained, "We haven't chosen our theme yet. We pride ourselves in not planning. Confusion will rule, but we'll just party through it. The ratio of fun to effort is supreme."

Rites of the Anglo-Saxon Swine

At first glance, the Krewe de Vieux would not seem to have much in common with the Mistick Krewe of Comus. But Comus, in its early days, before it lithified into its current form, had not been so different from the Krewe de Vieux and its spirit of iconoclastic fun. And in some ways, the Krewe de Vieux might be seen as a recent renegade offshoot of the Carnival that had begun evolving with the founding of Comus in 1857.

The original Comus celebration was less a timeless ritual than a social gauntlet, tossed in the face of Creole society by a group of Anglo-Saxon swells announcing their presence on the scene in a big way. Nevertheless, the krewe, which later formalized its membership into an actual club, called the Pickwick Club, followed a certain Anglo-Saxon penchant for order. Along with the pseudo-archaic secret-society mumbo jumbo, there was a clear chain of command. There was a captain, who ran things as a sort of benign despot, and various committees that took care of such matters as invitations and costumes. The members who were to take part in the tableau were all given numbers, to take their places in a chalked circle marked out on the floor, ready to move at the captain's whistle. To this day, krewe members are often referred to by number, with Comus himself each year becoming number one.

Comus succeeded, according to one account, not because of its "refinement," but because of its "happy combination of order with disorder, of pretentious gaiety with organizational pragmatism." And Comus, for all its carefree airs, soon became as elite and tradition-bound as the Creole cliques it had so annoyed, and in fact was soon embraced by a number of Creoles.

The Krewe of Rex, too, which began parading in 1872, soon developed its own peculiar traditions. Rex had been founded in anticipation of a visit to New Orleans by Grand Duke Alexis Romanov, the sybaritic Russian over whom Americans around the country had gone dotty. The grand duke had hunted buffalo in the West with General George Custer and Buffalo Bill prior to arriving in New Orleans for Carnival.

Romanov was said to be enamored of an actress named Lydia Thompson, who had serenaded him during a revue called "Bluebeard" with a silly ditty called "If Ever I Cease to Love." That song, with such lyrics as, "May oysters have legs and cows lay eggs," was performed ad infinitum for the duke during the first Rex parade, and it became the krewe's theme song.

Despite its frivolous origins, however, Rex took on a quasi-solemn aura, with its officious bows to public service, and subsequent balls and parades displayed a military influence.

For all their quaint, quasi-pagan rigmarole, the old-line Carnival krewes were American organizations. They were men's clubs, sharing a good deal in common with such groups as the Masons and the Mystic Knights of the Shrine, with their homegrown American exoticism. The theatrical flourishes of Carnival also reflected the influence of a city much enamored of the stage and of pageantry, where the beau monde regularly attended theater and opera.

New Orleans Carnival in its current form evolved during the growth of the debutante system and during the heyday of secretive men's clubs—two oddly undemocratic forms of social behavior that allowed Americans to indulge their furtive passion for aristocracy and cronyism. That passion for the trappings of royalty and secret brotherhoods was particularly strong in New Orleans, where nostalgia for the ancien régime was rampant.

During the Reconstruction era, the nostalgia for the glories of yesteryear was reinforced by a white populace that felt defeated and betrayed by Yankee Republican leadership. By bringing their daughters into the club activities as honorees or debutantes, krewe members could further rationalize the need for vigilance against outsiders. Undoubtedly, the martial cast to Rex was a response to the stigma of living in an occupied city ruled by a military government. I came to think of this defensive romanticism as the Liberty-Monument Syndrome.

In a sense, the history of Carnival in New Orleans can be viewed as an evolving pattern of order and disorder, of exclusion and expansion—of drawing circles and dancing around the limits. Because of its paradoxical nature—the urge toward wildness and disorder, forged with the penchant for exclusiveness and arbitrary ritual—Carnival has always tended to fracture and multiply. And because it deals with the creation of pseudoroyalty, it has also been ripe for mockery.

Over the years, would-be celebrants who were excluded from the increasingly rigid rites of the old-line krewes formed their own clubs or parades, often as spinoffs, parodies, or copies of the older groups. Zulu, the black Carnival club founded by day laborers and longshoremen as a parody of white clubs, is perhaps the most famous, while black Creoles had founded the Original Illinois Club as a serious dance club for black society, even earlier, in 1895.

There have come to be nearly as many Carnival organizations as there are ethnic groups and subcultures in New Orleans, each of them with their own hierarchies, their own rites, and their own constituencies.

From the beginning, there have always been two Carnivals—the formal Carnival and the shadow Carnival—the uptown Carnival and the Carnival of the fringe. The Mardi Gras Indian tradition, celebrated in the bars and on the backstreets of black neighborhoods, may be as old as Comus, and the scarlet Carnival of the demimonde, with its "painted Jezabels" and the floozies in bloomers known as Baby Dolls, extends back well before the Storyville era. During the 1970s, the gay krewes, as well as freelance drag displays, shifted the center of Carnival away from uptown to downtown.

There was another side, then, to the Mardi Gras Syndrome. In the economic shadows of the city, the orphans of Carnival—blacks, gays, artists, and musicians—continued to create a vibrant culture of celebration.

During the boom years of the 1980s, when the city grew out of the control of the city's old elite, the third category of Carnival, the "bourgeois" Carnival, expanded in the suburbs, and the newer krewes like Bacchus and Endymion outgrew and outshone the old ones, at least in terms of showbiz glitz.

Nevertheless, at the onset of the great Carnival war, Comus was still hanging on as the krewe de la crème, the reigning court to whom even the mighty Krewe of Rex paid homage with a royal toast on Mardi Gras night to end the season.

Comus, with its vestigial beauty and snobbery, had become symbolic of the last stand of old-line New Orleans, while the Krewe de Vieux, with its wide-open ragtag ribaldry, represented the possibilities for Carnival in the future.

10

The Illiterates of Joy

Although Mardi Gras day was still nearly three months away, the streets of the French Quarter were filled with a steady stream of revelers who seemed to think that in New Orleans, every day is Mardi Gras. I had hardly been able to sleep because of all the yahoo-ing beneath my balcony. These invaders, for the most part, were young men from out of town who drove, walked, or weaved through the streets of the Quarter yelling like stuck pigs and slamming their fists into street signs. They were the progeny of what Calvin Trillin has called the "Fort Lauderdale incubator"—the party animals who inherited the streets after the fading-away of the counterculture. Their idea of a good time was to drink hurricanes at Pat O'Brien's until they threw up and then to roam the streets of the Quarter, venting primal screams.

It was difficult to view these bands of young men, who reverted to the status of preverbal primates, as revelers filled with the Carnival spirit—as heirs, for example, of Nietzsche's "reveling throng of Dionysus." They were intoxicated, all right, but hardly transported, I thought, into the realms of rapture. In fact, I felt that they didn't have a clue. I had begun calling them the "illiterates of joy."

I was reminded of one Mardi Gras, when I had gotten laryngitis and hadn't been able to speak above a whisper and had to pantomime my wishes. As I was walking near Canal Street, I had gotten caught up in a crowd of young people who were oddly silent, too. They were gesticulating wildly, but no sounds came forth. And then I realized that they were deaf-mutes who were communicating in sign language. They managed to convey a great deal of exhilaration without speaking

127

a word aloud. I wondered if one could hoot or yell in sign language, or whether yahoo behavior is a function of working vocal cords.

New Orleans has a strange effect on people from out of town, based partly on their expectations, I suppose, and the effect isn't confined to college students. Tourists, young and old, come to New Orleans and behave in a way that they wouldn't dare in their own hometowns. Tennessee Williams had attributed this effect to the "lunar" quality of New Orleans.

Luigi Barzini had described a similar phenomenon with tourists in Italy: "A mild frenzy takes most of them and transforms them once across the Italian border."

This transformation, in New Orleans as in Italy, often involves drinking. Tourists in Italy, Barzini observed, drink with the indiscriminate enthusiasm of desert travelers reaching an oasis. Perhaps, Barzini theorized, "these people are trying to quench not a physiological but a psychological thirst. This may be an unconscious magic rite; they drink wine as if it were a potion necessary to acquire a new personality, or they drink it as one drinks champagne on New Year's eve, on the stroke of midnight."

In New Orleans, the bibulous pilgrims drink to the point of oblivion, as though they are drinking from the cup of Comus, thinking themselves, perhaps, more comely than before. Instead of turning into beasts with the souls of men, they become men with the souls of beasts. They drink until they drown those little inner voices of reason and restraint and listen to the louder voices urging them to dance as they have never danced before, to leer as they have never leered before, to boast as they have never boasted before, to weep as they have never wept before—to become wolves and jackasses.

The city itself acts as an intoxicant, and you can never predict what people might do, as the Duenna had observed. In a sense, every visitor to New Orleans is a potential Blanche DuBois, stepping off the streetcar named Desire. I had witnessed a number of bizarre transformations, particularly in academia. At Tulane, a conservative graduate student, known for his perfectly starched white shirts, bow ties, and retro crewcut, suddenly disappeared. He later turned up, according to one eyewitness, at a bar in the French Quarter, dancing on a table, wearing a kimono. Another graduate student I knew, a particularly macho type, wound up as the "companion" of a wealthy septuagenarian who had been sent into exile in New Orleans by her distinguished New York family. I walked into one of her parties one night to find "Jeff" strumming the guitar at her feet.

Perhaps the biggest surprise came when I was accompanying the rock group ELO around on a night on the town. The band wandered into a strip joint on Bourbon Street, where I saw a young woman who looked familiar doing a bump and grind on the stage. It was the daughter of an eminent historian who had arrived in town a few weeks earlier.

Barzini had observed that the travelers who arrive in Italy from cold climates or repressive cultures behave "as if they had shed the roles assigned to them and their personalities had suddenly become repugnant and alien to them; or as if all the rules of the game of life had been changed or suspended."

Carnival has had considerable bearing on this sort of behavior in New Orleans. There is something about the Carnival mentality that suggests a certain reluctance to grow up or get serious. The Duenna once noted that he and Henri and a number of their friends were a bit like Peter Pan, never seeming to age. And indeed, there was a notable lack of wrinkles or signs of decrepitude among a number of Carnival devotees I knew, despite their aversion to observing a healthy regimen of diet and exercise. Perhaps Carnival acted as a perpetual fountain of youth—or in some cases, of puerility.

A popular theory among French feminist anthropologists has to do with the influence of parades and the parade mentality on American culture. Men who march in parades, the theory goes, remain suspended in a kind of "liminal" adolescent state—the state that anthropologist Victor Turner has described as being in-between, or suspended between the categories of ordinary social life.

By Turner's definition, much of life in New Orleans is "liminal"—suspended in some kind of limbo from the real world. Often, there appear to be no ordinary rules governing behavior. People have been cut loose from ties and families elsewhere, or at least behave as if that were so. The ordinary boundaries between various categories seem to dissolve—between male and female, child and adult, reality and illusion, surface and depth. In most places, you have to go looking for the edge, for the far side, but in New Orleans, you can't get away from it.

Some people seem to fall apart in such an atmosphere, like Mann's Aschenbach in Venice, Conrad's Kurtz in the Congo, or like George Washington Cable's fictional Puritans, who tended to succumb rather rapidly to temptation in the enervating Louisiana climate.

Tennessee Williams, however, had found New Orleans a comfortable and comforting place, where he frequently returned to recuperate from life in other cities. The "lunar" quality of New Orleans, he once wrote, drew him back "whenever the waves of energy which removed me to more vital towns have spent themselves and a time of recession is called for. Each time I have felt some rather profound psychic wound, a loss or a failure, I have returned to this city. At such periods I would seem to belong there and no place else in the country."

It is perhaps telling that Williams described his need for New Orleans as being greatest when he felt most wounded. That "lunar" quality of life in New Orleans, which Tennessee Williams found so healing, and which others might perceive as mere tropical torpor, can be either a lure or a repellent, depending on your state of mind. And it can be either stifling or liberating, depending on your point of view.

One afternoon, as I was walking toward Josephine's studio on Saint Louis Street, I saw a scroungy little white dog break away from a drunk who was berating him. The dog scurried down the street, and the drunk stumbled futilely after him, cursing with each lurch. "Come back here, T-Bone," he yelled. The doorman at the spiffy Royal Orleans turned to watch the getaway, and a man putting out trash from Johnny's Po' boy sandwich shop urged the little dog on. The last I saw of T-Bone, he was headed down Decatur Street, free at last. If I saw him again, I thought, I might not even recognize him. Like so many other escapees into the fantasy life of the French Quarter, T-Bone would probably transform himself into the dog of his dreams—perhaps a French poodle in rhinestones or a bulldog in leather.

The Need for Extremes

One night at dinner, Dalt and Josephine and I had compared the merits of Boston and New Orleans, cities so perfectly antithetical in nature that they could be doppelgängers, representing opposite poles of the human spirit. The comparisons fell into rather obvious dualisms: yin and yang, fire and ice, summer and winter, pagans and Puritans, purple and gray, gaiety and gloom, gumbo and chowder.

Nathaniel Hawthorne had been intrigued by such dualities, by the tension in human nature between the dour rigors of the conscience and the impulses of the festive spirit. I liked to interpret his parable, "The Maypole of Merry Mount," as a tale of two cities, Boston and New Orleans, though it was written about two early New England settlements, the Puritan "New Zion" of the Massachusetts Bay Colony and the nearby renegade settlement, known as Merry Mount, where lawyer Thomas Morton served as master of revels to a crew of liquor-loving freethinkers and Indians.

In describing the festivities at Merry Mount, Hawthorne borrowed images from Milton's masque, *Comus*, the same source used by the New Orleans revelers who founded the Mistick Krewe of Comus: "Had a wanderer, bewildered in the melancholy forest, heard their mirth, and stolen a half affrighted glance, he might have fancied them the crew of Comus." In contrast, the "chief pastime" of the Puritans, for whom "festivals were fast days," was the "singing of psalms." The Puritans, who were made of "a sterner faith than the Maypole worshippers," prevailed in the end, suppressing not merely the dissident colony but the dissident impulses within their own hearts.

When I was living in New Orleans during the seventies, I shared Hawthorne's ambivalence about self-control and revelry. In New Orleans, as in Merry Mount, one tends to become either a reveler or a voyeur. I had never felt quite at ease in the subcultures I had wandered through in New Orleans, first as an academic on detour, and then as a journalist and ex-academic.

For too many evenings, I had sat on my balcony and watched the sun set over the gabled roofs of the French Quarter, feeling my life slip away. During the days before I packed up to leave New Orleans for good at the end of the seventies, I could have wept, like Lafcadio Hearn, over its ruined beauty. If only I could have lived on its ineffable riches, on its transient pleasures, its unexpected gifts of grace—Aaron Neville's glorious voice, the sounds of a brass band drifting on the balmy air, the smell of gardenias and the splash of a patio fountain, wild nights of transcendent harmonies.

I had sometimes felt, however, that I was out of place in New Orleans, among the drag queens, the uptown prima-donna debutantes, and the hard-drinking Southern femmes fatales ready to claw out the eyes of the competition. It had been a rather schizophrenic life for me in those days, teaching a feminist course in literature uptown at Tulane University, lecturing on the works of Kate Chopin, Virginia Woolf, and other avatars of doomed feminist valor, then riding downtown to the French Quarter on the streetcar and trying to figure out a place on the spectrum of sisterhood for the "gender illusionists" of Bourbon Street.

Almost everyone I knew then in New Orleans seemed to be harboring secrets or living a double life. I had a few secrets of my own, but amid this surreal sea of fluid identities, I felt something of an impostor, the plainclothesman at the masquerade.

I feared that if I stayed long enough, I might become another Quarter character, walking around with a parrot on my shoulder, growing more and more disheveled, like Blanche DuBois, or perhaps imperceptibly madder, like the Bead Lady. The Bead Lady was a Quarter regular who had appeared on the scene one year as a neatly dressed matron who came to parties, apparently uninvited, and stood quietly on a balcony. Her clothes gradually became more mismatched and dirty, although the tatters at first had a premeditated look, as though they were a kind of costume. The smears on her cloth coats appeared to be painted on.

Eventually the Bead Lady took to wearing either a crash helmet or an upturned tuna can (a minimalist pillbox) atop her head, and began carrying around a phantom supply of buttons and beads, which she offered for sale, singing out, "Lucky bead!" She would respond with a cackle of laughter and a muttered curse upon the unwary soul who agreed to buy one. Dalt said she had even spit on him once when he offered a price for a bead she felt was too low.

Boston had once seemed the perfect antidote for New Orleans nuttiness, although now I felt that there must be someplace in between, some middle ground between the Puritan ethic of Boston and the unrelenting revelry of New Orleans.

"There must be a perfect place, halfway between Boston and New Orleans," I said to Dalt and Josephine, imagining perhaps one of Italo Calvino's invisible cities, where the people might live both right-side up and upside down.

"Halfway between Boston and New Orleans?" asked Dalt. "That's Cleveland."

"You can't have it both ways," he reasoned. "Boston and New Orleans would neutralize each other. You have to have the extremes."

11

Family Circles in the Garden District

People had been drinking a lot less these days in some uptown circles and were venturing on more healthy regimens, according to Elizabeth Strachan Keenan. Elizabeth, a former queen of Comus, was considered by many of her peers to be the most sensible and gracious member of an uptown family with the most impeccable social credentials in town but which had gotten a bit dotty around the edges. Around age fifty, Elizabeth was a member of the generation that was on the verge of ruling Carnival. Both of Elizabeth's daughters had already ruled as queens of Carnival courts.

I had driven up to visit Elizabeth at her home in the Garden District. Most of the homes there had been built after 1830 in ornate Gothic and Victorian styles by nouveau riche Americans who had not been welcome in the Creole sections of town, in the Vieux Carré and below.

Here and there an old raised Creole cottage or stately Greek Revival mansion sat back amid the surrounding wonderland of imitation towers, stained-glass windows, and rococo gingerbread. Almost all the houses in the district are furbished with marble mantelpieces, bronze and crystal chandeliers, mahogany staircases, and inlaid flooring.

The houses are perhaps best known, however, for the gardens that gave the district its name. Streets are shaded by live oak and magnolia, some standing from the plantation era, and yards are lush with shrubs, flowers, and vines, many with heady scents: jasmine, gardenias, camellias, mimosa, crape myrtle, irises, and tea-olive roses.

As Carnival approached, many of the houses would also be bedecked with banners. Every year, the king and queen of Carnival are presented with flags, bearing the Rex logo of a crown on stripes of purple, green, and gold, which they display outside their houses on the Monday before Mardi Gras. In succeeding years, they put out the flags about ten days before Mardi Gras, so that on many Garden District blocks, there may be as many as two or three houses marked by Rex flags.

Elizabeth's home, painted a dark dove gray, appeared surprisingly modest amid its spectacular surroundings. She lived just off Prytania Street, two blocks from McGehee's school, whose oldest building had been constructed by one of her ancestors, Bradish Johnson. Johnson's grandfathers, Captain Bradish and Captain Johnson, were river pilots—possibly river pirates, said Elizabeth. The Strachan family was still in the ship business—specifically, the Lykes Brothers Steamship Company, where Henri and Paul worked.

Elizabeth had just returned from a funeral. A tall, handsome woman with short gray hair and a straightforward, no-nonsense air about her, she was dressed in a black suit with a short jacket. Elizabeth had the look of the headmistress of a good private school. Her husband Walter, a slight man, at first seemed to skitter around the room like a shadow. Then, as Elizabeth and I were seated in the main parlor, he sat at a table in the dining room, eating a light supper, occasionally shooting a comment through the archway, sometimes getting up to walk into the parlor to make a particularly important point. He did not so much echo her remarks as offer pointed asides, rather like a terrier who runs in to nip your heels and darts away before you're sure he has sunk his teeth in.

None of Elizabeth's siblings had ventured far from the family nexus. Elizabeth herself had attended McGehee's before making her debut. Most of the family had remained within a few blocks of the ancestral home. "My mother is just two blocks that way," she said, pointing toward First Street. One sister, she said, lived on Valence, the farthest away of any of the four children. Her brother Duncan resided on Coliseum Square, where he had been engaging in a quixotic crusade to revive the square, a rambling park laid out in the 1830s as the center of an envisioned revival of classical culture.

Duncan was a collector of Coliseum Square houses and of military regalia and weaponry, including, at one time, a German tank. He owned muskets, too, and he had revived the old colonial custom of shooting off a gun at midnight on New Year's Eve. He had engaged in this ritual at the old Half Moon Bar, near the square, one year, when the old musket misfired, nearly charbroiling one side of his face.

Elizabeth, as one of her friends had told me, had essentially been born into Carnival. As for belonging to those inner circles, Elizabeth observed, "You either are or you aren't, and you've known it since you were born. You become part of rituals that don't change. You have to renew the rites, like a tribal ritual. It's a family party, generation after generation.

"The little girls are decorative—just like potted palms. They're interchangeable from one year to the next. Everyone gets their fifteen minutes." Interjected Walter, "For fifty thousand dollars." Walter had recently footed the bill for two debutante daughters. "It's like a bullfight," continued Elizabeth. "You know the bull is going to be killed. You know she'll be a success."

Elizabeth herself started out in the process, she said, when she was around six years old. The usual procedure, she said, was to go from flower girl to maid to queen. For Carnival royalty, she said, there are not too many for whom it's their first time on the auditorium floor. It's not a frightening thing. It's like a room full of your mother's best friends. You know every face.

"They call you a week to ten days before the ball to let you know. Of course, they've been thinking about it since you were born. You get the phone call, and the next thing you know it's rehearsal at the Pickwick Club the Sunday before Mardi Gras."

There were a number of details involved in the ritual, she said, most of which she followed, a few of which she didn't. "There are these picayune little things that make you think, what a stuffy bunch. They say, This is where you go to get your dress made. I didn't do it."

The selection process, said Elizabeth, boiled down to choosing nice girls from nice families. "The thing is," she said, "it's so innocent." At that, Walter came into the room to clarify things. "A lot of conniving goes on, but we're not the connivers," he said. "They started asking me about my daughters almost right after they were born. They really watch. You have to be subtle. We were the opposite of campaigning. If you're too aggressive, they laugh at you."

Elizabeth observed, "Everybody says it's hard to break into these clubs. But I've found that anyone who goes the whole route, sending their children to the right schools and doing volunteer work for the school and making friends with other parents, gets invited as fast as anybody else. Of course, in New Orleans, it's where you eat lunch that counts. That's why all this matters so much to men, who lunch at the Pickwick Club or the Boston Club with these nice maids there taking care of them."

I asked Elizabeth if Carnival, with all its duties and details, had been fun. "If you like getting all dressed up. When you're in the court, your momma takes you to the beauty parlor, and you have your own spotlight.

"There's something to do every year of your life in Carnival. By the time you're fifty-five and you're going for the thirty-fifth year, you have to get yourself up for it—like football players or trial lawyers. But Mardi Gras has been good to me. My attitude is that, if you're bored by it, just stay home."

Elizabeth said she didn't know anyone in her circle who had given up on New Orleans. "I don't know anybody who has said, 'We just can't swing life in New Orleans anymore,' and moved out." A few people had moved into the country, though. And her own children had left town to go to school or take jobs elsewhere.

As she walked me to the door and then out into the warm dusk, we stood talking for a few more minutes. She had been reminiscing about her debut, when she had been surrounded by young men she had known all her life. "But that meant there were no surprises," I said. "That's the point," she said. The last thing you want at a coming-out party, I suppose, is a stranger.

Ghosts along the Mississippi

Later, as I talked to a friend about a crisis I was going through in my personal life, he observed, "You know, as you get older, you get worried about things that might be lurking around the corner." What was so disturbing, I thought, about those predictable uptown rituals that Elizabeth had described was that for all the secrecy, there were no surprises. The point of those uptown Carnival balls, it seemed to me, was not the element of mystery, but the ultimate lack of it. For all the suspense of guessing who the king might be behind the mask or who might be the next queen, the game had been rigged. The point was to ensure that there be no saboteurs of the social order lurking around the corner.

Imposing the rigid structure of the Carnival balls and the debut system on a previously chaotic and unorganized Carnival had created a way of life that could only have been invented by WASPs: rigid frivolity.

I was reminded of how I had sometimes felt short of air when I was seated in the parlors of the Garden District. Often, I had felt as though I were visiting a mausoleum, a society preserved under glass. It was something like visiting royal houses in England, where the residents seem to be marking time just long enough to pass things on to their descendants.

Clarence Laughlin had photographed the crumbling relics of old plantations, calling them the ghosts along the Mississippi. But here in New Orleans, it was not just houses themselves that were the ghosts. There were human relics, too, who were the specters of the past— people like Harry McCall who had made good lives for themselves, lives of considerable accomplishment, and yet still harkened to that old romance.

The past dies slowly in New Orleans, and that has been both good and bad. Forty years ago, Robert Tallant, a chronicler of New Orleans society, observed, "Both Creole and Anglo-Saxon, there are still New Orleanians living far out of their time."

There was a genuine sadness, Tallant observed, to the "New Orleanians who cannot adjust themselves to the changing times, a sadness that is as irritating as it is pathetic, but which is incurable and therefore tragic. . . . These people did and still do want another kind of world, a feudalistic society of a privileged class and slaves. . . . You may even come to look upon the beautiful relics of the past—the lovely plantation homes, the antiques—with loathing, for these things represent the dreadful civilization they fancy they cherish."

12

The Other Queens of Carnival

Wondering about the notion of exclusivity in other Carnival clubs, I met with John Dodt, the oldest member of Petronius, the oldest gay Carnival krewe. "We're the Comus of the gay set," said John, who had joined me at the Napoleon House for a glass of iced tea. John was something of a legend in the French Quarter. A former millionaire, he had once owned a beautiful stone house on Saint Louis Street and lived the good life. He had come down in station rather precipitously, however, and was now working as busboy and cook for Petunia's, a café on Saint Louis with its façade painted bright pink.

John, a slender man in his mid-sixties, but who looked younger, had reigned as queen of Petronius in 1966, he said, when the theme had been the Wizard of Oz. He had worn a headpiece on which the city of Oz had been displayed, all in green. At a recent ball, during a parade of past queens, however, he had tripped and fallen, and his hoop skirt flew up. He lay there for a few moments until someone finally realized he was not paralyzed from embarrassment, but had broken his hip.

John said that he had begun his participation in Carnival at straight Mardi Gras balls. "In the late 1940s and '50s, everybody had money and wanted to join the straight clubs, like the Virgilians." The now-defunct Krewe of Virgilians, begun by an Italian-American physician, was known for its glittering Ziegfeld-style extravaganzas. "But I finally put my tails in mothballs and said I'd never go to a straight ball again." He explained, "If a major international ballet comes in, you're not satisfied with some little day-school production."

Gay Mardi Gras, he said, had grown in fits and starts, beginning in the 1950s. "The first gay balls were in someone's home. We were

139

the Krewe of Yuga, and everyone dressed up like royalty. But it was difficult to socialize because you expected raids." The krewe soon grew too large for private homes. "The third ball was at Mama Lu's on the lakefront, and the fourth was at a day-school camp off Veterans Highway. In 1962, we had the first Petronius ball there." They named the krewe for the cynical author of the *Satyricon*, the phantasmagorical account of Nero's pleasure-loving Rome.

"The ball was all-male and all in costume," said John. "There was a tableau with a queen and a naked king. Everybody was really tacky. It was making fun of the pompousness of the straight balls. The following Saturday, the fifth ball of Yuga got raided by the Jefferson Parish cops, and all the names made the front page. Every window dresser who worked for Maison Blanche got fired. One of the men had a girl's first name, so everybody in the city thought it was a stag party that had been raided. I got home with a black eye. The people who were there when it was raided wouldn't go to Petronius for another ten years."

Nevertheless, he said, a group of Petronius members decided to try another ball. The rules changed, said John, and it was no longer a costume ball because of the archaic law regarding costuming in the streets. At the time, anyone caught on the street in costume on a day other than Mardi Gras was subject to arrest. "We decided to have a court, and the members of the court would dress at the ball. Other guests would be in black tie. Our next two balls were at the Italian Union Hall on Esplanade. We did a little tableau with about one hundred people there."

The next year, he said, the Italian Union Hall was closed. "The Italians had assimilated into society, and they didn't need it anymore. We needed a place, so we negotiated with the Jerusalem Temple. They found out we were a gay group and decided uh-uh. We settled on the Longshoremen's Hall on Claiborne, and we were there for ten, fifteen years."

Last year they had been able to rent the Municipal Auditorium because of the attrition of other krewes. "There was a time when every night between Twelfth Night and Mardi Gras was taken," said John. Some krewes had gone out of business, he said, and others had moved their activities to hotels. Now, he said, "They'll do anything to get people in the Auditorium."

In the early years, the costumes had been out of Greek mythology or Hollywood. "It had to be fun, and the costumes were cheap." The music was supplied by tapes, and spotlights were made by volunteers. The first dues were twenty dollars. Women had not been allowed at the early balls, a policy with which John concurred. Soon, however, there were members who wanted to bring their mothers, and the policy was relaxed.

During the fifth year, a splinter group calling itself Amon-Ra broke off. "There's always a feud, and some idiot always wants to be captain," said John. "Amon-Ra thought they should have more class." Later, in the early 1980s, a mixed-race krewe called Polyphemus was founded because blacks had not been welcomed as members by other gay krewes.

John said he had never spent much on his own costumes. "I steal the show anyway, but I won't piss away money because I think it's wrong," he said. Last year, he had spent only one hundred dollars on his costume for the ball. "I went as the Queen Mother." The previous year, he had gone as Kate Smith. One year, he said, he had slayed everybody with a tribute to stripper Sandra Sexton, with "tasseled tits." He asked, rhetorically, "What are you going to do to top that?"

For Mardi Gras day, John usually joined with a group of old friends to create ensemble costumes. "Last year we were seven Whistler's mothers," he said. "We went to Krauss and bought chairs because one of us had a bad heart and built our costumes around the chairs." He recalled, "One of our best years, we were eight Joan Crawfords beating the hell out of baby dolls with wire hangers. One year, we were singing nuns. We're running out of themes."

As he recounted the decades of costumes and balls and raids, John observed ruefully, "I feel like a war-weary vet." But he wanted to stress that the gay community, and gay Carnival, were alive and well. "It's totally different from the wild lifestyle of the past," he said. "But it's still a living, vital community and not a museum."

*   *   *

As for uptown Carnival, John observed, "I don't like the type of parties they have. I have my own lifestyle and I don't want to submit to theirs. There are a lot of uptown closet types who like the whole effect, but they grew into it. They've done it so long, it's part of them." The exclusivity of uptown Carnival, however, did not bother him. "I have a Rex attitude and a Comus attitude," he said. "I can understand how uptown people feel about their groups. Being exclusive makes you feel special. We can't really be an egalitarian society. People want to feel selected."

Gay krewes, he said, practice their own sort of exclusivity. "We're all desperate for members," he said, "but we draw the line. If someone is too trashy or hustling on the street, we don't want them. For one thing, they won't have the money to pay the dues. We have very few drag queens as members, and we haven't had any black men—but no one has come up for membership. One year, a dwarf wanted to join, but we said no. We didn't want to be a circus."

III

Preparations

13

Nostalgia for Lost Causes

On the docket at the City Council session on December 12 was an ordinance that gay activists in New Orleans had been pushing for nearly a decade. Despite its increasing tolerance of gay life, the city had never passed a gay-rights bill forbidding discrimination in public accommodations or employment. Although this bill would not apply to Carnival, a number of City Hall watchers regarded it as a kind of test of prevailing political winds—a preliminary skirmish before the battle over Carnival the following week.

The gay community in New Orleans, for all its flamboyance, was not known for its political clout. Most forms of political protest in New Orleans, for that matter, have tended toward the oblique and quixotic. In a city where parades and throngs are a way of life, ordinary political marches or demonstrations can go unnoticed. New Orleans gays had never mustered a protest or a cause on the order of New York's Stonewall. Probably the biggest gay protest march in New Orleans had come on the heels of the anti-gay crusade in Dade County, Florida, led by singer and orange-juice sweetheart Anita Bryant.

In 1977, on a hot June day, when Bryant arrived in town for a Summer Pops performance at the Municipal Auditorium, she found rival armies mustered on opposite sides of the French Quarter. At Jackson Square, the anti-Anita contingent was led by the Gertrude Stein Democratic Society and their guest speaker, former Air Force sergeant Leonard Matlovich, the controversial proponent for gays in the military, who had recently appeared on the cover of *Time* magazine. Frank Kameny, head of the New Orleans Human Rights Commission, had also addressed the crowd, declaring, "We will not continue to live in closets full of America's skeletons," while a transvestite known as Lady Russell carried a placard saying BAN SCREWDRIVERS.

The group of fifteen hundred or so protesters marched to the Municipal Auditorium, where they were met by a sanctimonious group called Christians for Anita, led by penitent transsexual Perry Desmond. Inside the Auditorium, Bryant was introduced to her fans by the Reverend Bob Harrington, another Bourbon Street preacher, who told the audience, "You conventioneers should watch out who you pick up in the Quarter, or you'll end up your brother's keeper."

In 1986, City Councilman Johnny Jackson had introduced an ordinance similar to the one now on the docket, inspiring a flood of testimonials on both sides. A number of civil rights veterans showed up to support the ordinance, although, on the whole, there had not been much solidarity between blacks and gays on the subject of civil rights, in part because the Catholic church had been a bulwark against gay rights, and a great number of blacks in New Orleans were Catholic. The ordinance had been strongly supported by Dorothy Mae Taylor and the women's activist group the Committee of 21. Rosa Keller, the eminent uptown grande dame, a strong civil rights proponent, had spoken eloquently in favor of the ordinance.

There had been much fire-and-brimstone rhetoric and quoting of scripture by opponents. Harry McCall, the prominent lawyer and doyen of old-line Carnival, had published a letter on the editorial page of the *Times-Picayune*, decrying the ordinance on the grounds that it would transform the city into a New Babylon like San Francisco and "encourage public demonstration of aberrant tendencies." This was, according to the Duenna, a "curious sentiment from a man who spends Mardi Gras dressed in plumes, wig, and sequins."

Dorothy Mae Taylor had answered the Bible thumpers, retorting that she understood the Bible, too, and quoted a directive for social justice from Jesus: "Inasmuch as you do it to these, the least of my brethren, so do you do it unto me." She had concluded, "In my heart, I do believe I should support this ordinance." Nevertheless, the ordinance was voted down.

This time, however, the handwriting was on the wall, and opponents of the ordinance had mustered only a token force in the City Council chamber. The two white women council members, Peggy Wilson and Jackie Clarkson, cast the only dissenting votes. Exceptions to the ordinance were made, however—one of them, I was told, because of the peculiar architecture of New Orleans. Double shotgun houses were exempt from the ordinance, presumably because the thin walls and close proximity of these narrow duplexes would mean not merely tolerance of one's gay neighbors, but unavoidable eavesdropping.

For those making book on the Carnival ordinance, the odds had just shifted from Comus and his krewe to Dorothy Mae Taylor.

Doing the Preservation Foxtrot

Following the council meeting, I went to visit artist George Schmidt in his studio in the roomy attic of a neatly restored row house on Julia Street, on the edge of the Central Business District. On the first two floors of the building were the offices of the Preservation Resource Center, the clearinghouse for the city's preservation groups. The PRC, which had once stood as a lone sanctuary of sobriety amid a welter of rescue missions and flophouses, was now the centerpiece in the revival of the surrounding neighborhood, known as the Warehouse District, which had once smelled of coffee and cigars and other commodities that filled the warehouses by the river.

George was considered the building's resident eccentric by the stylish uptown women of the center, who had been tenacious in their ongoing battles against developers, apathetic or corrupt city officials, general entropy, and the Formosan termites.

George was a kind of relic himself, a New Orleans character whose personality accumulated layers of eccentricity and flourishes of whimsy over the years, much like the multiperiod pieces of New Orleans architecture that were the pride of the PRC. George had already appeared, thinly disguised, in a novel about dissolute New Orleans society. George, however, like Henri, came from a family of German descent that had dwelled only on the periphery of genteel uptown life. His aunt had sung during the vaudeville era at the Saenger Theatre on Canal Street, his uncle had been a pianist in Storyville, and his grandfather had held the liquor concession at the Cotton Centennial.

George had grown up in his parents' boardinghouse on Saint Charles Avenue, whose corridors and porches were filled with faded gentry, eternal bachelors, and retired saleswomen, New Orleans characters whose faces later would come to fill the backgrounds of his paintings when he needed a crowd. There had been a Miss Hepler, head of ladies' foundations at Gus Mayer's Department Store, and a Miss Dauer, who sold girdles and brassieres door-to-door and attended Mass every day. Carnival would unfold every year practically in his front yard, as the parades passed by on Saint Charles, and spectators gathered on the banquettes and neutral ground.

In a recent television documentary about Saint Charles Avenue, George had positioned himself on the avenue in front of the spot where the old boardinghouse had stood. The house had been demolished, and George described the apartment building erected in its place: "It looks like a three-story Quonset hut." George, posing as an insufferable snob, recalled leaving New Orleans as a child to visit a subdivision in the suburbs, where he felt "suffocated" by the low ceilings and the "Tupperware fumes."

On most days, George resembled a disheveled preppie, in unpressed khaki pants and striped cotton dress shirt. His alter ego was something altogether more exotic—a flapper-era crooner. As vocalist for his band, the New Leviathan Foxtrot Orchestra, which resurrected campy levantine-influenced dance music of the 1920s, he wore a white suit and straw boater and sang through a megaphone in a quavery, Jolson tenor.

The attic studio resembled the aftermath of a small tornado, the floor littered with musical instruments, dust bunnies, a streetcar conductor's hat, stacks of academic journals, old newspaper clippings, boxes of props, piles of old photos, cuff links for his tuxedo shirt. It was the collection of an impulsive and compulsive antiquarian.

George was feeling besieged and embittered, with the kind of look in his eye and tone in his voice that would inspire a stranger who saw him on the street to cross to the other side. I had asked him about the proposed Carnival ordinance and stood out of the way for the resulting barrage. "Now they want to make everybody love each other," he said, waving his arms, "and so destroy the things that make life worth living in this city." George was quite conscious of the paradoxical nature of his remark. "They're going to destroy the last remaining true public festival," he raved. By "they," presumably, he meant Dorothy Mae Taylor, her black constituency, and her liberal white supporters.

George paused to sniff the air and then ran into the kitchen to turn off a toaster oven that had begun smoking.

"The Africans think because they have soul, they should belong," he continued. "But it's not their bag. It's not their thing. What everybody seems to forget is that Carnival in New Orleans was the invention of Anglo-Saxon Protestants who were stabilizing a Creole mishmash. But now they no longer have a right to their own invention. Now we're being told, You can't be with your own people. It's like a tribe of Apaches performing a sun dance, and some Washington official saying, 'I'd like to get in on that.'"

He shifted gears. "I don't care if I'm not invited to Comus. Applying the tools of civil rights to Carnival is absurd. Dorothy Mae thinks it's like integrating the school system. But the school system is a necessity. And things like Carnival—things that make life worth living—are unnecessary."

George had a theory that the ordinance was really a way of handing Carnival over to the tourists—to the rest of America, which possessed no more imagination, he said, than the "back lot of Warner Brothers."

When I first knew George, in the 1970s, he had been almost deliriously romantic in his view of New Orleans, particularly of its quirks and idiosyncracies. He had a jingoistic suspicion of outsiders, particularly of developers, and of local "philistines" threatening to turn the city's cultural artifacts into tourist attractions. He had been particularly vigilant about the intrusion of commercialism or bourgeois bad taste into Carnival. One year he had carried a sign on Mardi Gras day reading YANKEE GO HOME!

George had advocated an aggressive sort of provincialism, peculiar to New Orleans, that he envisioned as the antithesis of the artistic regionalism of the 1930s, which had been, he said, "Middle Western, democratic, optimistic, agrarian, populist." The sort of regionalism that should be developed in New Orleans, he said, was "urban, coastal, tragic, critical, and unpopular."

New Orleans, he told me once, was a "Scorpio" city, "furtive, secretive, damp, evil, capable of sensual gratification, liable to fall prey to its habits, dormant, able to hibernate a long time, with great survival power, likely to rise like a phoenix from its ashes."

He had linked the possibility of a social and artistic renaissance in New Orleans to the city's ties with the Third World. New Orleans, he would insist, was closer to the Caribbean than to Kansas City, mainly because its lifestyle was based on the principle of celebration. Modern education, he theorized, had erected a wall between the masses, tied to tradition, and the avant-garde elite. Carnival was a tradition that linked the peasant and the aristocrat, but that evaded the bourgeoisie. He quoted Octavio Paz: "The West must discover the secret of the incarnation of poetry and collective life: the fiesta."

George had been one of the city's early preservationists, although his choice of monuments to protect and his tactics had been considerably more quixotic than those of the well-organized PRC. When developers proposed to remove the ancient awning of the Café du Monde, the famous coffee-and-beignet oasis in the French Market, as part of the massive renovation that transformed the old market, teeming with produce and pungent smells, into tourist emporiums, George organized a spirited campaign to save the awning, shouting rabble-rousing slogans through his New Leviathan megaphone.

In 1974, when another venerable French Market coffeehouse, the Morning Call, was moved to a suburban shopping mall, in a development called Fat City, George mourned the loss by dressing on Mardi Gras day as the ghost of the transplanted café. He wore a Morning Call apron and waiter's cap over a grinning skull mask.

That day, he experienced a vision. "The mask," he said, "is like a limbic pot. You end up breathing your own exhaled breath. It isolates you and disguises you, and it acts as a ventilator. The intoxicating effect of the mask allows you to see things differently. That day, I went to the corner of Canal and Royal, and I saw the viewing stand of the Pickwick Club, filled with women, a sea of socialites, a nest of Babylonians. The women turned into jewel-like insects in front of my eyes. A friend told me I had seen the white goddess, the muse."

George had painted a series of pictures about Carnival that had a dark, ominous feel to them, verging on a George Grosz grotesqueness. The old men of the Carnival elite appeared as jaded sybarites, and the women as empty-headed mannequins. One of the paintings in that series hung on the wall of Dalt and Josephine's living room. It was set in the dimly lit backstage dressing room before the Comus ball, as a naked Comus reveler was waited on by a black attendant.

George had been wonderfully amusing in those days, cutting a romantic figure in his white suit and tousled blond hair. The New Leviathan, with its campy exoticism, had been one of the most popular party bands in town, and George's paintings were in considerable demand by the cognoscenti. His renderings of the dark interiors of Carnival, offering sardonic behind-the-scenes glimpses of the city's ancien régime, had the feeling of immediate classics. They seemed to become part of the cultural landscape, influencing forever the way people would look at Carnival.

In the intervening years, George's work had lightened, literally and figuratively, becoming more like that of the formal salon painters of the nineteenth century. His paintings now were brightly lit, realistically rendered, and precise in perspective, if bizarre in subject. George had adapted remarkably well, at first, to the commercial real estate boom, set off by the World's Fair, that created a growing market for local artists. George went on exhibit during the fair as an artist-in-residence, threatening to wear a pince-nez and dress like Whistler in a frock coat and beret, for the benefit of cotton-candy-carrying visitors fresh off the monorail or the world's largest Ferris wheel.

If the tourist industry was displacing indigenous culture with the culture of the marketplace, George reasoned, artists and musicians would have to serve as curators or keepers of the city's soul. "The old folk culture is going," George had told me in 1984. "There's no authenticity left. The only recourse to business and commercial interests who want to create that environment is the artist. Entrepreneurs can't recreate the past. But we can. You can't bring the old New Orleans back, but you can do it again in art. You can poeticize it."

He had begun painting a series of tableaux capturing odd moments in the history of New Orleans, particularly during the Storyville era, when the beau monde overlapped with the demimonde. In one painting, called *Sarah Bernhardt Meets the Razzy Dazzy Jazz Band*, based on an event early in the life of white jazz musician Emile "Stale Bread" Lacoume, the actress is bending down in front of Anderson's Saloon, on the edge of Storyville, to greet the ragamuffin boys of the street corner, or "spasm," band. Lacoume, considered by some jazz historians the first jazz musician, even predating trumpet player Buddy Bolden, played a homemade violin constructed from a cigar box.

In another painting, called *The Naked Dance*, based on a scene once mentioned in a memoir by Jelly Roll Morton, Morton can be seen playing the piano behind a screen in the mirrored ballroom of Josie Arlington's bordello. In the foreground, a Rubenesque nude dances with wild abandon, as men in white tie and tails watch, in various poses of smirking appreciation. For the faces of men in the background, George had used friends and relatives as models, including his father.

George was so absorbed in the past that his dreams began to merge with the subjects of his paintings. In one dream he described to me, he was riding on the Saint Charles streetcar holding a box of Cracker Jack's in his lap. In the bottom of the box was a man who invited him in. Suddenly he was riding in a much older streetcar. The man in the box, who was an antiquarian, told George it was the year 1910, and that they were on the way to the Rex parade. Suddenly they were in an old car, and the man said that they had to park it in Storyville before going to the parade. After parking on Iberville Street, the man said, "Josie Arlington is a friend of mine. Let's go have coffee with the girls." They went into the bordello, and all the women were dressed like baby dolls, carrying whips. The Cracker Jack man said to the girls, "I'd like you to meet George Schmidt, the painter." George was nonplussed by this gesture, feeling a bit like Alice in

Wonderland until one of the girls came up to him and rubbed her groin against his leg.

Last spring, when I had come to George's studio for a visit, he was at work on another painting in his series of New Orleans epiphanies. This one, commissioned by the owner of a chain of video stores, was a scene featuring Nick LaRocca, the Italian cornet player whose combo, the Dixieland Jazz Band, made the first jazz recording. According to George, the fact that a white man had made the first jazz recording had disconcerted a number of jazz historians. "Poor Nick had to be buried," he said. In the painting, LaRocca, who had been hired to promote a boxing match, was standing at the back of a wagon, playing his trumpet on Canal Street.

George had completed another series of Carnival paintings, also in a historical vein. He had done a painting of Louis Armstrong reigning as the king of Zulu in 1949 and another of the *boeuf gras* in the 1892 Rex parade. There was one of the Duke and Duchess of Windsor at the Comus ball—the juxtaposition of abdicated royalty with the trumped-up monarchs of Mardi Gras. There had been such a stir at the time, with questions of who would bow to whom—a game of royal chicken, perhaps. There had been general relief and awe when the real duke had taken the initiative and bowed to the anonymous Comus.

George realized now, he said, that the satirical paintings he had done of contemporary Carnival "were the tip of the iceberg. If I didn't go back in time, I would be excluding an important poetic element of Carnival. I wanted to do more than just be a documentarist of the empty lives of the upper class, which is basically a frustrating task."

George insisted that the past was not dead, but a living thing, disgorging facts and dreams. "Faulkner was right," he said, about "every Southern boy having that image of Pickett's charge in his head."

George's attitude toward Carnival and toward New Orleans had changed. "I was obsessed by Carnival," said George. "It was the source of my images. Those were the images I carried around with me. You're only attracted to the things that you love/hate. You disguise yourself, you create a persona, but it's still you, your obsessions."

He no longer loved Carnival, he said, but there was still a kind of afterglow. He freely admitted that he had been captivated by the subjects of his paintings, the uptown elite who made up Carnival aristocracy. "I realized I didn't really want to condemn those people. I became like an artistic quisling. I realized how much I really did dig it. I'm a closet socialite, like Proust. Instead of condemning it all, I became its champion."

He admitted, too, however, that he would forever be a kind of outsider, gazing at his obsession. "I'm not a part of it really. I'm on the outside looking in. People like me, we can never bring our gifts to it, but we can't keep our eyes off it."

Traditional Carnival, however, like uptown society, was withering away, a shadow of itself. "We're looking at mere vestiges of the past." The people actually responsible for putting on the show were very few. "Henri," he said, "bleeds over this festival. He's one of the few holding back the onslaught." In part, he said, it was a matter of attrition. The Atlanteans, the smallest and most secretive of the uptown krewes, he observed acidly, had been able to muster only two maids for its 1991 Carnival ball—"two bouillon cubes of social distillation."

An old-line captain had complained to George recently that all his children had left town. "There will be no one left," said George, "except those who didn't have the strength to flee." Uptown Carnival was dying of its own exclusivity. "It's like the Golden Book in twelfth-century Venice. These were the names of the Venetian nobility, and you were excluded if your family came along after that. That's what happened here. If your name didn't appear in a book, *New Orleans Masquerade*, in the list of queens and maids of Carnival before 1920, you're out." He had a close friend whose father "died regretting he had never been invited to Comus."

The old-line krewes, he said, were contributing to their own decline, "digging their own graves. There's nobody around clever enough to create the glamour. You need a Proust to glamorize the life. The very people who could help it aren't asked to belong. All the clever people have been snubbed or left town."

Worst of all, the most lethal enemies of Carnival had intruded: doubt and melancholy. "Our problem is that we have to share Carnival with Celts and their melancholy," said George balefully. "They think it has something to do with drunkenness." And now, too, there was irony. "Carnival used to be a time you never doubted. There was no sense of disbelief or irony. You never doubted you wanted to be there. Now we doubt everything about it."

A year later, the doubts seemed to have multiplied. George had grown weary of wringing his hands over the ruined beauty of New Orleans, and he seemed content to let it give up the ghost. He had "painted himself into a corner," he admitted, with his "provincialism," and retreating still further, into the past, he had still not been able to escape the increasing intrusions into his fantasy world of Carnival and old New Orleans. He felt, he said, that he had been "digging around an old corpse, a corpse that was beginning to smell." Wrinkling his nose, he said, "I've got to find some way out of this place in my imagination. I have developed a sensitivity to New Orleans that is killing me. I don't go down certain streets anymore because it breaks my heart."

George had long since stopped talking about a possible New Orleans renaissance, and now he was talking, instead, about Italy, where doubt and irony were still at bay, and about the Italian renaissance that "gave us the gift of seeing things as they really are, instead of being tyrannized by superstition." Said George, "I'd move to Italy if I could afford it."

He led me over to see his latest painting, of Cicero orating in the Forum, the first in a new series focusing on ancient Rome. His new passion, he said, was in the rise of the Roman code of law, from which the Napoleonic code descended.

And as for the dilemma facing Comus and the other uptown Carnival krewes, he said, "They've been so snobbish, nobody will come to their rescue. But those who are laughing about it are laughing at the edge of the grave."

The Queen of Queens

A session with George, the premature relic, was ideal preparation for a late afternoon visit with Susan Buck Mayer, who was known as the queen of queens. Susan had reigned as queen of Comus in 1937, and every year, all the living queens of Comus gathered at her home on the Friday before Mardi Gras day prior to walking over to the Pontchartrain Hotel for a luncheon. Susan was regarded by a number of my uptown acquaintances as the living embodiment of old-line Carnival, a true bon vivant.

Susan had just gotten a permanent wave, she confided, patting her short, neatly curled gray hair. A small, frail-looking woman, she was wearing a simple shirtwaist dress. She had set up her huge double parlor for a card party the next day, and there were card tables everywhere, as well as odd little decorations, which seemed to be left over from Halloween.

"I grew up in this house," she said. "My husband and I moved back here thirty-odd years ago." The house was a magnificent Greek revival mansion located just off Saint Charles Avenue, almost directly behind the Pontchartrain Hotel. Behind its tall, wrought iron fence, it stood as a lone relic of well-preserved grandeur, surrounded by ramshackle apartment houses and boarded-up ruins.

Susan fit the standard profile of Carnival royalty. Her father was sure that she would be queen of Comus the day she was born, she said. "I went to McGehee's and to Newcomb; I made my debut and didn't graduate." She met her husband George in college. George inherited the El Cuba Cigar plant in the Warehouse District. He had reigned, she said, as king of Oberon, of Twelfth Night, and of Mystic.

She pointed out the shadow boxes and display cases filled with Carnival memorabilia. There were favors from Twelfth Night and Proteus, including a silver bean from the court of Twelfth Night. "My sister got the gold bean," she said. Upstairs in the attic was a complete collection of Comus invitations.

The house had been robbed frequently, she said. The shadow box of Carnival trinkets had been taken off the wall three times and once wrapped up on a rug, but the thieves had never actually gotten out of the house with it.

"I've lived through everything," she said. "I've been held up and beat up." Her son still lived out back in the *garçonnière*, a sort of carriage house, a common arrangement in New Orleans. But her

daughter and grandchildren had all left town. "The younger generation, they don't like it here."

She herself still loved to walk the streets of the city, she said,
although it had gotten too dangerous. "I used to walk down to the
Boston Club as a child."

The afternoon was winding down, and Susan asked if I would
like a drink. I told her I'd just have whatever she was having, expecting a glass of lemonade or ice tea. From the pantry, she carried out
two tall glasses filled nearly to the brim with straight bourbon, no
water, no ice.

She brought out a scrapbook filled with photos and news clippings from various Carnival balls. There was a photo of herself as
queen of Comus: Miss Susan Olga Serena Buck. "I don't think the
Depression crimped our style much," she said. Her gown from that
year, she said, was now in the Cabildo museum.

There was even a yellowed clipping describing the Comus ball
held in 1891 at the Grand Opera House, the first year the krewe
elected a queen. There was a dance card, listing the order of dances
for the evening:

1. Royal quadrille
2. Waltz
3. Lancers
4. Polka
5. Waltz
6. Quadrille
7. Polka
8. Lancers
9. Waltz

The clipping from the next year's ball showed Winnie Davis,
daughter of Confederate president Jefferson Davis, as queen, dressed
in a Japanese kimono. The theme that year had been "Nippon, the
land of the Rising Sun." The real theme, however, as historian Clive
Hardy has since noted, was nostalgia for the Lost Cause, and this ball
represented "the high tide of Carnival homage to the old Confeder-

acy." In 1884, for its first court, Comus had already honored Winnie Davis, as well as Mildred Lee, daughter of Robert E. Lee, and Julia Jackson, daughter of Stonewall Jackson.

Since the subject of lost causes had come up, I asked Susan what she thought of Dorothy Mae Taylor's antidiscrimination ordinance. Susan retorted, "She's out of her mind. I don't see the point in dragging up these things." She felt, as did so many other traditional Carnival proponents, that if something was not broken, you shouldn't try to fix it.

I wondered if Susan and her husband had been tempted to move away after so many robberies and muggings. "I'll stay right here," said Susan. "They'll have to carry me out. There are too many memories here."

14

ReBirth in the Streets

It was a beautiful sunny day, perfect for a parade or a horse race, and I dropped off a friend at the Fairgrounds Racetrack, where he preferred to attend his own kind of Sunday worship services. Such pursuits were once a barrier between the pleasure-loving Creole population and the neo-Puritan Americans. The Creoles were given to testing their luck, rather than proving their virtue, and it was in New Orleans that two favorite American games of chance took root— poker, originally "pocque," and craps. Americans had once referred derisively to every Creole as Johnny Crapaud, and they had dubbed the Creoles' pastime of rolling dice as the game of Johnny Crapaud, later shortening the name to craps.

Particularly offensive to the Creoles had been the American attacks on the way the natives spent their Sundays—loitering in cafés or attending bullbaitings, horse races, theatrical performances, and dances. Transplanted New Englanders were forever posting signs beneath notices of Sunday balls admonishing the ungodly to REMEMBER THE SABBATH DAY TO KEEP IT HOLY! while Protestant newspapers and ministers fulminated against too much worldliness.

Some forms of black culture had managed to evade such schisms by combining the worldly with the sacred. I headed for Central City, where I was to meet up with a Sunday parade sponsored by the Just Stepping Social and Pleasure Club, and featuring ReBirth, the hottest young brass band in town. The ReBirth, as the band was known, was then the "house" band at the Glass House, a small, nondescript-looking bar on Saratoga Street, where the renowned Dirty Dozen Brass Band had gotten its start. Last year, ReBirth had been recorded at the Glass House on Mardi Gras day by Rounder Records, and the band had been getting invitations to play around the country.

I had gone to hear ReBirth play at the Glass House one night, a few weeks earlier, but I had had to gird up my nerve to venture into the neighborhood. If you arrived too early at the Glass House, say, around 11 P.M., you were tempted to keep driving. The deserted streets in that part of Central City can look ominous. But if you got there a little closer to midnight, it was as though you'd happened on a block party, with the crowd inside the bar spilling out into the street. Inside, the walls were lined with mirrors—hence "glass house"—and one end of the small barroom was occupied by a tiny stage, where ReBirth could hardly fit all eight musicians. They teetered there precariously, a clump of drums and brass, trombone slides poking out here and there, trumpet player Kermit Ruffins hamming it up in front, and bandleader Philip Frazier's tuba bell looming up behind and bobbing as the music got going.

Now, even in the bright noonday sun, I was feeling a bit nervous as I parked my car and found my way to the corner of Washington Avenue and Freret Street, on the edge of the Magnolia Housing Project, a place that had nothing about it to suggest that fragrant, easily bruised Southern bloom. Magnolia was the most ominous-looking of all the housing projects in the city, surrounded by abandoned shotgun cottages with boarded-up windows and signs announcing impending auction of foreclosed buildings.

The Just Stepping Social and Pleasure Club, however, made up for the drabness of the surroundings. Just Stepping was a women's club, and they had dressed in violet velveteen suits, with tight trousers and short jackets. One member carried a banner announcing the club's name in bright gold, and others carried ostrich-plumed scepters with their names spelled out in sequins.

I was reminded that uptown whites were not the only group in New Orleans who felt under siege, nor were white Carnival celebrants the only group trying to maintain their traditions, to keep the festive spirit alive, and to hold their families and community together in a crumbling city. In all of those endeavors, the black citizens of New Orleans had a long head-start.

*   *   *

Historically, the black residents of New Orleans have shown as strong a predilection as whites for clubs and societies and for lots of pomp and ceremony. Brass bands and "social and pleasure" clubs, whose origins were tied up together in the flowering of black culture in New Orleans following the Civil War, have been around the city at least as long as the Mistick Krewe of Comus. Long before the turn of the century, brass bands, dressed in bright uniforms, with the players reading music off little cards, were a common sight in the city, entertaining at conventions and parties and marching in parades. The legendary Excelsior Brass Band was known for its blue Prussian-style military uniforms and plumed hats.

During the nineteenth century, the black community in New Orleans, barred from using white banks or insuring their lives with white insurance companies, traditionally avoided charity from whites and turned to their own social and benevolent societies for their social security. In return for modest dues, black societies acted as a kind of social safety net, providing a sense of belonging and social status, in life and in death.

During the Reconstruction period, the mortality rates for poor blacks was very high, particularly for men, and the streets resounded with the mournful dirges of brass bands, hired by benevolent societies to follow horse-drawn hearses to the cemeteries, where young men, who had died before their time, were laid to rest in biers above ground. Behind or alongside the band, the parade of mourners, which came to be known as the second line, would follow, carrying umbrellas, good for sun or rain. Once the body was interred, it was time to celebrate.

Brass bands played so frequently for funeral processions that they became inextricably tied up with the notion of death in New Orleans. Even now, as Edgar Chase put it, "The dream of every black person in this city is to be sent off with a jazz funeral and a second line. Whether there's a heaven or not, you know you've made it, then."

Even more commonly than the bordellos of Storyville and the strip joints on Bourbon Street, the city streets, with their brass-band parades, became training grounds for black musicians. With a city so enamored of parties and parades, where even death required musical accompaniment, there was a lot of work for musicians. At times, there was so much music in the air that it seemed to come from everywhere at once.

Danny Barker, the great jazz guitarist and banjo player who grew up near the French Quarter not long after the turn of the century, once described hearing that ubiquitous music as a child: "A bunch of us kids, playing, would suddenly hear sounds. It was like a phenomenon, like the Aurora Borealis—maybe. The sounds of men playing would be so clear, but we wouldn't be sure where they were coming from. So we'd start trotting, start running—'It's this way! It's that way!' And sometimes after running for awhile you'd find you'd be nowhere near that music. But that music could come on you any time like that."

Edgar Chase, too, recalled being called away by music. "One afternoon, when I was going to Catholic school," he recounted, "we were having a May Day procession, with the Blessed Sacrament nuns and the Josephite fathers, carrying the statue of the Virgin Mary. At the same time, there was a jazz funeral for Paul Barbarin, and the children broke away from saying the Rosary and headed for the music."

Said Chase, "You'd be listening for that horn—*Da da Da-a-a-a*. The real second-liner will drop everything at the drop of the hat. That's the spirit of the second line."

By the 1970s, though, the average age of the musicians had crept up, and the brass-band tradition seemed on the brink of dying out, despite the growing interest of white musicians and musicologists. Jazz funerals for great old black musicians seemed to lament the passing of the tradition as much as the individuals themselves.

The Dirty Dozen Jazz Band, who infused the old tunes with contemporary sophistication, revived the tradition, introducing it to a new generation, and once they grew too big for the Glass House, ReBirth came along to keep things rolling.

As the Just Steppers lined up on Washington Avenue for the parade, I spotted Philip Frazier hoisting up his battered, taped-up tuba on the edge of the crowd and immediately felt more comfortable. Philip, who was twenty-four, seemed at first glance much too slight to bounce along for miles with a tuba slung around his torso like a big brass boa. But he was strong and sturdy—and an island of calm in any storm. Philip, whose smile was accentuated by a small diamond inset in a front tooth, radiated sweetness and light.

"This place is like a second home," said Philip, of the shattered neighborhood around the Magnolia project. I asked Philip how many years this particular parade had been going on. "It's been started since before we were born," he said.

Philip explained what the group would be playing today. For a funeral, the band would play a lot of "church songs," but for this occasion, he said, which was being held for pure fun, they would do a lot of "funky songs." Today, he said, would be "one big ole she-bang." The band had a flexible repertory. "Our material is loose and spontaneous," said Philip, "not the same old stuff." The band had already come up with twenty-two versions of their theme song, "Do Whatcha Wanna."

Philip and his brother Keith, who plays the bass drum in the band, and who also looks a bit slight for his instrument, were raised in the Ninth Ward. Their mother, whom they affectionately call Mama ReBirth, was a church organist. Philip started out playing the trombone and his brother the baritone sax in the school band. When they moved downtown to Tremé and heard a lot of brass bands, Philip switched to the tuba, despite his modest stature. "I was drawn to that big old horn," he once told me, because the tuba players "were having the most fun." In fact, most tuba players tended to be of the hefty, jolly sort. Now, playing the tuba, said Philip, was like "second nature, like breathing."

Keith Frazier was also a good dancer, and he had earned money dancing on the streets in the French Quarter. Philip, Keith, Kermit Ruffins, and five other friends started out as a street band in the French Quarter. They'd meet at the corner of Conti and Broad Street, at the Lafitte Housing Project, and walk all the way to the Quarter, playing on the way down.

"They came out of the public schools playing the hell out of those taped-up instruments," as their manager, Allison Miner Kaslow, a cofounder of the New Orleans Jazz and Heritage Festival, put it. At first, they had played with more raw energy and enthusiasm than sophistication. But as they combined traditional street music with funk, rhythm and blues, and even rap, they created their own brand of music. Metamorphosis, as James Booker would call it.

Philip, Keith, and their friends had named the band after a youth community center. But the name could stand for the miraculous way music is continually reinvented and replenished in New Orleans.

"That song of theirs, 'Do Whatcha Wanna,'" Edgar Chase observed, "is what the second line is all about. When Philip plays the tuba, all his lungs going out with that horn, it's as though they're saying, 'Nothing you can do will defeat my spirit.'"

This past year, they had gotten gigs around the country and around the world, but they still played local engagements, sometimes as many as two or three a day. Often that meant playing in the rain. "One time," said Philip, "it started raining harder and harder, and we just got wilder and wilder. I love playing in the rain. Our motto is, 'It's going to rain on the ReBirth Band.'"

For ReBirth, however, as for an entire generation of young men in New Orleans, the street parade had taken a sad new dimension. The crack epidemic had taken an early harvest here, as it has in other cities. Traditionally, the jazz funeral had been associated with old musicians being laid to rest after a long and distinguished life. But now, the jazz funeral was the ritual of choice for those murdered before their time—for drug dealers and their victims. It was like the days of the cholera and yellow-fever epidemics, when the brass bands could hardly keep up with all the bodies.

The drug epidemic had brought ReBirth a lot of work, sometimes as many as two jazz funerals in a single day. "I know a lot of people who chose the rough way out," said Philip. "I have a lot of friends who went that way. At one time I thought somebody would just go out and kill people so they could have a jazz funeral. The friends who went that way tell us it's a good thing we chose music."

At one funeral, ReBirth was playing at the back of the procession, while the more traditional Olympia Brass Band was leading up front. The young band members hadn't kept to the traditional pattern of slow dirges all the way to the cemetery and had begun to break out with their livelier numbers. "You can't play that," an Olympian told them. Said Philip, "They were playing that slow music in front, and we were in the back doing 'Shake Your Booty.'" They weren't being irreverent, Philip asserted. "In the Bible it says, 'Rejoice,' and we were rejoicing."

As the parade neared the corner of Washington and Loyola, I glanced up, facing the sun, and I could see the silhouettes of two young men dancing on the tops of the tombs in the Saint Joseph Cemetery. We continued marching, and turned right on Daneel Street.

I got lost in a sea of second-liners, but I felt confident as long as I could see Philip's bobbing tuba. As I got farther behind, I could hear little more than the throbbing beat, but that was enough to keep everybody dancing in the long second line. The sound was like bubbles popping at the surface of a merrily boiling cauldron of musical traditions. You could hear so many sounds and influences flowing through those taped-up horns. It was Louis Armstrong all over again, growing up in the Battlefield, learning to play the horn in the Colored Waifs Home band, starting with the standard brass-band repertory of the day—marches, spirituals—then cutting them up with a "beautiful attack"—the sharp stab of sound that could cut through skin and ice.

Across from a tiny building housing the Fats Shoe Shine Parlor, the band launched into "Let's Go Get 'Em," a song the Mardi Gras Indian tribes used as a challenge to their rivals, and as the only white face in the crowd, I was feeling more and more conspicuous. Two people had been shot on the street, near here, just two days ago. I had been to jazz funerals before that took me through housing projects, but that was more than a decade ago, when music seemed a kind of magic charm that offered its devotees immunity from all harm.

White people did have a way of intruding into the rituals of black celebrants in New Orleans. There was a time when white anthropologists, music aficionados, and photographers outnumbered black second-liners at jazz funerals. I still have a photograph taken at the cemetery during the funeral for piano legend Billie Pierce that shows a gaggle of photographers pushing and shoving for position atop a tomb.

The Glass House had been "discovered" a few years ago by white music fans, who began to take over the tiny dance floor, crowding out the regulars, who used to engage in legendary dance contests that put

New York "voguing" to shame. Before long, the cars belonging to the white intruders had begun to get trashed, and a few white patrons were mugged. According to Mike Smith, who knew a lot of the Glass House regulars, this was not random violence, but a kind of rough "community justice," which ended after community leaders and musicians called for tolerance.

Today, no one had made me feel unwelcome, nor had I felt any hostile undercurrents as I flowed along with the crowd. But I was still feeling nervous, and I jumped when I felt someone grab my shoulders from behind. I glanced behind me, ready to run, until I saw a skinny old man with a grizzled beard, wearing brown pants and an orange shirt, smiling at me, amused at my awkwardness. He moved my shoulders gently back and forth in a slow shimmy. "Just relax, young lady," he said.

We passed the Saint Mark Missionary Baptist Church, and elderly women in white suits and flowered hats peered out from the porch. We passed the Holy Ghost Center, with Coca-Cola signs painted on the side.

I thought about a story Philip had told me about going to play for a funeral and looking into the coffin to find an old friend, Blue Michael Till, lying there. "That made the music even better, even deeper" that day, said Philip. "It's the saddest but the best." At the funeral for Blue Michael, he said, when the procession reached the corner of Esplanade and North Roberts, the band launched into one of their trademark songs, "Freedom," and the procession stopped there. Philip looked up, and there was Blue Michael's brother on top of a building, dancing.

15

The Missing Links of Carnival

Gifts of grace and moments of transcendence in New Orleans come at strange times and in peculiar places. There is sometimes a very thin line here, particularly during Carnival, between saints and sinners, between the sacred and the profane. The origins of Carnival itself have been traced back, with varying credibility, to both sacred and pagan sources. Although the religious element has pretty well been "knocked out" of Carnival, the notion of Mardi Gras being cele-brated with as much verve in a Protestant or a completely secular city seems as implausible as New Orleans becoming the next Silicon Valley.

The population of New Orleans, as a whole, is now about 40 percent Catholic. The city is full of convents, surrounded by high walls like fortresses, most of them now deserted or converted to other uses. Some people, however, still consider New Orleans the last pagan city. Trying to resolve questions of either/or in New Orleans, how-ever, is usually futile. Walker Percy once remarked that, in New Orleans, "The tourist is apt to see more nuns and naked women than he ever saw before."

The outward manifestations of Catholicism—its rites, its altars, and vestments, if not the faith itself—have become a kind of obses-sion for many otherwise nondevout New Orleanians. The Duenna's other Carnival alter ego, for example, was that of a priest in a long cassock, and Henri's favorite Carnival costume, when he was not masking as Pulcinella, the hunchback clown, was that of a pope. I had noticed, too, that everyone in New Orleans seemed to use their man-telpieces as altars, strewn with various relics—feathers, statuary, old pictures, Mardi Gras beads.

I told the Duenna that I had been puzzled by the peculiar, inverted form of Catholicism that prevailed in some quarters of New Orleans. The Duenna replied, somewhat huffily, that it was not inverted—but that it was simply more like Catholicism in the Southern Hemisphere—that is, Catholicism tinged with voodoo and Santeria, a Catholicism of relics and strange saints and statues with miraculous powers.

The patroness of the city is Our Lady of Prompt Succor, whose statue was brought over to New Orleans from France by the Ursuline nuns. The former convent covers a square block in the French Quarter between Ursulines Street and Governor Nicholls. In 1815, shortly before the British attacked the city in the battle of New Orleans, the women of the city gathered with the nuns at the convent chapel to pray for protection from the Protestant dragons. The resounding victory by the ragtag New Orleanians was ascribed to intervention by Our Lady of Prompt Succor, and the citizens of the city vowed to celebrate a Mass in her honor every year. Even today, when hurricanes threaten the shores of Louisiana, supplicants pray to Our Lady for protection from the elements.

John Dodt had actually costumed one year as Our Lady. The theme for the Petronius ball that year was "New Orleans Institutions." He carried a baby doll as the baby Jesus, with the doll's brown hair dyed blond and a wire halo hovering above it. "It was like an eighteenth-century French statue," Dodt said. "Some people thought I should be excommunicated." A priest who had attended the ball told Dodt that he had said a quick Hail Mary but had stayed to enjoy the rest of the show.

The Duenna liked to collect odd saints, not merely from New Orleans, but from around the world. His favorite was the chaste young Spanish martyr who was courted by an odious suitor. She prayed for deliverance from the oaf and woke up the next morning with a full beard.

The most famous New Orleans saint, of course, was Saint Expedite, who now graces Our Lady of Guadalupe Church on North Rampart Street. The statue of the saint was apparently shipped to New Orleans without a name on the base, leaving those who unpacked the statue to guess the saint's identity. Someone decided that the word EXPEDITE, stamped on the outside of the crate, referred to the saint. There were rumors, too, of a Saint Fragile.

A remarkable show at the Contemporary Arts Center in 1977 reflected the odd confluence in New Orleans of the hallowed and the damned. The theme of the show was environments, and many of the exhibits were votive in one way or another, rather like hybrids of church altars and Mardi Gras tableaux. The Duenna put together a collaborative shrine with photographer Eric Bookhardt and Denise Vallon, founder of the Krewe of Clones.

The notes I took on the show at the time describe "the inverted reliquary of a mad apostate, a catechismic nightmare of flagellatory titillation, apostolic prodigality, unredemptive icons, and unconditional indulgences." As I recall, the wimpled Vallon had glided through the space sporadically, along with the Duenna, done up as a dancing prelate from *The Devils of Loudun*, and their friend Steve Duplantier, who posed as the renegade priest from Tennessee Williams's *Night of the Iguana*. The guardian saint of this "charnel house and hermitage" was, of course, Saint Expedite, "the saint whose time has come."

At the time, I felt that the real miracle being celebrated in these vatic spaces was the fleeting victory of art and creativity over Dionysian dissipation and entropy, forces that overwhelm almost everyone in the city at one time or another. In New Orleans, almost all of the angels are fallen, and one's demons tend to win most of the inner battles. Eric Bookhardt, however, emphasized that these "microcosms" were meant to be "geopsychic"—expressive of the peculiar consciousness and ambience of the local environment.

Hail and Farewell

Given the odd mixture in New Orleans of French, Catholic, Anglo-Saxon, and Afro-Caribbean cultures, the issues of influences and origins are quite muddled when you try to piece together a historical chronology leading to the creation of contemporary Carnival. More than half the krewes of Carnival, for example, are named for Greek, Roman, or Egyptian mythological figures.

Some historians of Carnival, following the lead of Sir James

Frazer's classic work, *The Golden Bough*, have turned to early pagan celebrations in Greece and Rome as ancient antecedents for contemporary Carnival. In this view, the church tamed the wild frenzies of the pagan hordes by incorporating them into its own calendar.

Perry Young offered the standard account of pagan practices taken in hand by church fathers, but then muddied the argument by pointing to pagan origins for nearly everything in our civilization. Young reasoned that our ancestors were "all pagans, unless Jews." While "morality, dogmas, and sacred mysteries" were "of Christ's life and teachings," he wrote, the rest of "Christian civilization—meat, drink, raiment on the street or in the pulpit, kisses, wedding-rings, sciences, kings, democracies, metals, machinery, and languages all go back to paganism for their fundamentalisms. Christianity refined those pagan things, gave them powers of progress and evolution. The church converted our usages as well as our souls."

Frazer had identified certain practices of Carnival with the Saturnalia, the Roman festival celebrated in December. The king of Saturnalia ruled over the revels as Lord of Misrule and was burned in effigy at the end of the festival. Frazer found an even stronger connection between Carnival and the Lupercalia, the fertility rite that Carnival historian Robert Tallant described as an "orgy of lust and pain."

In its early form, as described by Ovid, Arcadian shepherds sacrificed a goat and made whips of its skin, with which priests flagellated people of the village. The rite graduated in Rome to gladiatorial displays and general public debauchery, led by the worshippers of Attis who sacrificed their genitals and practiced male prostitution as a religious rite. Maskers dressed as women and offered themselves to other celebrants.

Contemporary scholars have not yet found convincing concrete evidence of a direct historical trail, from century to century, between the Lupercalia, last celebrated in the fifth century A.D., and the first mention of Carnival (as *carnelevare*) in church writings in the tenth century. There is a missing link, then, in Carnival evolution between pagan antiquity and the official church rite now called Shrove Tuesday, Mardi Gras, or Fat Tuesday.

The theory offered by some folklorists that the early forms of Carnival survived after the coming of Christianity as a kind of underground pastoral festival celebrated by peasants no longer seems very convincing. There is a chicken-and-egg question, too, whether the medieval church was simply reacting to the licentious excesses of the people in defining and setting the limits of Carnival—or whether the licentious excesses of the people might have been a reaction to the limits set by the church.

An entry in *The Catholic Encyclopedia* begged the question of pagan influences on Carnival and suggested that it was a natural sort of fleshly indulgence before the austerity of Lent: "It is intelligible enough that before a long period of deprivations human nature should allow itself some exceptional license in the way of frolic and good cheer. No appeal to vague and often inconsistent traces of earlier pagan customs seems needed to explain the general observances of a carnival celebration."

The word Carnival itself—that is, the Latin word *carnelevare*—appeared first in church writings in the year 965 A.D. Literally, the word *carnelevare* means to lift up, or relieve, from flesh or meat. The etymology of the word is somewhat confusing. Some scholars, for example, split the Italian word *carnevale* in two and translate it as "Hail, Meat!" or "Good-bye, Meat!" *The Catholic Dictionary* asserts that the word carnival was derived from the phrase, *carnem levare*, meaning the taking-away of flesh, which marked the beginning of Lent. But as Perry Young noted, that phrase could also mean elevation of the flesh or its relief, which would suggest that "carnival" derives from a phrase suggesting the consolation of the flesh.

I concluded that the word Carnival, in its root and current forms, implies both hail and farewell; that is, it means both a raising-up and a letting-go of the flesh, a brief embrace of that which we know we cannot keep. In Carnival, we celebrate what we must relinquish— which accounts for the strange mood of melancholy or the gallows humor that may invade the most festive of Carnival moments. Black historian John Rousseau once described Carnival most aptly as "the last fling of the flesh."

During early forms of Carnival, the flesh in question was not merely the bodies of the celebrants but the meat of a sacrificial bull. One of the chief processional figures in medieval French carnival and in later courtly celebrations was the *boeuf gras,* which was garlanded with flowers or laurel branches around his horns. Often the beast was butchered following these high honors and his meat served to the court. The *boeuf gras* was a staple of the Rex parade, which first marched in 1872. Perry Young listed the components of the first division of the inaugural Rex parade as follows: "A. Mounted police, section of artillery, lord marshal of the empire with state prisoners; troupe of Bedouins. B. Rex and attendants. Division I. Lord of the yeomanry, 300 maskers on foot; the pack; Boeuf Gras; music."

To play the part of the *boeuf gras* for its first parades, the Rex krewe enlisted a steer named Old Jeff, "well-known for many years as a decoy at the stockyards for beguiling beeves aboard ship." Old Jeff, however, was then replaced by young steers that were to be butchered to "furnish a feast for the immediate minions of the king and a quarter of choice cuts to be presented to the queen." The real steers were eventually replaced by inedible giant papier-mâché and fiberglass replicas.

For those who argued for the pagan origins of the *boeuf gras,* Perry Young offered a rather bloodthirsty shrug of the shoulders: "What difference . . . whether Boeuf-Gras was originally a Christian steer—that archetype of Carnival—or once the bull that raped Europa? Idolize him in any pagan form you will, he's an edible beast, beef to the heels, fattest that butchers' guild or public abattoir can yield, and the Queen (God save her) before the midnight chimes of mardi-gras, shall eat his filet mignon—the meat before Ash Wednesday."

It was fairly apparent, I thought, that by the time the Carnival bull had been transformed from sacrificial filet mignon to hollow fiberglass, the Catholic as well as the pagan elements of Carnival had simply become collections of images and symbols, some more highly charged than others, to be borrowed and embellished by the designers of parades and costumes.

Carnival is a constantly evolving rite of cultural accretion, which voraciously devours bits and pieces of the surrounding culture, incorporating themes and images from myth, literature, religion, theater, art, and society. Carnival is "geopsychic," to use Bookhardt's term, taking on the character of the city where it evolves and of the people who celebrate it, dramatizing or disguising the fears, dreams, and fantasies of its maskers.

16

The Fate of Bébé the Dancing Master

I couldn't help but notice all the sacral artifacts when I went to Henri Schindler's home for dinner one evening. Henri lived in a small, golden-yellow bungalow on Montegut Street in Bywater, the deteriorating neighborhood of homes and warehouses downriver from Faubourg Marigny. Montegut Street, lined with decaying Creole cottages, was located in the heart of Tennessee Williams's symbolic geography, between Elysian Fields and Desire Street, with Piety Street just two blocks away. Now there was a bus, rather than a streetcar, named Desire, but the mood of a fading culture, grown too refined and inbred to survive, was the same. Similar, too, was the sense of fragile illusions being invaded by vulgar reality.

Henri's house was set back from the street, behind an iron fence and a small yard that resembled a jungle, dense with banana trees and palmettos and ferns. Henri was feeling under siege these days; his house had been broken into repeatedly, his truck had been trashed, and he had been mugged on the street.

"This place is like Haiti," said Henri, "full of beautiful houses going to rack and ruin. I just have my postage-stamp dominion. But I'm like Susan Mayer. They'll have to carry me out, feet first."

Henri had invited his friend Paul Poché to join us, and when I arrived, they were in the kitchen whipping up a crawfish étouffée. I had been greeted at the door by Henri's two Pekinese dogs, Carlotta and Massa, the former named for the legendary float maker and the latter for an apocryphal gorilla. Henri had once read an account of a gorilla that had been captured and made to dress as a girl and which had developed the remarkable talent of making hats from canvas cloth.

Amid all the Carnival memorabilia were relics of Henri's obsession with popes, including a glass bust of Pius IX, issuer of the dogma of Immaculate Conception, and a papier-mâché bust Henri had commissioned of Pius XII. Henri also possessed a zucchetto worn by Pius XII. He had bid on it during a TV auction sponsored by the local channel owned by the Jesuits. Henri could get quite worked up on the subject of papal history. One night, Henri and the Duenna had called up Pasolini, the Italian poet and filmmaker who was later murdered by a hustler, to complain about a nasty sonnet he had written about Pope Pius.

Paul's house, a rambling Creole cottage a few streets away, was even more of a shrine. From porch to attic, it was one large votive offering to the gods of Carnival, with flowers and acanthus leaves and palm fronds from old Comus floats everywhere and a golden calf in the dining room. Hanging on a bedroom wall was his Whore of Babylon costume. "I like to make altars," said Paul. "I used to look at the clutter my grandmother had on her chest of drawers and say, 'I'll never have any of those crazy statues.' But you accumulate things that are dear to you, and you have to display them."

When I asked Paul about the mingling of the sacred and pagan during Carnival, he replied, "People get mixed up. Some say it's sacrilegious. But to me, Carnival is the sweetest religion. It gives me the balm most people imagine religion brings them."

"When I was young," said Paul, "the statues and saints and processions—those were my favorite parts of the Mass. I used to plan how I could make them more dramatic—have the statues come to life or maybe make them cry. You were desperate for anything to happen. Every now and then, a bird would fly in. I thought, if I could just be that white bird."

During the 1970s, after the Carnival parades stopped rolling through the French Quarter, Henri and Paul founded the Society of Saint Ann, a small marching club that met at Paul's house before walking up through Marigny and the Quarter to Canal Street. They named the society for a saintly statue Paul had found and placed on one of his altars, and the costumes were among the most beautiful and elaborate in the city.

Eric Bookhardt said the club reminded him of some ancient

cult—like the Eleusinians, perhaps. The membership, which had grown over the years, now included "everything but Martians." They had been distressed, however, by an influx of leather-clad S&M types, and while they did not ban them, they moved the starting point of the parade every year to discourage such unimaginatively costumed invaders.

More recently, a few members of the society had begun carrying along with them in the procession the ashes of friends who had died that year of AIDS and scattering them with a prayer over the waters of the Mississippi. Paul made special black velvet bags for the purpose, and he had already made one for himself, just in case.

At the end of the day, the remnants of the group returned to Paul's house, where they continued to party until midnight, when Paul opened up a hollow Corinthian column, where he stored a supply of nuns' veils. He passed them out for the celebrants to wear, and the mood immediately became sorrowful. Henri admitted that he used to shed a tear at the stroke of midnight, when Carnival was over for the year. The next day, Ash Wednesday, the celebrants dutifully went to the Saint Louis Cathedral to receive the penitential ashes on their foreheads.

Said Henri, "Carnival is all about Lent—ashes to ashes. If Carnival goes to ashes, then everything else is ashes." He repeated Perry Young's line about Carnival being a butterfly in winter.

Paul reminded us that in Spain, the butterfly is the symbol of the soul.

Said Henri, "Carnival has always been fragile. It has endured forever, but it's incredibly fragile."

Paul predicted, "It'll bob up and down. Affluence will rise and fall. But the people who live in New Orleans will always celebrate Carnival in their souls. The times they've tried to take Carnival away, they've just gotten more determined." Paul recalled that in 1979, during the police strike, when Carnival was canceled, people had turned out on the streets anyway on Mardi Gras day. Some people remember that spontaneous neighborhood Mardi Gras nostalgically as their best ever.

*   *   *

Henri and Paul had another theory about Carnival, which was that it was fueled as much by repressed royalism as by crypto-Catholicism. "A lot of the Catholics came here as aristocrats, not like the poor Catholics of Boston or other cities," said Henri. "They were orphaned twice from royal families—from France and then from Spain. We were passed from France to Spain to France and then to the United States. People who came here didn't want to be in the United States—they didn't want to be Puritans. So you have these people seeking fame and fortune. Louisiana was billed as the place of riches. You have John Law's bubble. France almost went broke. So here they are, lost in the swamps. What are they going to do? They were people of high spirits. They had a particular love affair with a sense of monarchy. There were lots of down-and-out aristocrats here, with all this pretense."

Henri loved to tell the story of Bébé the dancing master, the "Don Quixote of dancing," a quadroon who had been brought to New Orleans during the mid-eighteenth century by the marquis de Vaudreuil as part of the governor's campaign to transform a small, swampy outpost into a glittering center of society. "The marquis thought the people here were getting too common," said Henri. It was Bébé's mission to teach the children of the city how to comport themselves at soirees and balls.

Poor Bébé, however, was caught by Indians while out riding to a nearby plantation on a mule. Bébé was dressed in his court finery, and his long legs dangled over the side of his mount. As one account goes, the Indians, who were not given to smiling, burst out laughing at the sight of Bébé. They riddled him with arrows, however, despite their mirth. "Why?" asked Henri, quoting from an old history book. "Because they didn't like enigmas."

I suggested that Bébé, apparently done in by the extravagance of his costume, might be the first martyr of Mardi Gras.

"This gives you some notion of the marvelous frivolity of traditions here," said Henri. "We were bought in 1803 and dragged into this country. Since 1812, it's been downhill. During the transfer of Louisiana to the United States, the Creoles on the balcony of the Cabildo were weeping. They couldn't believe it. They thought they would shortly be returned to France or Spain." Henri thought a moment. "That wouldn't be a bad idea now."

He looked down at Carlotta, the Pekinese, and said, "You have to turn to royalty when everything is falling apart. Carlotta, you must walk with great strength. I'll put a tiny crown on your head."

Henri was now in an elegiac mood. Speaking of old, traditional Carnival, he mused, "I feel very much it's in the last days. Comus has one more year to parade, or they may choose not to parade. They'll just carry on with the ball, and they'll have their extremely private revelry. We're the losers in all this. I'd love to see it go out in a blaze of glory. The first year, they did Milton's *Paradise Lost*. I'd love to do a satirical version, 'Paradise Lost, 1993.'

"We must plan our last memorials—whole crowds of people with wreaths and scrolls at the Pickwick Club. They'll say in later years, 'The streets were so laden with scrolls.' "

The great pity, he felt, was that Carnival had never really been recognized as the remarkable art form it was, particularly at its height near the turn of the century. "Let's take the year 1893 as the point of comparison," he said. "The parade Comus did that year was based on Flaubert's *Salammbô*. That year, the great sensation in Paris in the salons was Rocheblave's 'Derniers Jours de Babylon.' I think if Comus had paraded through the streets of Paris in 1893, it would have been an event in art history. But it happened here. It rolled down Bourbon Street and passed into memory."

Henri observed wistfully, "So much that happened here was so fabulous the rest of the world would have swooned. It makes you crazy."

17

Day of the Pundits

For a more practical approach to the "geopsychic" nature of New Orleans, I consulted two experts on politics and demographics in New Orleans. One morning, I ventured out to the small suburb of Lakeview, near Lake Pontchartrain, to visit a Democratic sage named Joe Walker who was considered an expert on odds and probabilities—a horseplayer and a pollster with an uncanny ability to forecast political futures and winners of the daily double. Walker had projected the recent victory of Edwin Edwards in the gubernatorial election well before other anti-Duke operatives, and he had won a "nice bet" on the abysmal performance of David Duke. He predicted, too, that Edwin Edwards, for all his talk of reform, would soon revert to his gambling ways. "Edwin just likes living on the edge," he said. "He loves to tempt fate."

Joe, a heavyset man who looked uncomfortable in his loose-fitting dark suits, had the dry, gravelly wiseguy voice one would expect from someone who smokes cigars and spends part of the day at the racetrack. When I suggested a comparison between his two activities of divining, he replied, "I bet on probabilities at the track. And that's my business in politics—probabilities."

Joe's house was an ordinary two-story suburban box, with a large pile-carpeted downstairs living room turned over to his political consulting affairs. There were files piled everywhere. A large, affectionate dog kept trying to jump into my lap, only slightly dissuaded by Joe's halfhearted rebukes.

Lakeview, said Joe, was one of the first suburban areas in New Orleans, built during the late forties and early fifties on land claimed from Lake Pontchartrain. It was mostly middle class, he said, with some working-class residents scattered around. Lakeview, he said, was one of the three remaining middle-class strongholds in New Orleans. The others were in Algiers, across the river, and in New Orleans East, the collection of subdivisions reclaimed from low-lying swampland where upwardly mobile blacks as well as whites had been moving from Central City and other city neighborhoods.

"You have three pockets of wealth in the city," said Joe. One was "old uptown," which included the Garden District and the area near Audubon Park and Tulane University, the stronghold of old-line Mardi Gras krewes. Another was the lakefront, now lined with up-scale subdivisions—"Some call it nouveau riche," he said. And the third was the lower part of Algiers. "The white lower class of New Orleans is practically gone." They had moved, he said, to the neighboring parishes of Jefferson and Saint Bernard, leaving their old shot-gun houses boarded up.

Joe had grown up in Mid-City, he said, in a house across from a cemetery. His block was mostly white, while the adjacent block was black. "That pattern was repeated all over the city," he said. "That checkerboard pattern goes a long way to explain the nature of the city. In New Orleans, we've had racial tension, but never the riotous kind of binges that have erupted in other cities—which I think is due, in part, to our residential history."

Mardi Gras, he said, has also played a role in that history of live-and-let-live. "Even today, when they have a call for the flambeaux carriers, there are lots of volunteers. It's hard work—it's awful. It can't be an economic necessity—it's just one night's work."

He had not been surprised by informal surveys that were showing that a number of blacks were not particularly enthusiastic about Dorothy Mae Taylor's proposed ordinance. "They're saying, 'If it's not broke, why fix it?' If you look at the hoopla and symbolism of Mardi Gras, here are these elite groups—and they're toasting a black mayor."

The Mardi Gras elite, he said, don't run the city. "People like Jim Bob Moffett have more effect on the economy than the kings of Rex and Comus." What's more, he said, the old-line krewes, particularly Comus and Momus, "would be just as happy to call it quits. They've kept it going out of tradition—they felt obligated. But they may take this as an opportunity to fold up their tents. This was not a smart move from Dorothy Mae Taylor." Joe felt that Dorothy Mae was trying to lock up the black vote in a bid for mayor, and that it would backfire on her.

Joe had found that racism had been increasing in the last decade. "From the sixties through the seventies, there was progress being made. In my surveys, we saw less and less concern about racial issues. But all that progress is being lost." The recent alliance between uptown New Orleans and black New Orleans to defeat David Duke had not been enough of a catalyst, he said, to turn things around. "It was a togetherness against instead of a togetherness for."

The causes of increased racial tensions, he felt, were clear. "I blame Ronald Reagan and George Bush for not exercising proper moral leadership on these issues. The Republicans seem content to let the cities die in this country."

The real "nail in the coffin," he said, was money. "The state has been in terrible economic straits since the last half of the 1980s. Fifteen years ago, the city budget was four hundred million dollars, and it had twelve thousand employees. Today, there are six thousand employees and a budget of two hundred and twenty million dollars. The biggest hunk of decline is in federal and state assistance. Federal aid now is virtually nil. It's more conventional to say that there is bad leadership. But the problem is that there's just not enough money to run the city. You're at the practical limits of taxation. It's a problem that defies solution, short of state and federal governments taking more responsibility."

People were looking around for scapegoats, said Joe, and it was inevitable that demagogues like David Duke would arise.

There was another factor, too, that complicated race relations in New Orleans, and that was the unique position of the black Creole class, from which the city had drawn its first two black mayors. Originally known as the *gens de couleur libres*, the black Creoles, who were descended from the offspring of white Creole men and black women or women of mixed race, once made up as much as 28 percent of the population in New Orleans. Now, there were only about twenty thousand of them, said Joe, out of a total of one hundred and fifty thousand registered black voters.

During the nineteenth century, the *gens de couleur libres*, many of whom were sent to school in Paris, traditionally identified themselves with French culture. Many worked as artisans and small businessmen, but some went on to become wealthy and to own slaves of their own. They read French literature and their own French-language newspapers and attended theater and the opera. After the Civil War, they were referred to as "free men" as opposed to freed slaves, who were "freedmen."

Between the freedmen and the free men, there was a gap of culture, language, and religion. The free men, who lived in the Seventh Ward of the city, were Catholic, for the most part, and spoke French, while the freedmen, many of whom were rural and Protestant, were linked with African-American culture.

The relatively privileged life of the small community of *gens de couleur* was short-lived, however. In 1894, as part of the backlash against blacks, following Reconstruction, a law was passed in Louisiana that a person with any black blood whatsoever was to be considered black and treated accordingly. In a single stroke, the black Creoles were disenfranchised, left to tumble down the social scale among black stevedores and cotton-mill workers and other common laborers. As one historian put it, "They were pressed down onto the back mainstream, and by the beginning of the century they had been moved into the working class. Bitter, they continued to cling to their culture to distinguish themselves from the blacks only a small step below them." The black Creoles, despite their fall in station, remained as clannish as their white counterparts, with their own clubs and their own social circles.

The distinctions between freedmen and free men were undoubtedly exaggerated by white observers at the time. But there is evidence that black Creoles had a certain attitude of patronization toward freedmen, a sense of natural leadership and obligation. An article in the New Orleans *Tribune*, a black Creole newspaper, written in 1864, foreshadows the later role of political leadership to be played in New Orleans by black Creoles, who depended on their darker brothers for the power of numbers: "These two populations, equally rejected and deprived of their rights, cannot be well estranged from one another. The emancipated will find in the old free men, friends ready to guide them, to spread upon them the light of knowledge, and teach them their duties as well as their rights. But, at the same time, the free men will find in the recently liberated slaves a mass to uphold them; and with this mass behind them they will command the respect always bestowed to number and strength."

"I don't think the gap is as bad as it once was," said Joe, "but it's always going to be there because of the badge of skin color. It's a class distinction—social as well as financial. The Creole blacks are the parochial-school graduates—they go into the professions, into skilled labor. The plasterers and paperhangers and masons are dominated by Creole entrepreneurs. These people became well-off and sent their children to fancy colleges. There was always a feeling that the Creoles had it made, so they didn't give a damn about the rest of the blacks."

For black Creoles like Dutch Morial and Sidney Barthelemy, there were political advantages and liabilities in their heritage. When Barthelemy ran for mayor in 1986, his chief opponent was another black contender, of darker skin, a Protestant from North Louisiana named William Jefferson. In a race between two black candidates, it came down to degrees of blackness. While Jefferson, a graduate of Harvard Law School, campaigned for the black vote, as *the* black candidate, Sidney depended on the white vote for his margin of victory. He promised the electorate that his highest priority would be "to bring this divided city together."

Barthelemy paid a price, said Joe, for his white support, just as black Creoles had long paid a price for playing a mediating role between blacks and whites in New Orleans. "I think the Creole existence is the tougher one," said Joe. "Even though they are better off economically, it's always more difficult to straddle two worlds."

Whites may have paid a price, too, Joe suggested, for relying on black Creoles as their go-betweens and informants. "We get most of our information from the Creoles," said Joe. "But we don't know what crimes they're guilty of in the eyes of the black community."

Although Joe was a man of numbers and charts, he also relied on gut instincts, the kind of intuitions that propel a horseplayer or a political campaigner to tempt fate against unfavorable odds and inevitable losses. When I suggested that the problems facing New Orleans seemed insurmountable, he replied, "I don't believe that." For one thing, he said, there was the city's history of racial tolerance. "In the national surveys I do, you find that the greatest racial tolerance anywhere is in the city of New Orleans. It's like there is some cohesive force at work that's difficult to define. Part of it, I think, is that Catholicism breeds a greater tolerance. You hear people in New Orleans talking a lot of 'nigger' but no one actually behaving that way. You see them behaving civilly."

There were certain things about New Orleans that defied probability and statistics, he said. "People in New Orleans want it to work," he said. "They don't want to throw in the towel. People of my generation talk about leaving, but they never do. Those of us who live here have an irrational attachment to the place. It's difficult to explain why we're living in New Orleans. I can never explain to anybody what I like about New Orleans, but I wouldn't leave for anything. There's a personality to New Orleans that you don't find anywhere else. It's like the city has a personality, a soul. You can't grab hold of it, but you can feel it."

There was a problem of statistics, however, that all the optimism and determinism couldn't change, and that had to do with the exodus of the younger generation. "The white population in New Orleans is very old," said Joe. "I have six grown children, and five live outside Orleans Parish. Forty years ago, they'd still be within a half mile of their parents. There's no replenishment. You have some brave souls trying to rebuild part of Marigny and uptown, but you don't have the reserves of young people. What I worry about is the white population simply dying off."

The View from the Inner Circle

Later that day, I traveled back across the city and back across class and political boundaries to reach the office of the Pundit, as I've chosen to call the uptown savant who agreed to talk on the condition of anonymity. The Pundit was highly successful in business—a worthy "scion," as Sally Reeves would say—and he was an astute social observer who fancied himself a sort of Joseph Conrad of civic in-trigue. He balanced an almost insufferable smugness with an odd combination of realism and romanticism.

"I'm very deeply depressed about this place," said the Pundit, flatly. "You look for the hopeful signs in the ruins, but it's easy to get discouraged."

New Orleans, he said, mixing a few metaphors, "has undergone a huge metamorphosis in the political balance of power that holds the business and social and political fabric together. New Orleans is different from most places. In other cities, you have two different worlds sharing the same piece of geography—for example, Washing-ton, D.C., where the white and black communities live apart. That's true of most Southern cities, but not in New Orleans."

Like Joe Walker, he did not mind the mixed, "checkerboard" pattern of settlement and culture in the city. "I like the 'miscegenous' quality of life here," said the Pundit. "Most people do. But in the last ten or fifteen years, the rise of the drug culture has destroyed the fabric of the city. It's a nationwide trend. But it's even more acutely felt where people are living on top of each other. The best parts of New Orleans are adjacent to the most dangerous."

The Pundit, however, did not link the decline in the city's social fabric to draconian cutbacks in federal aid, but to a lack of capital, which he said was "the same problem of any Third World country," as well as to drugs. "The polarization between blacks and whites has become more extreme in the last three or four years. There has been a shift in demographics, with insecurity and fear for whites and a sense of futility about the future. You would be startled by the conservatism of my peers. There is a significant minority that has liberal views, but it *is* a minority."

For all the polarization, however, the Pundit agreed, like Joe Walker, that the "glue that still holds it all together is that people truly like being here. For all of its problems, New Orleans is more distinctive than other places. America is a very homogenized place. There's a lot to offer here. The more Third World it becomes, the more exotic it becomes—the more it becomes a locale for a Graham Greene novel, ever more darkly romantic."

*   *   *

185

Those who blamed the decline of New Orleans on Carnival or the Mardi Gras Syndrome, the Pundit felt, were being shortsighted. "A lot of people who criticize the Mardi Gras Syndrome," he said, "have an unfair perception about Carnival—that it's a pseudo-aristocracy trampling on those underneath. But what is more civilized—giving away beads or watching boxers beat each other's brains in or watching people trample each other on a football field? You really have to look at it in a broader context, of where it fits in with society and its values."

The Pundit agreed that the uptown krewes and clubs were highly selective. Recently, he had had to work very hard to get a mutual friend into a good luncheon club. "If you're a WASP whose parents came over on the Mayflower," he said, "it's still like climbing Everest to get into these things. People are very rarely put up for membership simply because they've achieved something. And the older you get, the more difficult it is to get in—you grate on people's nerves."

Nevertheless, the Pundit pointed out, old-line Carnival was only a small part of the overall Carnival pie. "It's only six or seven clubs out of the dozens that have balls every year. Look at how many balls there are—you have a portrait of a culture and the subcultures that comprise New Orleans." There were probably only about fourteen hundred men altogether who made up the membership of the top seven clubs. In Comus and Momus, for example, there were only about two hundred members and twice that many in Rex, with some overlap in club membership.

In addition, he said, "There are only a few people whose lives actually revolve around Mardi Gras. For them, it's a highlight every year. There's a ritual to each of the parades, of going to the den and having drinks. It can be lots of fun. There's nothing insidious about it. You're not killing animals or beating up on people. It's a benign thing, based on the spirit of giving. It's not an act of tyranny to stand on a float made of tinsel throwing glass beads to people in the streets. I don't think the people in the street feel inferior. It's an audience-participation event. It's as much fun for those throwing as those catching."

As for the influence of the elite krewes on the city, he agreed with Joe Walker that they had become largely irrelevant to political affairs or to the economy, but that they had retained a certain mystique out of proportion to their actual influence. "Thirty or forty years ago, it made a difference," he said. "Most of the money now is new money. What new money finds interesting about old money is the social cachet. There's a psychological attitude about it on the part of people. Personally, I don't see it as a big deal. It's irrelevant to business. It gives you a certain cachet, and if you're not a member, you could feel left out. But for myself, I never gave it a second thought. Although I'm part of this inner circle, my identity is hardly wrapped up with being at the core of the social structure."

Nevertheless, the Pundit found himself frequently in the company of friends who did not share his views. "I'm one of the few in my circle with black friends and clients," he said. "My black friends would say I'm too casual about these issues. All these blacks think there is this hidden network—a politburo—that gets together and makes decisions. These clubs are akin in their minds to the British raj in India."

He commented on the social ambitions of one prominent black Creole leader, observing that he was like a colonial administrator who wanted the queen to knight him. "There is no other place where that set of values exists. If we had real leadership in the city, we could fashion policies that would lead to some kind of balance." The political power of whites, he said, had been reduced to that of the veto, or the swing vote, and even that power was dwindling fast. "The ability of whites to veto has become less important, and when that becomes irrelevant, that is the end."

To understand the future of New Orleans, said the Pundit, "you have to spend a week in Nairobi, to see how things have changed there. Personally, I don't view a black society as a bad thing. I see the silver lining in the dark romance. I don't mind living in a black city." He paused, then added, "But I do mind living in a city out of control."

When I asked the Pundit how he dealt with his differences on racial matters with his ultraconservative white friends and colleagues, he replied, "I see no reason to cut myself off from people I grew up with. As Lloyd Bentsen said when he ran for vice president, 'I'm not going to stop eating lunch with my friends.'"

As I prepared to depart, he left me with this final puzzling assessment. "You come to the view that there are some things in life you can change," he said, "and some you can't. You can't fight every fight. Right now, I'm concentrating on saving sea mammals."

18

The Ladies of the Fan

I wanted to find out firsthand what it felt like to ride on a float in a Mardi Gras parade, and a friend recommended that I contact Irma Strode, the captain emeritus of Iris, an all-woman krewe. The krewe was named for the goddess of the rainbow, who was mentioned in the Aeneid as having saved the harpies, the winged tormentors, from the Argonauts. Iris also symbolized the bridge between heaven and earth.

This season would mark the seventy-fifth anniversary of the krewe, although they had been parading only since 1959. Iris, which began with small king-cake parties and graduated to major extravaganzas at the Municipal Auditorium, complete with hydraulic ministage, had been one of the first krewes to defy the uptown male monopoly on Carnival. The other major women's krewe, Venus, had been parading longer, since 1941, but its parade was considerably smaller.

I called Miss Irma, as she was known, and she said I could come by her house before lunchtime to discuss my participation in Iris, although she was going to be attending a last-minute meeting later in the afternoon for all the Carnival captains on the subject of "that ordinance." The next day would bring a vote from the City Council, and the captains were planning their strategy.

Miss Irma's small tan brick house was located in a remote corner of Lakeview, tucked away on a small street next to a canal. Her tiny entrance hall was jammed with plaques and citations, a fraction of the tributes she had received after thirty-three years as captain of Iris, which made her the longest-reigning krewe captain in Carnival history. Although the krewe sometimes tried to adhere to the traditional Carnival policy of maintaining anonymity for its captains, everyone knew that Iris was virtually synonymous with Irma Strode.

A friend who had been a member of Iris for a couple of years remembered the rehearsals for the Iris ball vividly, with Miss Irma barking out commands and blowing her whistle.

Miss Irma, a small woman with careful, charm-school bearing, was wearing a beautifully tailored white silk pants suit with a bright green silk shirt. Her wardrobe was known for its signature Mardi Gras colors—green, purple, and gold. She was said to have those colors running in her veins. With her rigorously coiffed black wig and bright dark eyes, she reminded me just a bit of my former neighbor Germaine Wells, another ageless grande dame who had created a dramatic persona for public view, but who was rather quiet in private.

Miss Irma apologized for being rather distracted, not only by all the fuss over the ordinance, but by a toothache. "I'm about to lose a tooth," she said, "although I'm glad at age eighty-four I still have a tooth to lose."

Miss Irma said that she had been active in Iris for forty years, that she had "loved every minute." She had been chosen as maid, back in 1950, she said, and Mrs. Aminthe Nungesser, founder of the krewe, asked her to take over the reins in 1952. "I've been busy ever since— fun, happiness, merriment," she said.

Miss Irma handed me a copy of a 1974 *Dixie Roto* magazine, the Sunday magazine of the *Times-Picayune*, with her picture on the cover. The photo had been taken during the 1973 ball, when the theme was "Your Hometown Newspaper." She was wearing a bright pink dress, glittering with sequins and rhinestones, the skirt billowing out with four layers of tulle. She was carrying her trademark of leadership, a double-plumed fan. The dress had cost her three thousand dollars, she said, and she had thirty-two dresses like it stored in various places. "I always went for the bouffant dress," she said. "My niece Joy goes for the slim look."

When she passed along the office of captain to her niece, Joy Oswald, in 1985, she had passed along the fan as well, presenting it to her niece during the ball in a dramatic gesture of royal succession. There was little doubt, however, who still retained the real power in the krewe.

Until recently, the krewe had a membership roster of six hundred. It was now limited to five hundred, which was still larger than

Rex or Comus. According to one member, the krewe had cut back because of all the uptown women who had suddenly decided it was a lark to ride in a parade, like their husbands, and they had inundated the largely middle-class and working-class krewe.

"We have attorneys, dentists, housewives, secretaries, everything," said Miss Irma. "We have Jewish, Irish, Italians." When I asked her about the criteria for membership, she said, "Friends invite friends, and that's what it's about. We choose people according to their character—not their skin color. Mardi Gras is happiness."

There was a place for men in the krewe, in supporting roles. Her husband, for example, was now "general chairman emeritus" of Iris. But on the issue of admitting men as regular members, she was absolutely against it, a stand that would put her in the category of sex discrimination, she feared, if the proposed ordinance were passed.

She had been very disturbed by the ordinance and by its implications of discrimination on the basis of race as well as gender. "With us, it's the person we're interested in—it's certainly not discrimination," she insisted. Miss Irma, like other Carnival captains, was used to a certain kind of autonomy in her decisions. And like other captains, she certainly wasn't used to having to answer to City Hall. "When we have a dictatorship like this," she said, "it's sad." She said she might consider someone like Sybil Morial, the aristocratic black Creole wife of the late mayor, as a member. "But I can't understand one person trying to control Carnival," she said. "You should be master of your own convictions." She sighed rather wistfully. "I hope we don't have to change."

As I was leaving, she wrote down my clothing size, and said that she would have to consult with the membership about my participation in the parade and ball, but I had a feeling I would be tossing beads to the throngs on the Saturday before Mardi Gras. She handed me a Carnival Christmas ornament, a little clown in a purple, green, and gold suit, saying no one should ever leave her house empty-handed, and I had an idea of how it was that a tiny woman with a quiet voice and a whistle had managed to rule a motley group of six hundred women for thirty-three years without a hint of rebellion.

19

The Fall of Humpty-Dumpty

On December 19, the day of the City Council meeting to decide the fate of Dorothy Mae Taylor's Carnival ordinance, tensions were mounting. During their hurried meeting the previous day, the Carnival captains had drawn up a statement, signed by all sixty-odd captains who attended, expressing unanimous opposition to the ordinance. Behind-the-scenes negotiations between Dorothy Mae Taylor, the mayor, and Carnival representatives had broken down.

Taylor later insisted that she had been ready to hammer out a compromise, which involved a year's delay in enforcing the ordinance and the appointment of a "blue ribbon committee" to study its impact. Representatives of the Carnival captains insisted, however, that they had not been given time to consider the compromise or to discuss it with their membership. There were a series of missed connections, miscues, and misunderstandings during the last hours, and krewe representatives felt that 144 years of tradition had come down to a game of hide-and-seek in the corridors of City Hall.

The City Council had been moved temporarily from its spacious quarters in the Municipal Court building into a cramped room in the basement of City Hall. The previous week, Joe Giarrusso had opened the council session with the quip, "Welcome to the dungeon." The room was lined with rows of folding metal chairs, and a dais had been fashioned at the front of the room for the council members, with a small cordoned section for the city attorneys. As people filed in, the regular council-meeting pianist, Lillian Dunn Perry, a frail-looking older black woman, president emeritus of the B Sharp Music Club, played jazzy versions of Christmas songs. She segued from "Santa Claus Is Coming to Town" to "Silent Night."

The crowd was restive, however, as clusters of allies and advocates grouped together in the hallway, looking around conspiratorially. Peggy Wilson, the council member from the heart of uptown, from the Garden District to Audubon Park and Tulane University, was wearing a bright red dress. She was surrounded by Carnival royalty, like Queen Elizabeth I and her nobles. Among them were past and current captains of Comus, Rex, and Proteus, although no one was supposed to know their secret Carnival rank. The scene would have been more effective, of course, if the men, who were wearing business suits, had been wearing their Carnival regalia, the captains in their plumed helmets, as though mustering for a council of war.

There was a time when some of these same Carnival muckety-mucks had played a more powerful—and more enlightened, some would say—role in the political and economic affairs of the city, particularly in the matter of race relations. During the school segregation crisis of the 1960s, three men who ruled as Rex—Darwin Fenner, attorney Harry Kelleher, and attorney Harry McCall—helped steer a moderate course among the city's white leadership.

In 1960, following a legal duel between the Louisiana legislature and the federal courts, four black girls entered two white schools in the city's Ninth Ward, to a chorus of abuse by a white crowd. The following night, Leander Perez, the political boss of Plaquemines Parish, downriver from New Orleans, exhorted the five thousand members of the Citizens' Council to rise up, in one of the most shameful speeches in the history of Louisiana: "Don't wait for your daughters to be raped by these Congolese," he had urged.

Darwin Fenner stepped forward and organized three hundred people to publish a paid advertisement supporting the School Board and integration headlined A DECLARATION OF PRINCIPLES. Two committees, black and white, were formed to bring about a peaceful resolution to problems of desegregation. The key figures on the white committee had been the Carnival triumvirate of Fenner, Harry Kelleher, and Harry McCall.

In the summer of 1962, the two committees, with the leadership of Kelleher and McCall, brought pressure on Canal Street merchants to desegregate their lunch counters. The next year, the black Citizens'

Committee and its white allies negotiated a compromise by which the city agreed to amend its hiring practices and remove the signs restricting black access to public facilities.

As some black leaders pointed out, of course, it had been of little personal concern to Fenner, Kelleher, and McCall, who dined further down on Canal at the exclusive Boston Club, to open the lunch counter at McCrory's. Nevertheless, the men had risen to the occasion.

Now, however, the conflict had come to the front doors of their clubs and dens, and the captains of Carnival had been placed in the untenable position of appearing to support discrimination. And because of the krewes' strict policy of secrecy, they could not even reveal their actual roles in Carnival. If they let the masks slip, the battle would already be lost.

Inside the makeshift council room, an odd collection of spectators had gathered. A cluster of uptown dignitaries was seated in front of a homeless man wearing a purple wool woman's coat and carrying a Bible. On the same row were two artists from the Momus den in paint-spattered jeans and T-shirts. Sitting near the front row was Blaine Kern, Mr. Mardi Gras, who, according to one observer, had had his toupee recently restyled into a more blow-dried look.

I found a seat in a middle row, next to Henri, Paul, and the Duenna. Paul leaned over and whispered, "I've brought a holy relic." He handed me a red amber bead embedded with gold stars and told me to say a prayer to save Carnival. "This is not really a bead," said Paul. "It's a stolen kiss."

Council President Joe Giarrusso called the session to order and waited as Dan King, pastor of the Nazarene and Mount Olive Baptist churches, led the group in prayer. Johnny Jackson, Jr., led the Pledge of Allegiance to the flag.

Council members picked up the agenda for the day, a hefty twenty-two-page document, which included the usual petitions protesting decisions by the Historic District Landmarks Commission, requests for liquor licenses, and a number of disputes over the legality of charitable bingo games. On the top of the docket, moved from its initial position in the middle of the stack, was Calendar No. 17,611, an ordinance to "amend and reordain section 42-101 and section 42-102 of Chapter 42 relative to the Human Relations Commission and City policy with respect to invidious discrimination, to prohibit such discrimination in public accommodations, resorts and amusements; to amend the definitions of public accommodations and discrimination so as to include certain classes of persons and certain types of clubs and other institutions not distinctly private in character."

Disguised in the legalese was a time bomb, ticking away, ready to blast away at the very foundations of traditional Carnival. The ordinance would yank the masks from Carnival royalty and revelers and remove the most cherished traditions of the old-line krewes: the power to select their members according to their own arbitrary standards and to operate in secret.

Joe Falls, a prominent member of Zulu, came over to say hello. "It's bad," he said, shaking his head. A Zulu representative had signed the unanimous statement of opposition by the Carnival captains, but club members had been uneasy about it, and Roy Glapion, the president of Zulu, had come to the meeting to speak in favor of the ordinance. "We can't say we're against it," said Joe, "because we have all races in our club. With us, we're all blue bloods. But we're not in compliance about the females."

Joe Giarrusso continued, "We realize this is a serious and emotional issue. We're not going to permit the hearing to go awry." He announced that major speakers chosen for each side would be given ten minutes, and all other speakers would be limited to three minutes. One onlooker declared loudly that the meeting should be adjourned to the Superdome.

Before the debate could go forward, there was a question about the inclusion of physical disability as one of the criteria that could not be used to discriminate against prospective members. Blaine Kern had protested this particular provision, saying that insurance costs to the krewes would be prohibitive if they were forced to let disabled people ride the floats.

One city attorney responded that there were "people already

riding who meet the definition of disabled without even knowing it.''

"Yeah," muttered the Duenna. "Being blind drunk would fit that definition."

Sidney Barthelemy arrived, looking grave, but rather cool and noncommittal. "This morning we met with the krewes," he said, "trying to get an agreement. I'm sorry to say the krewes did not agree. I'm here today to support the ordinance."

It was clear that Sidney, like Dutch Morial, had decided to step away from the neutral ground of black Creole tradition and side with his black constituency. Rather than speaking from a solid moral stance, however, he argued from a position of civic insecurity. It was the same kind of argument that had convinced white voters as well as black to vote against David Duke. For New Orleans to appear to condone discrimination would be yet one more reason for conventioneers to stay away and for other cities to regard New Orleans as small-time.

Ironically, an economic argument was also being used by those opposed to the ordinance, with Carnival held up as the golden-egg-laying goose of tourism that shouldn't be killed for the sake of political correctness.

"As a city," said Sidney, "we can't send a signal that we support any practices that further discrimination. We are being watched by the entire nation. We've become a big-league city with regard to conventions and sporting events. There are those who would like to stop us from being competition. We can't appear to be a city that supports discrimination. This is the modern age, and we are being watched. As a member of the administration, as a policy maker, I have to take a strong stand. We don't have a choice. The rest of the nation will see we're a big-league city. It's in the best interest of our economy."

A low murmur of anger in the crowd steadily grew louder as Dorothy Mae Taylor took the microphone. "There was no olive branch coming from the other side," she said, then rapped on the table, as the murmur grew louder. "I'm going to ask the police to go out in the room and circulate. Those who can't adjust themselves will be escorted out. We're here for business."

Dorothy Mae tried to regain the moral high ground. "I hope that all of us can come together as we did in the recent gubernatorial election," she said. "Discrimination in any form is intolerable. I believe everyone should question the city's participation in any way in perpetuating discrimination of any kind. I leave you with a question: Why is there a need to discriminate?"

There was not even a ripple of applause in response to her rhetorical question.

The first speaker on behalf of the ordinance was Dwight McKenna, a member of the School Board recently convicted of tax evasion. A black Creole with a distinguished career, he had accused the white establishment of the city of singling him out for persecution.

An obese white man sitting in front of me made a disparaging remark as McKenna began to speak, and a well-dressed black woman sitting next to him turned to him and said, "You're lucky they don't discriminate against fat people." He retorted, unintelligibly, and she replied, "You're lucky I don't hit you with my pocketbook. I'll show you about David Duke."

A policeman made his way back to the fat man, pulled him up by the arm, and escorted him out of the room, as the black woman nodded in satisfaction. It was clear who ruled City Hall now, if not the city, if not Carnival. White men, particularly obese white men of redneck origins, were in a minority.

James Gray, a young black attorney who worked in Juvenile Court, took the microphone and began to speak quietly, his voice gradually gathering strength. Gray was a member of the Louis A. Martinet Society, named for the managing editor of the New Orleans *Crusader*, a vehicle for racial protest and the only black daily newspaper in the United States during the 1890s. Martinet, a lawyer, had argued at the time that well-chosen legal suits offered more hope than the corrupt politics of the state for blacks to recapture their basic constitutional rights.

"This ordinance," said Gray, "says you cannot do two things at once—discriminate and use public money." He looked out at the crowd. "It seems incredible to me that people can come into this council and argue for the right to continue discriminating and that the public should continue to subsidize them."

He looked at individuals in the crowd, whom he clearly recognized. "I'm amazed at the faces here, faces of people who talk about being friends. I'm amazed to see people here that I've dealt with in other places and who talked about needing to pull together in this city. And now you've come here, saying, 'By the way, there has been a little tradition in place since your ancestors were slaves, and we'd like to keep it in place, and if you don't, you may lose some money.' Well, there were those back then who argued that if slavery was done away with, the economy would suffer. My great-grandfather would have said, 'I don't care. Right is right.' "

Gray's voice broke, and he had to pause before going on. "I cannot go home and look at my children and say we decided today to let people discriminate on special occasions because it's good for the economy. Some things are more important than if we make a dollar."

Gray concluded with a burst of remarkable candor, speaking to the whites in the audience with a heartfelt directness that put Sidney Barthelemy, Dorothy Mae Taylor, and most of the other speakers of the day to shame. "I realize there are people here," he said, "who feel that things are changing from what their fathers and grandfathers knew. They feel a sense of losing something significant. The truth is that things *are* changing." He paused a moment, then continued. "We can live in this changing city, working together, or we can fight each other on a daily basis. I'm not going anywhere, and most of the black people of New Orleans are not going anywhere. For the rest of you, you have a choice. You can decide whether or not we can live together and work together in peace. But you can't decide that you can discriminate the way you have in the past."

It was now up to Beau Bassich, representing the Mardi Gras Coordinating Committee, to outline the case against the ordinance. It was a poorly kept secret that Beau was also the longtime captain of Proteus. He sometimes carried around in his pocket a list of prospective future maids and queens of Proteus through the first years of the next century. An ancestor on his wife's side, Jacques McLoughlin, had been a member of the first Krewe of Proteus back in 1882. Beau was also one of the most civic-minded men in New Orleans—the savior of City Park, the benefactor of various city museums. He hardly fit the image of imperious Carnival despot. But he was faced with the unenviable task of trying to defend old-line Carnival without giving up its cherished secrets.

Not surprisingly, Beau argued against the ordinance on the basis of preserving a valuable city tradition. His reference to constitutional rights was brief. "Carnival," he said, "is a community celebration based on unique customs and traditions that have evolved spontaneously for 150 years as an integral part of the history of the city. New Orleans Carnival owes its uniqueness and charm and its integrity as an expression of the life of the city to traditional rituals created over the long period by private social groups. If government attempts to intervene, the result will almost certainly be something different, much less interesting and attractive to anyone. Carnival organizations have a constitutional right to associate, to select members as they wish. This ordinance sends a message that Carnival krewes that have paraded since 1857 may no longer be welcome to do so."

James McLain, the UNO professor and author of the study commissioned by the Carnival captains on the economic impact of Carnival on New Orleans, buttressed the anti-ordinance position with some numbers, but first acknowledged the unique nature of the New Orleans economy. "I'm from West Virginia," said McLain, "and I was immediately struck by the contrast to cities I knew, like Pittsburgh, with smokestack industries and workers carrying lunches to work. It wasn't evident at first where the activity in the New Orleans economy was generated. I was surprised to find that what seemed papier-mâché and makeup had such a tremendous impact on the city."

Later in the afternoon, Blaine Kern, Mr. Mardi Gras, straightened the lapels of his expensive-looking dark blue suit and took the microphone for an odd, rambling disquisition that kept returning to his own thriving float-building business. Kern had recently won a contract to work on EuroDisney. He had once told Henri, "I'm the only man outside Disney who has the right to make Goofy." Currently, his son was at work on Mount Mickeymore.

Kern had the manner of a nervous first-time stand-up comic waiting in vain for applause or guffaws. He had already gotten in hot water by telling a reporter that he would allow girls to ride his floats "if they were young and pretty." Said Kern, his eyes darting around the room, "I'm glad to be here today. I'm sorry the occasion is as it is. I've been in the business of Mardi Gras for forty years. I'm proud of my background. I never had a black/white sign in old Algiers, where I live, and I cofounded Bacchus nearly twenty-five years ago. It's open to everybody. Thank God for Mardi Gras and its great reputation. My company is now worldwide. We're in Atlanta, Dallas, and Galveston. We're even doing EuroDisney. Mardi Gras has had an effect all over the world. We're doing a hotel in Florida—at Epcot; it has thirty-six hundred rooms—the main room is called Port Orleans. It's a float factory. It all goes back to Mardi Gras.

"I've started Mardi Gras in twenty other cities, and it's open to everyone. I want you to know that. It's changing here, too, and it's changing on its own. But this thing is a big sword hanging over the captains' heads. How can they stay captain of the krewe? It's a unique baby we have here. It's gotta be nurtured. Why are we rushing to do this today?"

Finally running out of steam, Kern turned to Dorothy Mae Taylor, Peggy Wilson, and Jackie Clarkson. "Okay, girls," he said. Dorothy Mae rolled her eyes, and the women enjoyed a brief moment of solidarity.

Following another handful of speakers, James Bassich, Beau Bassich's son, a blond, sturdily built young man, took the microphone, looking very nervous. He hemmed and hawed and sweated as he spoke, but there was a look of desperate sincerity on his face. "When I was growing up," he said, "I came from three different ethnic backgrounds. My father's background is German. I had Irish and Quakers, too. I had to understand my heritage to learn who I was. I had to respect everybody's heritage. Mine is not better than yours."

He cast about for a way to explain how he felt about the city and his role in it. "Not long ago," he recalled, "I was standing on a ladder in front of my house, cleaning my gutters. A tourist came walking by, lost, and asked if I worked there. He said, 'The streets are in terrible shape. The city must be having problems.' He asked me, 'Why do you live here? Just look at this city.' I told him, 'This is New Orleans. There's history here. We are real. We're really real.'"

Said Bassich, "There are people who have worked for years to pass this down to their families. My father has done everything— Gallier House, the State Museum, the Cabildo, the Cub Scouts. He has done this for history."

Bassich concluded, "Be very careful of history. Mutual respect is necessary on both sides."

Jimmy Bassich, I thought, might well have been speaking for the dwindling younger generation of white upper-class residents of New Orleans who had chosen not to flee, but to stay and dig in, to try to carry on the things that their parents had passed along to them.

It was difficult for them to articulate what it meant—this burden, this heritage, this history, as Jimmy put it. But it was clear, too, that there was a deep, abiding love among them for the city. Why live here, indeed, with the potholes and the crime and the heat and the humidity? Jimmy, cleaning out his gutters, and pondering the question posed to him by the tourist, had found his love for the city questioned, and now he was finding that love tested even more.

Young New Orleanians, I thought, may love the city even more than their forebears. It is certainly not a complacent sort of love, given all the fear and insecurity and inconvenience. After all, young men like Jimmy were inheriting considerably less than their fathers. Their fathers had inherited a virtual Carnival kingdom whose boundaries seemed to coincide with those of the city. This generation of white Carnival scions were like dauphins without thrones, but who chose not to go into exile. They had to figure out, like everyone else, how to make a living and raise a family in a place that was falling apart. And if Jimmy and those like him were forced to leave, some blacks might say good riddance, but the city would be that much poorer for it.

Jimmy Bassich and young black men like James Gray should have a lot to say to each other, I thought, and it would be better said over dinner and drinks than over a yawning gulf of political rhetoric in a claustrophobic council room.

Things began to get considerably more bitter as the afternoon wore on, and opponents of the ordinance began to feel that the deck had been stacked against them. A number of opponents were never called upon to speak. A tone of self-righteous thunder for proponents of the ordinance was set by lawyer Henry Julien, a black Creole whose angry speech belied his cultivated, elegant appearance. His light-skinned face told of a mingling of races, and his name indicated a mingling of cultures. But Henry Julien had cast himself today as an unflinching prophet, foretelling the doom of the Carnival of his white ancestors, hammering the last nails in the coffin. There was a note of steely triumph in his voice.

"The truth of the matter," concluded Julien, "is that the horse is out of the barn, and Humpty-Dumpty is off the wall. Because the Mardi Gras that we're talking about is dead and gone. The Mardi Gras of segregated clubs. It may not be buried for another couple of years. But it's dead."

Dorothy Mae Taylor proceeded to grill Beau Bassich on the membership policies of the uptown krewes, trying to pin down in black and white something that was subjective, unwritten, and unspoken. Beau kept trying politely to evade her, and I thought of the mythical Proteus, master of changes, shifting in the grasp of Odysseus.

It was already getting dark outside, and it was long past the cocktail hour and dinner time. Dorothy Mae requested a recess, and the hall again broke up into whispering and gesticulating clusters in the hallways and back rooms of the City Hall basement. The Carnival captains, along with their allies, Peggy Wilson and Jackie Clarkson, agreed that they had little choice but to assent to the compromise suggested by the mayor, which allowed a delay in enforcement and the setting up of a "blue ribbon committee" to study the implementation and possible amendments to the ordinance. Dorothy Mae Taylor requested a vote on the ordinance, and there were seven green lights on the vote-counting machine on the wall.

The ordinance had passed. Comus, Momus, Proteus, and all the gods of Carnival had been exiled from their independent pantheon and placed under the roof of City Hall. The element of doubt—the most dangerous enemy of Carnival—had been admitted to the celebration, and the very future of Mardi Gras was in jeopardy.

20

Moon over Mardi Gras

In the days following the fateful council meeting, everyone seemed stunned by the sudden end of civility in New Orleans. Things had been said during the meeting that couldn't be glossed over or forgotten. At one point during the meeting, Peggy Wilson had interrupted Dorothy Mae Taylor during her questioning of Beau Bassich, pointing out that the meeting was not, after all, an inquisition. Wilson later told a friend that the meeting had not had the usual cathartic effect she had witnessed in previous controversial sessions. This was the first time, said Wilson, that feelings were worse instead of better at the end of the day. And wounds continued to fester.

Most New Orleanians, however, hadn't needed a weatherman to tell them which way the wind was blowing. This painful changing of the guard had been predicted months earlier by Moon Landrieu, the city's last white mayor, who had become a kind of elder statesman in New Orleans. Landrieu had presided over an earlier political upheaval, during the 1970s, by building an unprecedented coalition between uptown whites and black political groups. Landrieu had run independently of the two rival Democratic organizations, the Regular Democratic Organization and the Crescent City Democratic Organization, and he had been supported by young black political organizations that were coming of age—SOUL, BOLD, and COUP—who thought the older black politicians, particularly the church ministers, had sold out. Landrieu had maintained a link to uptown society through an adviser whose father and grandfather had ruled over Rex.

Landrieu, who had kept a rather low profile in the city since his glory days, when he had been mentioned as a possible vice presidential candidate, had just won the late Jim Garrison's judgeship. Always

203

edgy and impatient, even curt, with anyone he thought was wasting his time, Landrieu had become even more bristly.

Carnival had remained immune from change for so long, he told me, because of the shared history among uptown whites and blacks. "This is a small town," said Landrieu, "maybe the smallest big town in America." He speculated, "I think elite Mardi Gras had been ignored by blacks because uptown people had been the ones involved in civil rights. Their position had been moderation if not activism." It was the "ethnic types" like former mayor Vic Schiro, he said, who were the most virulent racists. "It was not 'seemly' for uptown types to be racists." What's more, it had been the more moderate of the uptown crowd, including lawyer George Denegre and two former captains of Rex, who had recently sponsored anti-Duke rallies. "I think they felt betrayed," said Landrieu. "There was deep hurt and feeling of betrayal on both sides."

The position of uptown whites on the question of race, however, left a great deal to be desired. "When you got into that uptown group, there was still a plantation mentality. They were good to their servants. They were thoughtful. They were not anti-black. They wouldn't throw rocks at a black because it might be their maid or maid's son."

Landrieu himself had never felt quite at home with the uptown crowd, and he had given them reason to feel uneasy, too. The first real challenges to their Carnival exclusivity had come during his administration. One of the first things Landrieu had done as mayor was put a black woman in the receptionist's desk at City Hall, as a signal that things were about to change.

In 1975, a member of Rex had submitted an invitation list to the club hierarchy that included the names of several black citizens and their wives. Among them were the Reverend A. L. Davis, the city's first black councilman, and Dutch Morial, who was then an appellate-court judge. When the Rex hierarchy balked, Landrieu let it be known that if black guests were not welcome at the Rex ball, Landrieu would not be present in the city's Gallier Hall reviewing stands on Mardi Gras day to offer the traditional greeting to Rex, who that year was Harry McCall, Jr., the prominent lawyer.

Now, almost twenty years later, a few blacks were regularly

invited to Rex balls, although by the 1992 season, none had yet been invited as members. In 1991, when the name of a prominent ambassador from an Asian country was submitted as a guest to ride on a float in the Rex parade, there was an inquiry about the shade of the ambassador's skin before the invitation was approved.

Landrieu observed, "Both sides still have a lot to learn. When you're in a period of transition from white to black control, power bases are being dislodged. In an expanding economy, you can live with losing a piece of what you had. But where the pie is shrinking, that makes it very tough. There's a general feeling among whites of fear where the city is going. Whites have never learned to be a minority, and it's a difficult transition. It may be equally difficult for blacks to learn to be a majority."

Unplanned Obsolescence

The treatment of blacks by upper-class whites in New Orleans, as Landrieu noted, had been based, for the most part, on a principle of noblesse oblige rather than on a recognition of the innate rights and the innate worth of black citizens. And thus, for all its good intentions, such a code of genteel patronization was bound to fall short of true social justice. It was inevitable, too, that the patrician proponents of noblesse oblige would feel bewilderment and betrayal when their gestures of generosity and their long-standing sympathies for black New Orleanians were found to be lacking. It was as puzzling as having the beads they tossed to black children in the crowd during a Carnival parade tossed back at them with an epithet. Where was the gratitude?

Not all uptown Carnival rulers were puzzled, however, or taken aback by recent developments. Landrieu's analysis had been echoed, surprisingly, by a former captain of an uptown krewe. A realist and something of a fatalist, the former captain had remarked, mildly, during an interview the previous spring, that he had been expecting some changes in Carnival. "We can't keep having lily white parades through a black city," he said. "It just won't fly." Carnival had changed before, he said, "and I expect we'll be going through another metamorphosis."

When I asked if Carnival would survive, he replied, "My lord, yes." The next Carnival, he said, "will be a less patrician festival, and that's not all bad. I think it will go back to its real roots, back to more of a rites-of-spring festival. That's where it started originally, before it got formalized with the Anglo-Saxon debutante system. I don't think white satin dresses are the essence of Mardi Gras. These things change. And the next metamorphosis after this one will be easier."

IV

Epiphany

21

The Land of the Wild Magnolias

Despite rumors flying around uptown that Comus and Momus and perhaps another krewe or two were going to cancel their parades, Henri had been told by the captain of Comus to carry on with his work on the floats. Beau Bassich was said to be trying to hold Proteus together, and the captain of Rex was determined not to fold, although parading now seemed a matter of duty rather than pleasure. There were reports of some krewes inquiring about parade permits in Jefferson Parish, although no one seriously believed that the aristocrats of the Garden District would care to parade past suburban shopping malls and subdivisions.

All the turmoil and tension in uptown Carnival circles, however, had little effect on another Carnival subculture that was as old as many of the elite white krewes and just as given to rituals and symbols of power. The season had just begun heating up for the Mardi Gras Indians, the "tribes" of black men who dressed as Indians on Mardi Gras day and again on Saint Joseph's day in March.

There were around a dozen tribes in New Orleans, divided between uptown and downtown, and on Mardi Gras day, the uptown tribes set out downtown to confront their downtown rivals, with stops at their favorite watering holes along the way. In the old days, rival gangs would meet on the "battlefront," with knives and guns. These days, the confrontation was one of ritual chants and dances, with the rivalry a matter of one-upmanship in costumes and voice.

With their elaborate costumes, chants, signals, and tribal hierarchy—big chief, second or third chiefs, spy boy, wild man, flag boy, and second line—the Mardi Gras Indians are the most "folkloric" of all Carnival celebrants. And they are also the most self-reliant and autonomous, since they make their own costumes and their own music, and they make their own way down the streets, with no trac-tor-pulled floats, no police escort or blockades.

Although the notion of blacks posing as Indians might appear to be an example of fanciful cultural cross-dressing, there is a strong historical connection between blacks and Native Americans in Louisi-ana. Runaway slaves often took refuge with Indian tribes, and inter-marriage between the groups was common enough at the turn of the century to give rise to yet another term of ethnic identity in New Orleans: the "griffon," or cross between black and Native American. Brother Timber, legendary chief of the Wild Squatoolas tribe early in the century, was said to be part Indian.

Photographer Mike Smith, who has been following the Indians for decades, regards the Indian gangs in New Orleans as a kind of "maroon" culture—a variation of the culture of runaway slaves that emerged in the swamps around New Orleans. "It's a submerged cul-ture," Mike said, "that has survived in the urban wilderness." Simi-larly, New Orleans music historians Jason Berry, Jonathan Foose, and Tad Jones have traced a line of influences and ancestral spirit figures from the songs and dances and voodoo ceremonies of Congo Square down to the Mardi Gras Indians.

The first known Mardi Gras "tribe" was the Creole Wild West, which appeared during the 1880s. Various origins have been sug-gested for the Mardi Gras Indians, including the traveling Wild West shows of the time. There was undoubtedly a Caribbean influence, too, since Indian-inspired Carnival costumes appeared as early as the 1840s in Trinidad.

Mike Smith has also found a connection between the Mardi Gras Indians and the black "spiritualist" churches of New Orleans, which engage in ceremonies invoking the spirit of Black Hawk, the Native American warrior venerated as an icon of peace and justice.

Believe It or Not

As Carnival season approaches, the weekly rehearsal sessions for the Mardi Gras Indians pick up in intensity. "Practice is serious," one

Indian told me. "Serious as a heart attack. Being at rehearsal pays off. You find out who is who and what is what. You learn the codes, the signals, the verbal response, and whatever way to communicate."

Every Sunday, the uptown "chiefs" gather with their followers at bars in Central City, while the downtown tribes congregate in their familiar haunts in Tremé and the lower Ninth Ward. Like uptown white krewes, the tribes tend to be secretive enclaves, with a distinct hierarchy, who demonstrate deep roots in family and neighborhood, who wear extravagant costumes each year, who mythologize themselves as heirs to an ancient festive tradition, and who celebrate their lineage and their forebears, real and mythic.

The resemblance between the two subcultures ends there, however. You could hardly get as far away from the Boston Club or the Comus den as the H & R Bar, the headquarters of the Wild Magnolias. Although the H & R, which occupies an unmarked, ramshackle white frame building in the heart of Central City, lies only three blocks from Saint Charles Avenue, there are times when it seems a continent away.

I ventured out to the H & R one afternoon to meet Emile "Bo" Dollis, the chief of the Wild Magnolias. I learned that Bo could be found at the bar, near the corner of Dryades and Second, almost every afternoon. Bo, a powerful-looking man of forty-seven, appeared more than strong enough to carry the considerable weight of a chief's costume. The crown alone was so heavy it sometimes cut deeply into his forehead. Bo said that he had sold one of his suits to the Ripley's Believe It or Not Museum in the French Quarter that weighed almost two hundred pounds.

All the Mardi Gras Indian chiefs exude a kind of charisma, although some of the greatest chiefs have actually been rather slight of build. When Bo walked into the barroom, with an air of low-key command and the presence of a matinee idol, there was little doubt about his ability to physically dominate a scene. All the patrons of the bar roused themselves from their stools or from their tables to pay their respects. Bo's picture was hanging behind the bar, and his recordings were on the jukebox, so that he was always there, in spirit at least.

"Bo is the big man with the big voice," a second-liner told me once. "And he's been some big places."

Bo cut his first recordings of Indian songs back in the early seventies, and he had recorded an album recently for Rounder Records, but there were long periods of drought between tours and recordings. Performing as a kind of cultural curiosity for the outside world was only sporadically rewarding. He would travel to New York, for example, to play Town Hall, or to Europe to star in jazz festivals, then find himself back home in New Orleans with empty pockets.

"You can never make a living from it," said Bo. Recently, he said, he had come up with an idea to supplement his concert engagements. He had invented a portable car-wash which he hoped to patent. "I got a tow truck," he said, "a car-washer on wheels. If I get a job, I've got my own electricity and water."

Bo's first job had been as a busboy at the cafeteria at Tulane University about the time of the assassination of JFK. Since then, he said, he had been a city bus driver and he had worked with steel. He drove trucks for a liquor company. Since he started traveling with his music, he had worked at house painting and as a contractor. "All the guys around here," said Bo, "are good at certain things—electricians and plumbers. But there just hasn't been enough steady work." As a result, Bo, like his second-liners, spent many an afternoon at the H & R, waiting for opportunity to stroll by. In the opinion of some of his friends, Bo, despite his robust constitution, was in danger of drinking himself into an early grave.

Bo's father had been a cabinetmaker for Dixie Furniture, and his mother was a nurse. One brother was a versatile designer who had recently done a floral design of a motorcycle for a funeral. Another brother, he said, was an artist in New York.

Carnival had always been a big thing when he was growing up, recalled Bo. "On Carnival day we had all different kinds of organizations around us. We had the skeleton men (young men from the projects who dyed their union suits black and painted white bones on them). We had the Baby Dolls (prostitutes who dressed in little-girl frills and ruffles). We had Zulu. But when it got to the neighborhood thing, you couldn't mask as a gladiator or a Viking. What we had were the Indians."

A neighbor, George King, had been an Indian, and Bo tried to emulate him by having his brother draw a design on an apron that he filled in with watercolors. It wasn't until he was thirteen or fourteen that he began to learn the craft of sewing beads, sequins, feathers, and rhinestones, he said.

His mother hadn't wanted him to follow the Indians at first because it was too dangerous. In the early days, he said, he saw a lot of confrontations, mostly between the spy boys who had been sent out by the chiefs to scout out rival gangs. "The attitude of the different tribes changed," said Bo. "Then there wasn't so much confrontation with knives and guns and razors. Now they outdo each other with needle and thread." The most trouble nowadays, he said, came from the second-liners. "I tell them, 'If you're trouble, I don't want you out there. I'm not going to spend all that time and money and get my day messed up.' "

The styles of the suits had changed, too. In the early days, the Indians would go to the poultry yards to get feathers and pieces of bone and shell. These salvaged elements soon evolved into expensive plumes and rhinestones. Tradition calls for a new suit, with a new color scheme, every year, which can cost thousands of dollars, although beaded sections of a suit can be recycled into other parts of the costume the following year.

As teenagers, Bo and a friend went first to the White Eagles tribe, but there was a long wait to move up in the ranks. "We wanted big positions," he said. "We went to the Magnolias because they had positions opened up. I was the first flag boy."

"My first costume I put on was gold. The suit was stones on top of sequins. We used to go from uptown down to Elysian Fields and back. Now the costumes are so heavy we can hardly make it to Elysian Fields. Now we use a lot of velvet, and that makes us uncomfortable too." Even so, he said, "When you put that costume on, you feel the energy. You always overdo it. Once you put it on that morning on Carnival, you just get the energy and strength. You're having so much fun with it. This is your work that you did."

The Wrong Neighborhood, Baby

Bo invited me to a practice session of the Wild Magnolias, and I brought a friend along to the H & R on a Sunday night shortly before Christmas. We parked just off Dryades Street, and as we walked toward the bar, a young black man drove by and shouted, "You're in the wrong neighborhood, baby!" His tone was playful, suggesting less of a threat than a friendly warning.

Once you were inside the H & R, after running the dangerous gauntlet outside, you were home free. "You're safe here," a Wild Magnolia drummer once told me. "The Wild Magnolias don't stand for any trouble. We don't shoot here. We don't fight. There's been no killing here. There's no blood on the floor. You can come here with your finest jewelry and clothes and walk back out again."

We walked into the bar to find a crowd of men gathered in a corner, many of them rattling tambourines. There were a few women sitting at the bar. One of them had brought a big sack full of chicken wings, which she began distributing around the bar. A large man walked in with a big drum, and began contributing to the rhythm. Bo still hadn't arrived, and after waiting another hour or so, the men finally decided to start without him. They began chanting, "Let's go get 'em," and my friend and I edged back into the opposite corner.

They did Bo's "Handa Wanda," the chant that means the tribe isn't looking for trouble. Nevertheless, I was a little nervous without Bo there to give us his stamp of approval. We couldn't help but feel like the white voyeurs who used to go to Congo Square to marvel at the wild bamboula. A tall, skinny man named Slim who was standing next to us at the bar asked us if we were scared. I shook my head, not very convincingly, and he said, "Hey, this is all in fun."

Slim was concerned that I couldn't see the action, and he lifted me up on top of a cigarette machine and handed me a cowbell so I could join in.

The drums and cowbells heated up, with bystanders at the tables beating on wine bottles or glasses. Two young men, the regular spy boy and an aspiring spy boy, faced off in ritual combat. "They're finding out who's the best," said Slim. The spy boy pantomimed looking off into the distance, hands over his eyes. The challenger

214

circled him, and the two rushed each other, dancing back only at the last minute. The aura of violence was convincing, and eventually one of the men had to be escorted out of the bar to cool down.

Bo never did show up, and as the fires beneath the drums began to burn down, we decided to leave. It was quite late, and the deserted street looked menacing. Slim followed us out to the car, and leaned in the window. He said, "If y'all come back, don't worry. I'll look out for you."

We drove over to Saint Charles, where the lights in the parlors of most of the mansions had been turned off for the night, and we felt that we had just crossed an ocean of sorts.

22

The End of the Mardi Gras Mystique

There was a small riot in New Orleans a few nights after Christmas, on the edge of the Central Business District, following a concert by a rap group from out of town. By Los Angeles standards, the melee was really quite tame. But genuine anarchy is unusual in New Orleans, where crowds get raucous but seldom get too far out of control.

Sally Reeves theorized that there was a "Mardi Gras mystique," some kind of benign subliminal force, that had been the key factor in keeping the peace in New Orleans during so many years of jostling, drunken crowds. There was a question now of whether the "mystique," which had certainly not protected the Carnival captains at the council meeting, had dissipated for good.

I went to check in with Sally in her dungeon below City Hall, where she had been stewing over the passing of the new Carnival ordinance and what it meant for the end of privacy and secrecy. Was Carnival no longer to be a masquerade, but a politically correct charade? At a Christmas party, she had told Beau Bassich, "Thank God it was you who was there representing the krewes." Beau, she said, "never lost his cool or his geniality."

"The symbol of Mardi Gras," said Sally, "seemed to draw out the frustrations of each side—the frustration of blacks who feel they are the have-nots and the frustration of those who have worked hard only to have the government take it away."

Mardi Gras, said Sally, "may seem robust and profitable. But this has made people realize that it's a delicate mechanism. It could all be gone with a fire or an explosion or a riot."

She asked, rhetorically, "Why has a riot never occurred to snuff out Mardi Gras?" The answer, she said, was "the mystique." She pointed out, "The rap group that ended up in a riot last night did not have the cohesive force of a mystique to hold behavior in line."

Sally elaborated. "I think the mystique of the whole thing has kept people from feeling the resentment of class consciousness," she said. "Just think of the heterogeneity of it all. The people who celebrate on La Salle and Rampart, in Central City, know they're having more fun than people on ladders on Saint Charles and Napoleon. Everybody does their own thing. What this ordinance says is that we can have the lowest common denominator, but we can't have the highest."

Sally was particularly concerned in her role as archivist, she said. "We have impersonal economic and democratic forces coming to bear against the survival of things as we once knew them. These developments change everything," she said. "When something goes into decline, people rush to document it. For example, I wanted to document the oil industry, just as someone from the University of Michigan wanted to do the auto industry." With so many cats out of the bag now, however, and so many secret rituals brought out into the open, her fellow archivists wanted to do Carnival. But the idea of putting the secret inner workings of Carnival into the public record was heresy, somehow. "The whole cachet of Carnival," she said, "has been that when people called you out, you didn't know who it was. It was just for the pleasure of the moment.

"It doesn't seem to occur to anyone," said Sally, "that there is another way philosophically to deal with these things. Consult Tocqueville and see if he predicts that the rabble will devour the elite within a democratic system.

"My husband, a man of goodwill and passion, says he wishes the krewes would give it a try. The only problem, it's just like the French Revolution or *perestroika*. You can't open a crack in the door—the genie will get out of the bottle."

Sally pointed out that it was actually Henri Schindler who would be most affected by the ordinance, if Comus were to cease parading. "His existence is the most threatened of all," said Sally. "Henri's particular renaissance of Comus would be ended. It's a peculiar irony that in the midst of his one-man revival, his conversion of this transitory form into an art would be snuffed out."

The audience for Comus had been diminishing over the years, she acknowledged. "If they decided to convert it into a slide show, an imaginary parade, not that many people would know they had missed it." But Mardi Gras would not be the same without Comus, she said. "After you have thrown yourself into the throngs all day and participated with verve and worn a silly costume and tromped the streets, and you think it's all over, you have this last lovely hurrah at the end of the day. It comes out like so many phantom figures, passes quickly, and disappears. Then and only then can Mardi Gras be over."

As Sally spoke, I thought of the line from Alexander Pope: "Who breaks a butterfly upon a wheel?" You could make a good case on aesthetic grounds for preserving traditional Carnival, although the newer parades like Bacchus and Endymion were greater crowd pleasers. But what kind of art did Carnival parades represent? If floats were an art form, they lay somewhere between folk art and theatrical scenery. They were made to be disposable, solid enough only to be glimpsed for a few moments by the light of flambeaux. Their duration in the public view was not much longer that that of a fireworks display. In that sense, the art of Carnival was the art of illusion.

23

High Rolling and a Mardi Gras Mugging

Aside from all the bickering over Carnival, the year did not end auspiciously for the citizens of New Orleans, nor did it bode well for the future, unless you were a compulsive gambler. The governor-elect of Louisiana had traveled to Las Vegas for the holidays and was spotted on New Year's Eve by a reporter for the *Times-Picayune* at the gaming tables of Caesar's Palace. Edwards, who avoided the roulette wheel in favor of the old Creole game of Johnny Crapaud, got lucky that night, and left the craps table several thousand dollars richer. As Joe Walker predicted, it was the same old Edwards playing the same old game. Before long, Edwards would also win his long crusade to bring casino gambling and his friends from Caesar's Palace and other Las Vegas establishments to New Orleans.

While Edwin Edwards was rolling the dice in Las Vegas, back in New Orleans an eighteen-year-old black man was running amok through a historic mansion on Saint Charles Avenue and terrorizing the young nephews of the captain of Comus.

Shortly before midnight, two men armed with a semiautomatic pistol hijacked a pickup truck stopped for a traffic light and took off on a crime spree. They robbed four pedestrians on Third Street, in the Garden District, then held up two revelers leaving a party on the other side of Saint Charles. They abandoned the truck after being pursued by the police, and one of the robbers jumped a twelve-foot fence and landed beside the swimming pool on the grounds of a mansion near the corner of Third and Saint Charles. The thief had unknowingly invaded the ancestral home of the captain of Comus, where the king of Carnival stopped every year during the Rex parade for a toast.

That night, the captain's elderly arthritic sister had been staying at home with her two grandnephews. She locked herself into her bedroom, and the two boys took refuge in an adjoining room, as the invader crashed through a kitchen window and began rampaging through the house, smashing more windows and leaving smears of blood and mud on the cream carpets and white walls. He wreaked particular havoc in the Carnival trophy room, full of memorabilia, including the cup used to toast Rex. The robber soon found himself lost and trapped, however, feeling perhaps as though he had entered a Carnival fun house, with Parish Prison at the exit.

It was as though the robber, during his helter-skelter New Year's Eve, had set out deliberately to assault old-line Carnival. If one were prone to such symbolism, one might suggest that any residual illusions of isolation or safety on the part of Comus and his krewe were shattered along with the windows of the mansion on Saint Charles Avenue. A few days later, Susan Buck Mayer, the queen of queens, was mugged again, brutally knocked to the sidewalk near her house.

Requiem for a City

The next day, at a New Year's gathering I attended with Dalt and Josephine, the festivities ended with a series of toasts. The final word of the day went to a bookstore owner who offered a toast that suited all of us, in our elegiac mood.

"There's decay and deterioration all around," said the bookstore owner, swinging his glass in a circle that seemed to encompass the French Quarter, uptown New Orleans, the state of Louisiana, and America at large. "But there are people here who are trying to do good things. Decay and deterioration are just the way of the world now, and we have to make the best of it."

24

A Dose of Wisdom

There was something so obdurate and abstract about Dorothy Mae Taylor's campaign against old-line Carnival that she and her followers appeared at times to have been caught up in the wave of political correctness that had swept the nation. As one observer remarked contemptuously, Mardi Gras was foundering on the shoals of abstract principle, while the city was falling apart with very real problems. The notion of public space, of places and things to which everyone should have access, had become so attenuated and the feeling of victimization so expanded that people who knew nothing about Comus or Rex suddenly felt hurt by being excluded from them.

For a dose of Solomonic wisdom on the Carnival dispute, I went to see the man who had been credited with the key role in the Civil Rights revolution in New Orleans during the 1960s. Judge John Minor Wisdom had agreed to meet me on the day after New Year's in his office at the Court of Appeals, an enormous Italian Renaissance building, a former post office, embellished with what the judge called a "Tootsie Roll" columned façade.

Judge Wisdom, aged eighty-six, was a tiny man with very bright eyes and a brisk, no-nonsense manner. He was a well-known collector of historical documents, and his walls were covered with framed letters and memorabilia. The judge owned a decree signed by the Sieur de Bienville, as well as a letter from Judah P. Benjamin to General Beauregard, upon his bombarding of Fort Sumter. There was a large Audubon print, too, of a white pelican, the state bird of Louisiana.

Judge Wisdom's grasp of Louisiana history and his own extensive library had helped him in imparting a historical sweep and solidity to his landmark opinion, in *The United States* v. *Louisiana*, striking down discrimination in voting rights. The judge had analyzed in considerable detail the historical methods by which black political participation had been contained and restrained.

"A wall stands in Louisiana between registered voters and unregistered, eligible Negro voters," wrote Judge Wisdom in 1967. "The wall is the State constitutional requirement that an applicant for registration 'understand and give a reasonable interpretation of any section' of the Constitution of Louisiana or of the United States. It is not the only wall of its kind, but since the Supreme Court's demolishment of the white primary, the interpretation test has been the highest, best-guarded, most effective barrier to Negro voting in Louisiana . . . We hold: this wall, built to bar Negroes from access to the franchise, must come down."

The wall barring blacks from the Boston Club, the Krewe of Comus, and other all-white private organizations, however, was a different matter. The judge, who was seated behind his big antique desk, leaned forward in his chair, fixing me with an eagle eye, as he explained. The issue of integration in schools and voting booths had been a fairly straightforward one, he said. "I had always realized that things had to change in Louisiana. It was apparent to me that something was coming. African-Americans didn't have decent schooling. They were not permitted in good hotels or restaurants. They were not even permitted to have interracial athletic contests. This was a social injustice that had to be corrected. But when it comes to personal relationships of a social nature, you have a different problem that will take years to settle—more than I have to live, and more than you have to live."

The Carnival ordinance, he said, had left the city more polarized than he had seen it since the 1970s. Legally, he said, the issue of integrating private clubs was a close call. "If you use state facilities such as the Municipal Auditorium for the ball or police or firemen, you have a very close case. In order for discrimination to be unlawful, the state must be involved in some form—cities, counties, state agencies. But by definition, a private club has a right of exclusion by virtue of the right of association—the right to choose one's friends."

*   *   *

The judge himself, who came from a patrician family, had been an avid participant in Carnival and in private clubs, particularly the Louisiana Club, known formally as the Louisiana Debating and Literary Society, whose membership was synonymous with that of the Knights of Momus, the krewe founded in 1872. When he was young, the judge had ridden in Comus, Momus, Proteus, and Rex parades. His sister had been queen of Twelfth Night, and his brother Ben had been a noted Carnival historian. One of his daughters had been chosen queen of Comus and the other, who became a lawyer, could have been queen of Momus, except that "she was very independent," according to the judge, and "didn't approve of it."

Judge Wisdom had reluctantly quit riding in parades thirty-five years ago, in 1957, when he joined the court, for the sake of appearances. "Riders had been known to fall off the floats. They used to start and stop suddenly, and a rider could be taken by surprise. The public would never believe that the rider did not have too much to drink, and I didn't want to bring discredit to the federal judiciary."

He did not relinquish his memberships in his private clubs and Carnival krewes, however. Even as he was incurring the wrath of many of his peers with his landmark decisions against segregation, he retained his lifelong conservative friends and maintained his membership in organizations that discriminated against blacks and Jews. Perhaps, just as remarkably, he hadn't been asked to leave. Said the judge, "I felt I could do more good by staying than by getting out. A lot of my friends didn't like what I was doing, but most of them respected me for my decision."

One day, in the bar at the Boston Club, he ran into a lifelong conservative friend, who asked, "Well, John, what have you done to us white folks today?" Wisdom retorted, "Oh, just put a few Neanderthals like you in jail for contempt!"

Judge Wisdom's wife Bonnie, a grande dame, had grown up on her family's sugar plantation. Her great-grandfather, George Mathews, presiding justice of the Louisiana Supreme Court, had issued one of the most remarkable rulings in the history of black-white relationships. A free woman of color had sued for the freedom of her daughter, Josephine, who had been born a slave. Josephine's owners had taken her with them to France, where slavery was outlawed, and returned with her to Louisiana. Justice Mathews had upheld the decision of the jury to free the child, declaring, "Being free for one moment in France, it was not in the power of her former owner to reduce her again to slavery."

The Wisdoms were subject to considerable harassment for the judge's stand on civil rights. One night, Bonnie Wisdom had answered the phone to hear a caller shout, "Nigger lover!" Before hanging up, she shouted back, "White trash!"

The Wisdoms continued to get threatening calls, as well as warnings that their pets would be poisoned. Eventually they moved out of their mansion in the Garden District, one of the most beautiful in the city. The house on First Street was bought by John Mmahat, whose savings and loan business had thrived during the boom of the early 1980s. When the economy crashed, the Mmahats put their house on the market, and it was purchased by novelist Anne Rice, who then used it as the setting for her thriller *The Witching Hour*. In Rice's novel, there are grisly scenes involving blood and murder in almost every room.

25

Playing Genetic Lotto on Twelfth Night

On the church calendar, January 6, the twelfth day of Christmas, marks the Epiphany—the showing forth of the divinity of the baby Jesus to the magi. The magi were said to have followed a star over great distances to find the holy child and shower him with gifts. In New Orleans, however, this short winter day marks the beginning of Carnival season, the season of the flesh, and there is not much left of the sacred about Twelfth Night. As observed by the elite krewe known as the Twelfth Night Revelers, the occasion has become an odd hybrid cross between the British Twelfth Night festival, in which a monarch of merriment is chosen by means of a golden bean, and the French tradition of the *bal du roi*.

In New Orleans, no one of humble birth or exotic origins is likely to be sought out by the captains of uptown Carnival; they usually search no further for the recipient of their homage and their gifts than the edge of the Garden District.

Ordinarily, the Twelfth Night ball, the first official event of the Carnival season in New Orleans, wouldn't have been a big deal, worth biting one's fingernails over. As a kickoff event, Twelfth Night was notorious for leading its revelers into Carnival with more of a yawn than a bang.

The Twelfth Night Revelers could claim, technically, that they were the second-oldest surviving Carnival organization, since the first incarnation of the club put on a ball and a parade in 1870, during the height of Reconstruction. The early Twelfth Night celebrations, involving a giant cake, and presided over by a Lord of Misrule, were said to have rivaled those of Comus. But the organization, which had long since dropped the parade and now put on a ball and tableau, had been declining in importance over the years. A number of influential society matrons had lost interest and stopped attending.

I would rather have spent the evening riding with the Phorty Phunny Phellows on the Saint Charles streetcar. An early Carnival tradition, the streetcar ride on the day of Epiphany, or Twelfth Night, had been revived by Errol Laborde, editor of *New Orleans* magazine and another "guardian of culture." But this year, Twelfth Night, as the curtain opener onto a season of uncertainty, had taken on a certain symbolic importance, and I had had to fish for an invitation with a rather unbecoming urgency.

In order to acquire my invitation, I had done the unthinkable. I had actually called and asked for one. I had telephoned the "baker," the krewe member who plays a sort of zany counterpart during the ball to the more dignified Lord of Misrule. According to rumor, the baker's daughter had recently been on tap to be queen of Comus, but because his business had foundered so badly during the recession, she had to forgo the expensive honor.

The baker, a Creole descendant of Governor Claiborne, seemed shocked at my effrontery. He said it was not in his power to grant me an invitation, but that he would refer it to the "invitation committee." Meanwhile, at the behest of one of my uptown allies, I also contacted a kindly, genteel couple, Stewart and Betty Maunsell, who resided on the Mississippi Gulf Coast, and who were highly regarded in Carnival's aristocratic circles. Betty Maunsell was prominent in preservation causes and in the Colonial Dames. The Maunsells' granddaughter had been chosen queen the previous year.

"It's strictly up to the men," Betty Maunsell told me, when it came to issuing invitations, although I had a feeling her opinion carried some weight. My invitation arrived on the day of the ball.

I arrived at the Municipal Auditorium and proceeded through the side entrance to the upstairs function room, where a preliminary cocktail party for special guests was to be held prior to the ball. The debutantes making up the court of Twelfth Night were visions of white satin and tulle floating around the room, greeting friends and relatives, some of them tugging surreptitiously at the tops of their strapless gowns.

Former court members were distinguished by the silver or gold beans they wore on chains around their necks. I spoke to Mary Virginia Weinmann Kaufman, a beautiful young woman in a blue taffeta dress, who was wearing a silver bean around her neck, relic of the court of 1985. Mary Virginia's father had just been named chief of protocol in the Bush White House after his predecessor had flubbed badly during Queen Elizabeth's recent visit to America by allowing Her Majesty to address an audience with only her hat poking over the podium.

Carnival, observed Mary Virginia, "is archaic—no, it's more like an air bubble. But it's a memory I treasure." As for the current crisis, she observed, "There are things that should have been worked out a long time ago—so maybe it's a good thing. It should be more open. But the old krewes are the glue that holds everything together. Without them, everything would fall apart."

I spotted Beau Bassich, who was indeed still trying to hold things together. Looking relaxed and at home in this setting, he sighed and shrugged philosophically when I asked how things were going. "We still don't know what Mardi Gras this year is going to be. But we'll keep playing the game."

I asked an older woman in a dated-looking dress and a rather moth-eaten fur wrap if she had seen my hostess, Betty Maunsell. The woman said she didn't really know anyone in the room. She hadn't been to Twelfth Night in years, she said. "Ordinarily, I can't be bothered." But this year, with traditional Carnival under fire, she felt obliged to show up.

I found Betty Maunsell, who led me to a side room, where her daughter, Beth Smith, wearing a gold bean from her reign as queen two decades earlier, was coaching her granddaughter, Sally Dart Hughes, last year's queen. Sally would reign briefly tonight before turning over crown and scepter to the new queen. Sally was waving her scepter gracefully toward a phantom crowd. She smiled, then made a funny face.

The lights began blinking, a signal to repair to the Auditorium for the ball. As I walked in, a group of little boys, the hope of Carnival future, were capering about, dressed as cooks, and handing out yellow and green tickets for the "Twelfth Night Revelers Lotto." The tickets said "Win your chance—to be Queen of the Dance" and "The Hell with Cake and Beans."

The theme for the ball, appropriately enough, was chance, in honor of the newly elected governor's passion and the inevitable arrival of gambling in Louisiana. According to a humorous poem in the program, written by some anonymous Twelfth Night Revelers bard, the cooks of TNR had decided to forgo their usual means of choosing their queen and had decided to leave it to the lottery: "This year we'll offer each young lady a chance / to serve as our King's consort at our Twelfth Night Dance."

Unlike most guests who were not "to the manner born," I had not been banished to the upper rows of the Auditorium to squint down at the action. I was among the lucky elite seated in the crowded call-out section, who were actually eligible to be called out later for a dance. "This is the biggest crowd we've had in years," said a young woman sitting next to me.

The evening began with "The Star-Spangled Banner," played by the orchestra seated near the stage. The curtain rose over the stage, revealing the masked king, the new Lord of Misrule, seated on a settee. Behind him was a banner proclaiming the club logo, TNR, in huge gold letters. A masked centurion then led the previous year's king, also masked, and his queen, Sally Dart Hughes, to the dais, where everyone raised their scepters in tribute.

A bevy of cooks, dressed in white, purple, and blue satin suits, came dancing out onto the floor, leading what appeared to be a giant slot machine. According to the program, this was the lotto machine that was supposed to pick the queen. The machine, however, started smoking and shaking, and it appeared to fall apart. The cooks then decided to return to their old method of choosing the queen—the cake, with its predestined bean.

The original Twelfth Night ball featured a giant cake, into which a golden bean had been baked. The cake was to be cut and distributed at random to a group of young women, with the lucky recipient of the piece with the golden bean to be designated as queen. As it happened, however, the revelers, dressed as spear-carrying barbarians, began tossing the cake on their spears, and the bean was never found.

Subsequently, the queen was selected in advance, although she was kept in the dark until the ball, and the progress of the bean was carefully orchestrated.

Eventually the real cake was replaced by an artificial replica, a development that represented, according to Sally Reeves, the growing artificiality and stylization of old Carnival. "Like all of culture that's old," she had told me, "its usages have become more stylized, maybe decadent. There was a real cake, and then one day, the cake came out, and it was a cardboard cake with electric lights. The chef only pantomimes cutting it. My husband contends that it's a stylization that reflects age and culture—not a degeneration, but a crystallization." The idea, she explained, is that "you no longer need the actual cake. All you need is a pretense."

Tonight, as the orchestra launched into "New York, New York," the debutantes in their white dresses seemed as delighted by their cardboard boxes as they might have been by real cake. I recognized two of the debutantes who received silver beans, Elizabeth Kelleher and Julie Learned Phelps, as my friend Judy's early winter-book favorites to reign as queens of Rex and Comus.

Following another procession by the newly beaned court maids and their escorts around the dance floor, it was time for dancing, and an unmasked man in white tie and tails began calling names from a list for the first number. The masked revelers, apparently unembarrassed by appearing in public in bright satin costumes that looked like pajamas, were hovering eagerly around the call-out section.

There was something vaguely obscene about a group of masked men looking over the array of women in their low-cut gowns. On the society pages of the *Times-Picayune*, the photos of the old-line balls, with young women posing next to anonymous masked men, are usually accompanied by captions that listed the names of the young women, followed by "and masker" or "and reveler." As an uptown friend once suggested, there is something about the photos that suggests vintage French erotica. Tonight, even the masks and loose-fitting costumes couldn't entirely hide the men's paunches and jowls and eyeglasses. Like the king, who is usually at least a generation older than his young queen, many of the men were obviously older than the women they chose to dance with.

Nevertheless, I felt a flutter of hope that I would be called out to dance, although I knew that most women got to dance only once or twice, usually with their fathers, their uncles, or a friend of the family. What's more, as my Texan friend had pointed out, these were scions of families whose dance cards had actually been filled generations before I arrived. I thought of Sally Reeves's description of the "enigmatic men" who had called her out for a "magic moment on the floor."

Of course, if the men had lifted their masks, the moment might have been spoiled, for beneath the masks were men she had known all her life. Behind the masks, there were very few surprises, and that was by design.

The broken lottery machine had been toted to the edge of the dance floor, and I couldn't help but think how little these faux cooks and bakers actually left to chance when it came to choosing their friends, their dancing partners, their club-mates, and most of all, the prospective mates for their daughters. Most young girls in New Orleans had already lost the genetic lottery, by their standards, and stood less chance of reigning as queen of Twelfth Night than they did of picking a winning lotto number.

Following yet another procession, winding up the evening, the orchestra launched into "Dixie." I saw the Pundit, unmasked, talking to a group of grandes dames. He walked over, as someone let out a rebel yell. "You certainly picked the time to be here," he said. "Mardi Gras, as we've known it, is over."

I felt as though I were in a scene from *Gone with the Wind*, the one where Rhett tells Scarlett, as they dance in an Atlanta ballroom, that the South is doomed.

These revelers had not rallied here tonight, I thought, out of racism, but out of class solidarity. It was not just their Carnival, but their entire way of life that was threatened by the notion of opening their doors to strangers. Theirs was a small world that was growing smaller by the day. Their children were leaving town, and familiar comforts were slipping away.

There was a kind of twisted romanticism tied in with these old Carnival frivolities that had lithified into stylized rituals. Carnival depends, as Sally Reeves had pointed out, on a "suspension of disbelief," a "veil of make-believe," and the City Council had pulled aside that veil and yanked off the masks.

Things had not changed much since Mark Twain remarked on the compulsive romanticism of Southerners and observed that Carnival could never exist in "the practical North." Wrote Twain, "The very feature that keeps it alive in the South—girly-girly romance— would kill it in the North . . . In our South . . . the genuine and wholesome civilization of the nineteenth century is curiously confused and commingled with the Walter Scott Middle-Age sham civilization and so you have practical, progressive ideas and progressive works mixed up with . . . the jejune romanticism of an absurd past."

Instead of defending the Old South, however, against Lincoln and those who would crush the dream of antebellum greatness, these New Orleanians had rallied under the banner of Carnival against those who would crush their dreams of exclusive frivolity. Dorothy Mae Taylor, with her stern calls for morality and fairness, had somehow been transformed into the ultimate enemy of Carnival, the Puritan with a pursed, disapproving mouth.

In Shakespeare's *Twelfth Night*, Sir Toby Belch, the veteran reveler, inquires of Malvolio, the Puritan steward, who is later driven by shame from the stage: "Dost thou think, because thou art virtuous, there shall be no more cakes and ale?"

26

Swimming with the Club Ghosts

I was still thinking about clubs and exclusivity when my friend Josephine called to ask if I wanted to join her at the New Orleans Athletic Club, the former all-male, all-white bastion of power and political connections on Rampart Street. I felt as though I had been invited to pump iron in the ruins of the Roman forum.

When I was living in New Orleans during the 1970s, the NOAC still maintained a reputation as the healthy equivalent of smoke-filled rooms, the place where you went if you wanted to swim and steam and box with men of influence—district attorneys, judges, ward heelers. In recent years, however, the club had fallen down on its luck, and now women were seen as its primary hope of salvation. The huge, bare men's locker room was being transformed into the women's locker room, with spiffy new lockers and new carpeting. The men had been moved elsewhere.

When we arrived, women were everywhere, on the stationary bikes, around the pool tables, on the Nautilus machines, sweating and puffing in the faded elegance of high-ceilinged rooms. We passed by the bar and by the card room, still monopolized by men. We eased ourselves into the beautiful heated pool, surrounded by fluted columns, where Jim Garrison and other men of political muscle had once swum nude in the security of their all-male preserve, not realizing that they were the last of the dinosaurs.

While there was a sense of satisfaction in having invaded forbidden ground, there was also a sense of anticlimax that even the barbarians at the gate must have felt when they stormed the city and lolled about the empty banquet rooms.

I wondered if the Boston Club and the other exclusive men's

luncheon and card clubs in New Orleans, which were now under the same scrutiny as the Carnival krewes with which they were affiliated, would go the way of the NOAC and such clubs around the country.

Clubs, as Tocqueville noted more than a century and a half earlier, appear to be as deeply ingrained in American culture as religion. "The Americans who mix so easily in the sphere of law and politics," he wrote, "are, on the contrary, very careful to break up into small and very distinct groups to taste the pleasures of private life."

Men's luncheon clubs had actually been rather slow to catch on in New Orleans, probably, as one historian noted, because "the French are not club-minded as are the English-speaking peoples." And in fact, it was the city's ambitious Anglo-Saxon businessmen who were the leaders in establishing clubs modeled after the English and New York organizations, which combined wood-paneled stuffiness with hard drinking and compulsive card-playing.

The Boston Club, the third oldest such club in the country, was founded in 1841, only five years after New York's Union Club, with which the New Orleans club felt a strong kinship. The Boston Club was not named after the Yankee city, however, but after the card game that obsessed its members. The popularity of the game of boston was soon superceded at the club by whist, poker, and a game called "brag."

The Boston Club, like the Pickwick and Louisiana clubs, followed the pattern of Northern clubs like the Union Club until the Civil War, when the issue of slavery divided clubs in the North as well as the South. During the Reconstruction years, club members in New Orleans became even more tightly knit. The clubs affiliated with Carnival krewes, particularly the Pickwick, Louisiana, and Boston clubs, were described at the time as "close" clubs. A number of members of those clubs joined the Crescent City White League, the paramilitary organization that led the uprising of 1875, which temporarily overthrew the Republican state government.

By the 1880s, the Boston Club, for all its airs of casual bonhomie, soon became synonymous with the city's small, elite ruling class. That it had become restrictive in its membership policies was apparent in an article written about the city's clubs in 1881 in the *Daily Picayune.*

"As for the Boston," noted the author diplomatically, "although it is composed of first-class material and is in every way a delightful resort for its members and their guests, there is a doubt whether it possesses the elasticity to meet the demands of the occasion. The conservative element prevails so largely in its composition and the exigencies of space are so exacting that doubt is justified. In fact, we recognize the general impression that New Orleans needs another club—a social, open, liberal, cosmopolitan organization, with abundance of elbow room and the necessary spirit of progress as its animating motive."

There seemed to be some sort of Darwinian principle at work in the evolution of the city's clubs. In a history of the Boston Club, written nearly fifty years ago, in honor of the club's one-hundredth anniversary, the writer had suggested that clubs should follow Darwin's law of natural selection. "In club life as in all other activities only the fittest survive," the writer had observed. Accordingly, just as "nature invisibly selects and rejects for generations before a species becomes perfectly adapted, so must a club membership select the members to fill vacancies with a care to the future. It should select only the fittest in the hope that they will become 'adaptable,' or the club might not survive."

A club should be like a life insurance company, argued the writer. "If it is too strict in its regulations, it cannot find enough insurers who can qualify, its total volume of insurance will decline, and the company will soon cease to operate. If it is too liberal in selecting insurers, taking too many bad risks, the mortality will be excessive and the company will fail just the same."

Perhaps members of the Boston Club, as well as the other exclusive white men's clubs in town, should have taken these observations as a warning. Black opponents of all-white Carnival had begun using a similar Darwinian argument to suggest the inevitable extinction of the city's dinosaurs of exclusivity. As the majority population in the city, blacks could afford to treat Comus and other relics of bygone days as the social equivalent of dodo birds.

In a sense, theories of social Darwinism had come full circle. The notion of evolution, at first lampooned in white Carnival parades and used ironically by white aristocrats to ridicule the aspirations of blacks, had been dusted off in recent years by conservative Republicans as a rationale for ignoring the needs of the poor and under-privileged—the losers in social Darwinism. Now, however, the black citizens of New Orleans, the social survivors, at least in terms of numbers, could use the same rationale to ignore the needs and fears of whites.

V

Gotterdämmerung

27

Momus Regrets

Only a few days into the Carnival season, the forces of merriment were making a hasty retreat. The gotterdämmerung of traditional Carnival had begun with Momus, the most mischievous of Carnival deities and also the most persnickety. There is a passage in the writings of the Greek satirist Lucian describing a rather haughty Momus, who complains to Zeus about the upstart deities that have been installed in the Pantheon: "However did Attis and Corybus ever get trundled in upon us?"

This year, the Knights of Momus would remain mum on their traditional night, the Thursday before Mardi Gras. They would hold their ball and anoint their queen, but they would not parade. The horses would remain unsaddled, the tractors silent, and the floats empty of riders, parked in the uptown den they shared with Comus.

Momus members had met to discuss the ordinance, and found that all the controversy and rancor had left them with little spirit for revelry. "You don't go where you're not wanted," one member told a reporter. Some members said their wives feared for their safety and refused to let them parade. Momus, it seemed, had expanded his role from the god of mirth to the patron of excuses.

In announcing their defection from the streets of New Orleans, the Knights of Momus issued a brief statement devoid of their customary mannered levity: "Momus, Son of Night, God of Mockery and Ridicule, regretfully and respectfully informs his friends, supporters and his public that he will not parade the streets of New Orleans on the Thursday evening before Shrove Tuesday, 1992, as he has customarily since 1872."

On the Thursday night before Mardi Gras, when Momus ordinarily would have paraded past Gallier Hall for a toast to the mayor, Saint Charles Avenue and Canal Street would remain dark and crowdless, and the politicians who had assembled for the mayor's annual Carnival party would not have to grit their teeth and smile at the floats that poked fun at them.

In recent years, Momus, which had once been known for producing drunken riders prone to falling off their floats, had revived its reputation for political satire. Last year's parade theme, "Momus Brews a Toxic Roux," applied the motif of Cajun cooking to political corruption and other toxic effluents abundant in Louisiana. One float had decked out City Hall as a po'boy sandwich stand, with a sign reading SIDNEY'S PO'BOYS and MORE BALONEY. Another float had gone after David Duke, with a *DuKKKe Soup* tableau depicting Duke in his Klan robes being boiled in a kettle. A "Mutant Ninja Turtle Soup" float had lampooned the city's sewer system.

For those familiar with the history of Momus, the current defection from the streets brought a sense of déjà vu. In its early years, Momus had been known for its whimsy. In 1880, the krewe's theme had been "A Dream of Fair Women," marking one of the city's earliest experiments in cross-dressing. The men of Momus had portrayed Dido on the funeral pyre, Samson and Delilah, Sappho, and Joan of Arc, among others. A scornful woman observer had remarked at the time: "They attempted to portray a 'Dream of Fair Women,' but I confess my imagination was not vivid enough to fancy 'fair women' in the lot of gorgeously appareled brawny men who hid their beards and moustaches behind false faces. Adieu! It was a perfect nightmare. The disillusion was most complete."

During the Reconstruction years, however, Carnival became a means for local aristocrats to protest the rule of carpetbaggers and Republicans and express their bitterness over their loss of sovereignty. Following the federal putdown of the White League rebellion of 1875, Momus had failed to parade. The following year, however, Momus came back with a vengeance. Some Carnival historians consider the bitter Momus parade of 1877 the most important in Carnival history. Without doubt, it was the most controversial Carnival parade ever, and it reflected the divided status of the city. By comparison, the Comus parade of that year, titled "The Aryan Race," was a model of restraint.

The theme of the Momus parade was "Hades: A Dream of Momus." The maskers portrayed New Orleans as the outskirts of hell, populated primarily by the Grant administration and by state and local figures who had incurred the wrath of the White League. Ulysses S. Grant was portrayed as Beelzebub on his imperial throne. The cabinet secretaries were devils, while General Philip Sheridan was Eurynome, Prince of Death, seated amid writhing "Ethiop monsters." As Perry Young described it, "Hellish decorations shimmered in the leaping glare of torches on ghostly freedmen shoulders that toiled beside infernal palaces of Reconstruction—flames of green, blue, sulphur, gold, and red blazed over the haunts of the unclean, the wicked, and the hideous." The final float in the parade, titled "Ship of State," portrayed the Republican party as a sinking ship on a sea of fire.

Among the maskers was Edward D. White, who would later become chief justice of the Supreme Court, appointed by President Taft, whose father had been caricatured in the parade. The immediate reaction from local Republicans, however, was stronger than indignation. According to one source, the masker who portrayed President Grant as Beelzebub was threatened with death if he were ever identified, a threat that reinforced the Carnival krewes' attachment to secrecy.

The Other Face of Carnival

With the defection of Momus, it was now up to the Krewe de Vieux to take up the satirical slack. "We're the poor man's Momus," said Ray Kern, the captain of the moment. Ray had listened to the council proceedings on the radio, and he had thought to himself, "Dorothy Mae, have I got a krewe for you." Not only did the Krewe de Vieux not discriminate against blacks, noted Ray, but most of the krewe's black members were also gay, which doubled the club's political-correctness rating. During a meeting of subkrewe captains at an uptown bar called Beachball Bennie's, Ray presented his views on the controversy. He had jotted down his thoughts on the nearest paper at hand, which had happened to be a page of the *Times-Picayune* featuring an ad for a sale on intimate apparel. He xeroxed his notes, ad copy and all, for the benefit of the krewe.

In the spaces between bras and girdles, Ray had written: "We, as a people, are just as responsible for this divisive situation if we let this hatred creep into our own hearts. Each of us must look inward and decide if the beating of one heart is also the beating of many hearts, that we are somehow all related and connected as a community, and that we can affirm this unity without the rancor of hatred and the politics of our differences. Individually and collectively, we must answer to the theme song of Mardi Gras, 'If Ever I Cease to Love.' " Ray added that since he had written his thoughts on an underwear ad, the krewe should also answer to the anthem, "If Ever I Cease to Laugh."

The club's only prejudices, as Vivian Cahn admitted, were against lawyers and Republicans. The subkrewe of Mama Roux had one lawyer as a member, she said, "so we're already over our quota." Disturbed one year by the inordinate number of Republicans in the club, she said, Mama Roux "picked a theme so offensive they dropped out."

The main theme for this year's parade, "The Krewe de Vieux Rights the News," had already been established, and the subkrewes were finally deciding on their own complementary themes. The idea was to turn the headlines upside down, to redress old grievances, to solve mysteries involving famous people, or to prod sacred cows.

The Krewe of Underwear, the oldest subkrewe, had adopted a permanent basic costume of red long johns, to which they added variations every year. The tradition had begun in 1980, when the parade coincided with a cold Valentine's Day. During the oil boom, the krewe had been made up predominantly of geologists, but after losing half their membership, they broadened their base. For this year's theme, they had toyed with solving the JFK assassination ("The Krewe of Underwear Rewrites the Conspiracy"), and with rewriting the Bill of Rights (to include the right to "bear ass"), but decided to go with a theme of homeless Russians. Their red underwear was already a start, and they would acquire shopping carts from Schwegman's grocery stores.

The Krewe of CRUDE (the Committee for the Revival of Urban Decadent Entertainment) had just switched themes. One member had generated support for the theme of "Cereal Killers," with such variations as "Rape Nuts," "Guts 'n' Honey," and "Special KKK." Another member, however, had countered with the more general theme of "Krewe of CRUDE gives good Headlines," with the emphasis on "head." Examples offered were MAGIC JOHNSON GIVES AIDS TO DAVID DUKE and WATCH OUT FOR THE GAG RULE. A general theme would allow more leeway for individual creativity, which suited the subkrewe's varied membership. CRUDE included among its ranks a professor of art at the University of New Orleans, a geologist at Exxon, and a computer specialist who ran the electronic imaging lab at the University of New Orleans.

The most elaborate theme had been suggested by the Krewe of Kaos, which proposed to enact a Vatican IV conference, in which Madonna would be elected pope and ride in the popemobile. The conference would be held in Las Vegas and would address such issues of reform as adding a twenty-four-hour Vatican shopping channel and introducing a 900-number hotline for administering the sacrament of confession by telephone.

My own subkrewe, Mama Roux, had met a few days earlier at the home of Pat and Butch Gonzalez in Mid-City to decide on its theme and costumes. Pat ran a family praline-making business called Aunt Sallie's, and her husband was a musician who managed the Tremé Brass Band and performed as its only white member. I was astonished to discover that one of my Texas high school classmates, Linda Gautreaux, a former barrel racer, was also in the krewe.

A core of krewe members had already decided on an Egyptian theme, with Dorothy Mae Taylor to reign as "Dorotiti, Queen of Denial"—or "de Nile," as one less enlightened member pronounced it. For inspiration, someone had brought along a video of Charlton Heston starring as a beefcake Antony in a campy production of Shakespeare's *Antony and Cleopatra*.

"Let's make it a royal procession," said Pat Gonzalez, "with

maidens throwing petals and men in loincloths beating drums."
Someone else suggested palmetto-bearing slaves and whip-cracking
slave masters. Frank Cole asked, "Can I whip somebody?"

Pat Gonzalez intervened. "I'd like to see us be completely nonra-
cist. Let's make it colorless and highlight Dorothy Mae's pomposity,
not her skin color."

We decided that we'd have some uptown society folk dressed in
formal wear chained to Dorotiti's barge. Pat Gonzalez demonstrated
how an exasperated Comus member might behave. She threw some
imaginary grapes (sour, of course), and announced, petulantly, "This
is my city. My father founded it eight generations ago. I won't
parade."

Ray Kern managed to attend most of the subkrewe meetings, but
his role appeared to be more of coordinator than dictator. During the
meeting at Beachball Bennie's, he explained that his concept of being
captain was considerably different from that of uptown autocrats.
"This thing has a magic and a momentum all its own," he said. "The
best thing I can do is get out of the way. I tried to impose my will on
it one year, and I got trampled." He was feeling burned out, nevertheless, and he declared that this was his last year. "Putting this on is like
swimming upstream. There are forces that don't want it to happen,
and they throw all kinds of obstacles at you. It's like a test—how bad
do you want to do this?"

When I asked Ray how the other subkrewes were progressing
with their themes, he mentioned that the Krewe of Mystic Inane, the
gay subkrewe, was having a difficult time. The captain, Jeffrey, was in
the hospital, wasting away from AIDS. "He just wants to live through
another Mardi Gras," said Ray. "You know, there are two faces of
Carnival, two masks. We don't always see the other mask clearly."

Last year, he said, just two weeks before Carnival, the captain of
the Krewe of Underwear had committed suicide. "God is not going
to let us forget the flip side of the face," said Ray.

28

The Disappearing City

Within a week after Momus officially withdrew from the streets, the leadership of Comus sent out letters to krewe members stating that, unless the ordinance were repealed, the krewe would not parade. Instead of a parade, there would be an open house at the den on the Saturday before Mardi Gras, and the krewe would view the floats there. The Comus floats were designed for streetlights and flambeaux, their loosely attached acanthus leaves and pendulous figures designed for movement as the rickety wagons moved down the potholed streets. But the krewe would view them, instead, as exhibits in a museum, crowded together and static in the light of day.

Henri's friend Paul had suggested that Comus simply parade down Audubon Place, a private street across from Audubon Park closed off from the pedestrian public by a gate and a security guard.

I met Henri for dinner at Galatoire's, the favorite restaurant of the uptown elite, to commiserate. There are no reservations at Galatoire's, and even the king of Carnival has to stand in line out on Bourbon Street for a table. And so we stood out on the sidewalk, in a light mist, under umbrellas, talking again about loss and decay.

Comus krewe members, said Henri, were practically in mourning. "It's like losing a family of twelve all at once." A former captain was said to be disconsolate. Henri pointed out the sad coincidence of two major stories that had appeared together on the front page of the *Times-Picayune*, one on the pullout by Momus, the other about the decline of housing stock in New Orleans and the abandonment of the city by the middle class. "Everything is in ruins," said Henri.

The hard-hitting *Times-Picayune* story noted that one out of six houses in New Orleans was vacant, giving New Orleans the dubious distinction of the highest vacancy rate of any major city in the country. "The cycle of flight and vacancy and abandonment has turned New Orleans into a disappearing city," wrote the authors. Middle-class couples, discouraged by the decline of their neighborhoods and schools and frightened by crime and encroaching urban blight, were giving up the charms of their cypress cottages with generous verandas and columns for undistinguished tract houses. One vacant house led to another and then another, and the crack dealers moved in.

During the 1970s, baby boomers had discovered the charm of the city and began restoring the old cottages and shotguns. But when federal money for housing dried up during the 1980s, the city's funding dropped nearly half, from twenty-two million dollars to fourteen million dollars. Once the boomers started having babies, they followed their parents to the suburbs.

Frederick Starr, president of Oberlin College, jazz expert, and the author of a book about the Garden District, told the reporters, "Someday, we'll be seen as the generation that let this city go down the drain. Every citizen and every official should fear being viewed by posterity as one of those who allowed New Orleans architecture to perish."

It appeared that this generation would witness not only the decline and fall of traditional Carnival, but the disappearance of much of the city's old architecture. And this was not mere coincidence.

City Hall had not done much to save the old architecture of New Orleans. So far, the most effective efforts at preservation had been carried out by privately funded programs operating under the umbrella of the Preservation Resource Center. And once Carnival came under the control of City Hall, said Henri, it was all over. "What amazes people about Carnival is that so many events can take place over that many days without any central authority. But that's why it works." He tried out a phrase. "Carnival bureaucracy," he said, contemptuously. "Have you ever heard such an oxymoron?" And he wondered how you would police secret organizations. "With secret police?" he inquired.

Henri said that he and Paul were calling off the official walking parade for the Society of Saint Ann. "I don't feel like dancing in the streets this year."

29

Planning the Potlatch

Cracks had begun to appear in the façade of the Mardi Gras elite. There was said to be bad blood between the captain of Rex, who had rallied his krewe to carry on, and the captain of Comus, who had called on his krewe to retreat to the den. The disagreement carried through to the card tables at the Boston Club, whose inner circle was affiliated closely with Comus. The club, located at 824 Canal Street, where Rex had stopped to greet his queen and her court for more than one hundred years, sent a notice to its members that it would not erect a viewing stand in front of the building on Mardi Gras day, thus, in effect, evicting Rex's queen and tossing a gauntlet in the face of Rex.

So far, Iris was still planning to roll. Miss Irma had made a brief appearance at the City Council meeting on December 19, stating that Iris liked its all-women status and would prefer to keep men out of the club.

Meanwhile I went to a warehouse in an industrial suburb to pick up my "throws" for Iris.

Tossing things at the crowd had been a part of Carnival since the nineteenth century, when revelers scattered bags of flour—or worse, lime—on unwitting onlookers. The first known trinkets to be tossed from a float were the gifts bestowed on the crowd by a Twelfth Night masker posing as Santa Claus in the krewe's 1871 parade.

Beads became the measure of a krewe's generosity by the 1950s. Most Mardi Gras beads were imported initially from Japan, then from Czechoslovakia. Now most of them are imported from China.

Doubloons embossed with the crest of the krewe on one side and the parade theme on the other were first introduced by Rex in 1960.

Doubloons soon became collectors' items, particularly the special doubloons made of silver, bronze, or cloisonné. In recent years, however, doubloons had become less desirable than plastic go-cups or Frisbees sporting the krewe insignia.

The Iris warehouse had undoubtedly been chosen for its location on Iris Boulevard. When I arrived, it was packed with women wearing Iris T-shirts. Miss Irma was wearing her customary silk suit, this time in emerald green. Before ordering my throws, I picked up a copy of rules and regulations for the parade. I discovered that I would not be able to drink liquor on the float, nor show any skin. Even though this was Carnival, the ladies of Iris were no floozies. What's more, I would have to be tied onto my float with a specially designed belt, required by city law. The rule had been added following a number of accidents involving male riders.

I was startled by the array of items laid out on the tables. There were Iris umbrellas, Iris key chains, Iris coasters, Iris Frisbees. Special turquoise Iris doubloons were going for $10.50 per 100, while a package of 250 Iris cups cost $60.

"You'd think you were throwing them gold," said Miss Irma, picking up a long strand of fake pearls, the kind onlookers would fight for during a parade. "It's worth a million dollars till you catch it."

One Iris member warned of overenthusiastic onlookers who would simply reach up and grab the goodies out of your hands before you could even throw them. Others, she said, would taunt your aim because you were a woman. If they didn't like what they caught, she said, they might toss it back at you. Some hooligans would toss beer cans and such at the riders.

Iris float riders, I was told, spent an average of seven hundred dollars each for their throws, which was about seven times what my budget allowed. Since hardly anyone in the krewe was rich, Iris krewe members were spending a much greater proportion of their income on giveaways than the wealthy male krewes. For Iris, and the less prosperous krewes, the Carnival parade and its giveaways were a charade of abundance.

Although some critics of Carnival likened the scenario of rich float riders hurling beads at the crowd to aristocrats tossing crumbs to the peasants, the ritual of throwing seemed closer to the potlatch ceremonies of the Kwakiutl Indians. The Kwakiutl chiefs invited onlookers to their ceremonies in order to acknowledge and validate their rank and their inherited privileges—the right to use certain masks, relate specific legends, and perform certain dances. As the potlatch ended, the chief paid the guests for witnessing his displays of the privileges he claimed. Accepting the gifts affirmed his claim. In other words, the chiefs, like Carnival maskers, bought their positions with trinkets. They needed the onlookers, for without them, they would be kings without subjects, trees falling in the forest without witnesses.

For old-line krewes, the tossing of beads also suggested the principle that anthropologist Annette Weiner has called "keeping while giving." If giving, as Weiner suggests, can bridge a social gulf, it can also reinforce status differences, particularly when a group retains its most valuable property and gives away only less valuable things.

One of the reasons Comus had declined in popularity, according to a number of observers, was the krewe's notorious stinginess with beads, when compared to the profligate Endymion and Bacchus. A legendary Comus skinflint used to go so far as to tease the crowds with a paddle and a ball. He would slam the ball out into the crowd. But just as the lucky recipient would reach out to grab the ball, the darned thing would fly back to the rider.

The Vieux Carré Artists

Rehearsal for the Iris ball had been scheduled on the morning of the Super Bowl, and as one of the krewe members, I was expected to wear my float costume at the ball and participate in the program of entertainment that preceded the general dancing.

I walked into a ballroom at the Hilton Hotel, and plunged into the crowd of women milling around. The most popular outfits were warmup suits or jeans worn with an Iris T-shirt. Eventually, I could see that there was some order to the chaos, and each float captain was holding up a sign with her name and the number of her float. Although there were no black women members of Iris, the last names of the float captains suggested a variety of ethnic groups: Landry, Akkaya, Gore, Halloran, Bernstein, Ancona, Jumonville, Leblanc.

I had been assigned to Float 15, whose theme, according to one of my float-mates, was to be the "Vieux Carré Artists." My float captain and line lieutenant was Dottie Ancona, who worked in "government procurement." This year, she would be one of the maids in the Iris court, so her float captain's duties would be carried out by her friend Anna May Hudson, who worked as a clerk at a local hotel. Anna May, a good-hearted sort, promised to show me the ropes.

Miss Irma was sitting quietly on a chair at the edge of the crowd, while her niece Joy took charge of the proceedings, asking us to line up by groups. We formed two long lines, and we were asked to dance out into the middle, do-si-do, join hands, and dance to the end of the row.

Said Joy, "Ladies, this is a lot of fun and I hope it all works out." She even provided the music, humming the theme from *Cabaret* and singing a few bars.

During a break, I joined the women of Float 18, which I immediately recognized as an uptown group, with that understated, perfectly-put-together, Junior League look. They were to be jesters in the parade, and they appeared to be having a lot of fun. Sybil Lawson, whose husband is a doctor, said that this was her first year in Iris. When I asked her why she joined, she replied, mockingly, "Women's lib, of course." Her husband is a member of Momus, she said, and she had decided that this year, it was her turn to ride. Now that Momus had decided not to roll, she said, her husband was a bit jealous, but she had told him, "No men on the float."

"Iris used to be all Y'at," said Sybil, using the old-fashioned epithet for the lower-middle-class and blue-collar New Orleanians who have now largely vanished from the core of the city. "Where y'at," the all-purpose greeting, now has a nostalgic ring to it. "In recent years," Sybil continued, "there has been more of the uptown crowd involved in Iris. You can tell by the hairdos on the day of the parade. You have the sprayed bouffant look versus the flat, more casual look."

When I asked her about the antidiscrimination ordinance, she surprised me with her reply. "If I were a black person, I'd be for it," she said. She had often found the barriers between blacks and whites in New Orleans to be artificial, she said. "It has come home to me recently," she said. "My mother has been sick, and Rosalie, the woman who has been working for me for twenty years, is taking care of her. I was just there today, and my mother was upstairs alone, eating her lunch on a tray, and Rosalie was downstairs, eating a pork chop in the kitchen. If it was me, I'd have lunch with Rosalie. It's demeaning to both of them to have to eat alone."

As for the exclusive men's clubs, she said, "The world is passing them by, anyway. They're withering on the vine. They're saying, 'If you don't like the way we party, go ahead and pass us by.'" Her husband had been invited to join the Boston Club, she said, much to his delight. "But it wasn't fun. It was just a bunch of old men having lunch. They had lost their chef. And my husband can't take those three-martini lunches. We decided to quit and go to Europe instead."

Women, she said, would be the last group to break the club and Carnival barrier. "I feel that a black or Japanese businessman has a much better chance of joining the Boston Club than I do. They don't want us there."

I rejoined my fellow Vieux Carré artists, and I found that during the ball, we'd also be playing the role of "Southern belles." Anna May Hudson advised me, "The crazier you act, the better you'll be."

The groups were getting ready to practice the second line that would come as a finale for the ball program. "You're gonna love this," said Anna May.

Most of the women were doing a pretty poor imitation of the black second-liners I had seen. Bringing up the rear, with Group 19, however, was Sadie Leblanc, float lieutenant and born second-liner. Sadie, a stocky little woman of sixty-one was making everybody laugh with her antics. When she paused to take a break, I asked her where she had learned to dance like that. Sadie, a fifteen-year Iris veteran, said that she had retired as a nurse at Charity Hospital six years ago, and she now worked with the elderly. Some of her black patients had shown her how to do the second line.

She said that she saved every week during the year for her Iris dues and throws. On her small income, she couldn't just write out a check at the last minute. Her favorite throws, she said, were tiny teddy bears. Iris kept her young: "I feel like I'm in my thirties. You can't let anything get in your way."

Apparition on Royal Street

That night, following a Super Bowl party, I parked my car on a quiet block on Burgundy Street and hurried over to Royal Street, feeling nervous about the lateness of the hour and the deserted streets. I was about to round the corner of Saint Louis Street, when I saw some movement in an alcove out of the corner of my eye, and I stopped, transfixed at the bizarre tableau. There was an old black man standing in the doorway of an antique shop, next to a tattered-looking white man, considerably younger. A young white woman in some sort of gypsy garb was bending over a small portable table that looked like a TV tray. She appeared to be changing the diaper on a baby, but as I looked closer, I noticed long reddish hair on the arms and legs of the baby, which were waving in the air, and which seemed to be unnaturally long. And then I realized that baby was some sort of ape. But it appeared to be unlike any ape I'd ever seen—more like a baby Sasquatch, some sort of mythical missing link.

I dismissed the sight as some kind of hallucination until the next fall, when I was having dinner in Boston with a friend who was describing a recent visit to New Orleans. This friend is a computer scientist not given to flights of fantasy. He had seen the strangest thing in New Orleans, he said. "There was this old black man and a white man and a white woman and a baby orangutan, sitting together on a stoop."

30

Carnival in Blackface

After a while, you simply get used to seeing strange things in the streets of New Orleans: cultural cross-dressing, interspecies confusion, religious transvestism, and even outrageous stereotypes. Just as disorienting as orangutan babies, black Indians, or old men in drag is a black Carnival krewe who paint themselves even blacker on Mardi Gras day and daub white rings around their eyes and lips. They wear grass skirts and enormous Afro wigs and hand out gilded coconuts to beckoning crowds.

The trademark blackface disguises sported by the float riders of the Zulu Social Aid and Pleasure Club work as a kind of double mockery—a black parody of white Carnival as well as a black takeoff on whites who caricature blacks.

These days, Zulu, for all its exaggerated blackness, is the most multicultural of all the Carnival krewes in the city. The club began accepting whites as members without any ado back during the 1970s. My friend Bill, who was among the first small group of white members, simply asked a friend in the club if he could join, and before he knew it, he was painting coconuts and practicing applying black theatrical makeup. Within the past two decades, black membership has broadened from a working-class base to include politicians and black Creole professionals.

Zulu now enjoys the exalted position of leading off the festivities on Carnival day, preceding the Rex parade on Saint Charles Avenue past the mayor's reviewing stand at Gallier Hall. The Zulu ball, held at the New Orleans Convention Center, on the Friday night preceding Mardi Gras, is the largest Carnival ball in New Orleans. But Zulu, which celebrated its seventy-fifth anniversary in 1991, has already weathered a number of controversies, including derision and scorn by whites and a boycott by the black community. There was a time when the future of the club was in serious doubt.

The club got its start unofficially in 1909, when a group of laborers who called themselves the Tramps went to the Pythian Temple Theater, owned by another black organization, the Black Knights of Pythias, to watch a musical comedy that included a skit about the Zulu tribe, called "There Never Was and Never Will Be a King Like Me." After the show, the Tramps retired to their clubhouse, a woodshed behind a saloon on Perdido Street, and emerged as the Zulus. That year, their king, William Story, wore a lard can for a crown and carried a banana stalk as a scepter. Pete Williams, named king in 1913, added a necktie made of Italian bread and an onion stickpin to his royal regalia.

In 1916, the club was incorporated as the Zulu Social Aid and Pleasure Club. To the foot parade, they added a float, a spring wagon built up with dry-goods boxes, for the king, and their reviewing stand was set up in front of a funeral parlor, the Geddes and Moss Funeral Home, now the Gertrude Geddes-Willis Funeral Home, on Jackson Avenue. The parade stopped there so that the king could toast his queen, just as Rex toasted his queen at the Boston Club. The following Mardi Gras, spoofing the arrival of Rex on a yacht at the foot of Canal Street, King Zulu, aka James Robertson, journeyed on a barge down the New Basin Canal, waving a ham-bone scepter.

Zulu was closer to Huey Long's populist anthem, "Every man a king," than any other krewe. Until Louis Armstrong reigned in 1949, the kings of Zulu had been chosen from among the club's regular membership. They were men of humble origins and station—porters, day laborers, dock workers. For a time, even the Queen of Zulu was chosen from those same ranks. From 1923 through 1932, a male Zulu club member played the role of queen. The tradition began, according to legend, when Joseph Kahoe, king Zulu of 1923, couldn't make up his mind between two women and chose instead a man named Alex, who was crowned as Queen Corinne.

As it happened, Louis Armstrong, who had grown up in black Storyville, near the Zulu clubhouse, dreamed as a boy of becoming

King Zulu, and when he returned to the city to reign, it was a double triumph, for Armstrong as well as for the club.

During the mid-1940s, Armstrong's career had been in slow decline. Wearing blackface and reigning as a caricature of an African king might have reinforced the view of Armstrong's critics, who compared him unfavorably to the new beacons of bebop and swing and who saw him as a throwback to the minstrel show. But when Armstrong appeared on the cover of *Time* magazine as a king wearing a crown of cornets, accompanied by a story detailing his rough coming-of-age in New Orleans, it was apparent that Armstrong and the New Orleans he had known were becoming part of American mythology: the ragtime professors and pretty babies of Storyville, the riverboats, the blues played for prostitutes and pimps in funky dance halls, the jazz funerals that turned into dance parties on the way home from the graveyard. Zulu, too, was a part of that heritage.

Following the reign of Armstrong, Zulu returned to its ordinary kings, who traditionally had to campaign for the job. There was nothing secret about Zulu's selection process, which involved a vote by the general membership. Would-be candidates for positions of royalty went all-out to win, holding fish fries and barbecues and giving away favors to woo voters.

The previous spring, I had gone over to the Zulu clubhouse during election day, and the campaign was still going on. There were tents set up out on the neutral ground across from the clubhouse on Broad Street, which served as campaign headquarters for each candidate. Candidates were passing out leaflets, giving speeches, while their supporters attempted to sway voters with such blandishments as bowls of red beans and rice and fried chicken. Joe Falls, the chairman of Carnival activities, a recently retired investigator for the Equal Opportunity Employment Commission, explained that it cost a member two hundred dollars to run for an office, which would be refunded if he lost.

Lionel Daggs, a candidate for witch doctor, who worked in the quality control department of the post office, said that the main duty of the witch doctor was to ensure good weather. He had run the previous year but had lost by thirty-four votes. This year, he had campaigned very hard, he said. "My catch word is accountability."

By comparison, Jim Russell, a candidate for king, seemed to be taking a more low-key approach. Russell, at age seventy-four, was one of the oldest living active members of Zulu. Hanging in the clubhouse was a photograph of a young Russell riding on a Zulu float during the 1920s as a page. Russell, who had also ridden with Louis Armstrong, had served as president of the club during its most troubled years, in the 1960s, and he was credited by a number of members with keeping the club going. In recent years, he had ridden in the parade as "Mr. Big Stuff," another Zulu bigwig, but finally decided it was time to go for the crown.

At the end of the day, after vats of red beans and rice had been dispensed and coolers had been emptied of beer and soft drinks, Lionel Daggs had won the title of witch doctor, and Jim Russell had been designated the next king of Zulu.

Pride of Ownership

In order to talk about the ups and downs of Zulu history, I went to see Dr. Morris F. X. Jeff, Jr., director of social services at City Hall, who was perhaps the last person you could imagine dressing up in a fright wig and a grass skirt. Morris Jeff was an imposing-looking man with a gray-streaked beard and a deep, commanding voice. Dr. Jeff had been a member of Zulu since 1972, and his father, Morris, Sr., had reigned as king in 1974 and currently held the positions of toast-master and head of protocol. Dr. Jeff, with his dramatic voice, served as narrator for the program during the Zulu balls, and he always took the opportunity to remind the celebrants of their African heritage, of the proud history of the Zulus in Africa.

That heritage, he said, had been problematic for Zulu during the 1960s, when the Civil Rights movement and the growing emphasis on black pride called into question a club that featured black men in blackface and grass skirts. "We were at the peak of the Civil Rights movement," said Jeff. "Pride in ourselves as Negroes was the order of the day. So anything that belittled us was looked down on. This was not the time to take any part of the past that was not complimentary and expose it."

At the same time, he said, nations in Africa were struggling for independence. "The whole concept of Zulus and Africa began to take on a different meaning. The true history of the Zulus would have been something to be proud of." Even now, said Jeff, when he traveled around the country and mentioned that he was a member of Zulu, people thought he was referring to a radical organization.

The membership of Zulu dwindled during the 1960s, and professional blacks, for the most part, shunned the club. Jeff's father, however, who had earned a master's degree from the University of Michigan and worked as a director of the New Orleans Recreation Department, was one of the first professionals to join the club. "I can remember him sending out invitations to his professional friends and them sending them back. Now the same people are tearing the doors down to get in."

Jeff's father had also moved his family into the public housing projects, he said. "Being with his people and those on the bottom rung always was his love. There was no condescension there. He saw himself as lucky." Morris Jeff, Sr.'s parents had been illiterate, his father a longshoreman and his mother a housewife.

His family had been living in the projects, at the corner of Orleans and Galvez, said Jeff, when Louis Armstrong was king. He had been ten years old at the time. The parade was on its way down Orleans Street to stop at Dooky Chase's restaurant, a landmark in the black community. "All the parades, funerals, and second-line clubs came by there," said Jeff. A block from Dooky Chase's, Armstrong's float, which was overloaded with officials, admirers, and hangers-on, broke down. Armstrong later recalled that he had been happily tossing coconuts hither and thither, including one that missed its mark and "fell down on a brand new Cadillac," when his float "commenced to crumbling down to pieces."

Armstrong might have enjoyed knowing that the Zulu floats were later built in a shed attached to the former Colored Waifs Home, where he had gotten his first cornet.

*   *   *

Despite the bad rap that Zulu had gotten from some elements of the black community during the 1960s, Jeff said that he had never looked down on Zulu, nor on the all-black schools he had attended. "I was a sophomore in high school when that separate-but-equal decision came down in 1954. All those descriptions about how awful segregation was—I had mixed feelings about the notion that everything I had been exposed to was inferior." He had gone to an elementary school on the edge of Congo Square, across from the area of Tremé later razed to create Armstrong Park, and he had attended Booker T. Washington High School during what he regarded as its golden years. "I felt that I had the best nurturing and the best teaching," said Jeff. "I had the best of what the black community had to offer. I didn't feel deprived."

Zulu was part of that. "It was ours. It was our Rex. Those who had wealth had better resources, but they were not necessarily better spent. We had Louis Armstrong. We had the gift and the spirit, and that changed the world."

I asked Jeff what he foresaw for the future of Carnival and the future of New Orleans. "I think the city is in search of its destiny," he said. "When I studied biology, I learned that when a species is bombarded by changes, you have to do something to strengthen yourself to survive in a hostile environment. In Mardi Gras, we've seen some of that taking place. I think Mardi Gras will survive, that they will make the internal changes necessary to be there tomorrow. If they don't, they'll die. Mardi Gras is going to go on, with or without Comus and Momus and the Boston Club."

31

The Purple Knights

One of the big drawing cards for Zulu and other Carnival parades were the flashy high school marching bands that were now in as much demand as the traditional brass bands. It was in these school bands that so many young musicians, including most of the members of ReBirth, got their start. The uptown white parades, however, had to import most of their bands from other cities, since the leading black high school bands now marched with Zulu. That had not always been the case, however, particularly for the Saint Augustine Purple Knights, the best high school band in the city and perhaps the South.

Saint Augustine High School had been founded in the early 1950s as a black Catholic boys' school designed to offer its students a good education, discipline, and leadership training within a school system that was still segregated. The young men who had attended Saint Aug, as it was known, during the 1950s and '60s, including Mayor Sidney Barthelemy and City Councilman Lambert Boissiere, were now among the city's black political and social elite.

Edwin Hampton, the school's music director, arrived at Saint Aug in its second year of operation. Hampton, who had a strong classical background in music, had recently been discharged from the army, where he had participated in a drill squad that specialized in what he called "monkey" drills. His squad had used a Harlem Globetrotters approach to embellish their regular army drills, including a "lost man" routine, in which one man would go the wrong way.

Hampton brought that sense of showmanship as well as strict military discipline to the Saint Aug band. The idea, said Hampton, was a "combination of the dignity of a military band and the music of a show band." Their first uniforms had short Eisenhower bomber jackets, a military look reminiscent of World War II. After a priest suggested the "Purple Knights" as the school mascot, Hampton located a uniform company that specialized in "Hollywood things," and they devised a Crusader-style helmet and gold uniforms with purple capes.

The marching Purple Knights soon became recognized as readily as the school football team. They were a double-barreled threat, the Saint Aug football team and the band. I once attended a landmark state championship game between Saint Aug and the Covington Lions, a white team from across Lake Pontchartrain. It was the first such high-level confrontation between a white and a black team. The Saint Aug team had been leading at halftime, and when the Purple Knights came marching out onto the infield, stepping high and swinging their instruments to the theme from *Shaft*, they seemed invincible.

Saint Aug was a school whose leaders were conscious of the need for black pride and dignity, and in the early 1960s, the school had been a leading opponent of Zulu's undignified capering. In 1961, teachers in the school had begun a petition to prevent Zulu from rolling. One year, students printed a cartoon in the school paper showing the Zulu parade as an Uncle Tom's Cabin on wheels.

By 1965, however, Zulu convinced Saint Aug to march with the parade, on the condition that they become more like a "real" Carnival parade, with a set schedule and predetermined route. "We brought Zulu out of the trenches," said Hampton. In 1967, the band was invited to march with Rex, and school officials accepted, with a certain ambivalence. It was a great honor, but band members would risk being ridiculed and even harmed by white onlookers.

For more than twenty years, Saint Aug marched with Rex, until pressures from the black community convinced school officials to switch back to Zulu, and Hampton agreed reluctantly. Zulu had changed by then, said Hampton, and it now included a number of politicians and school alumni who could bring considerable influence to bear. Even now, said Hampton, he felt a little sentimental about those years with Rex.

Marching for the Community

One afternoon, I went to see Ken Ferdinand, who had marched as a member of the Purple Knights band in the 1967 Rex parade. Ken was exactly the kind of success story that the priests who founded Saint Aug had in mind. At age forty-three, he was now working as manager of the French Market, the thriving marketplace along the river at the bottom of Decatur Street, and he was highly regarded in both black and white political circles. He was also an astute historian and observer of social mores in New Orleans.

We met at Ferdinand's office, and he was a little late because he had been showing Julia Child and a group of celebrity chefs through the market.

Ferdinand was delighted to talk about Saint Aug and the Purple Knights, about which he had fond memories. Like Morris Jeff, he had not resented attending an all-black school. "Saint Aug always represented the best the black community could provide for its children," said Ferdinand. "When you marched, people on the street were seeing several decades of attention paid to the details of molding young men to be respectable members of the community."

Saint Aug, he said, and Edwin Hampton in particular, "stood for progressive values in the black community. They tried to avoid things like the second line, the funkier styles. We weren't allowed to do that. Musically, we were supposed to be playing more progressive music than gutbucket funk and soul. I remember when we turned down Zulu because we didn't want to deal with the second-line rowdiness. We had to represent the black community. We were well ordered and controlled and disciplined because it was an image thing."

Observed Ferdinand, "It was like our grandparents who used to say, 'I'm your color, not your kind.' They wanted to be something better than plantation slaves or the 'nigger on the street.' "

Like so many black families in New Orleans, Ken and his family had celebrated Carnival at the junction of Orleans and Claiborne Avenue. He had made his first visit to the Canal Street parades and the white crowds in 1963. "I thought then that going to Bourbon Street was like Cairo, Egypt. It was the worst experience I ever had.

I was called all kinds of names." Consequently, four years later, marching for Rex as the first black band to march with a white parade, "was an honor, a kind of obligation, as opposed to a lark. We were marching for the whole community, and we didn't want to fail."

Ferdinand served as band captain that year, he said. "You feel very important. You're performing for thousands of people. You're marching for miles, and it's a hard little romp, but you're aware of so many people observing you, so you have that extra adrenaline. You can't step out of place or lay your instrument down. You have to be strong to meet the expectations. It's not just school spirit—it's a higher calling. The whole community is riding on your shoulders, the way you march and play your horn. You practice your music, shine your instrument, stay up all night because you're scared and excited. You're told to be prepared for trouble. You take that quiet bus ride from the school to the parade. You keep looking straight ahead and keep marching and don't miss a step when they call you names."

Ferdinand recalled that day with pride and satisfaction. "It was our little contribution to the movement," he said. "If they could do it in Birmingham, we could do it on Canal Street."

The Emperor's Clothes

Carnival had changed since those days, said Ferdinand, but he felt that the issue of race had been played up excessively as the source of the current Carnival crisis. Class, rather than race, he felt, was the key to Carnival. And as the city had changed, so had Carnival. "I'm forty-three years old," said Ferdinand, "and in my memory, Carnival has gone through several changes and transformations. With this ordinance, the transformation is more complete."

Not all the changes, he said, had been obvious at first. "People have seized on race as the agent of change," he said, "but there are other, less 'sexy,' less sensational changes. Like the creation of Endymion and Bacchus. These were almost unconscious changes. Like what happened with the American economy. People didn't set out with a conscious decision to buy imported goods. It's an unconscious will. And with Carnival, I think most of the changes occurred without anybody taking much notice. I don't think Blaine Kern set out to change the look of Mardi Gras, but he did.

"It's obvious that elitism plays a role in the backbone of our social interactions. The City Hall thing has brought issues to the surface. It's not that they were hidden, but that they were accepted. We do an elite little jig in the black community, too—the lights from the darks. Divisiveness is a feature of New Orleans. That doesn't mean we're always fighting, but that there are boxes, and people get placed in these boxes. Stratification has always been clear and apparent, and people accepted it. Carnival has been a very stratified, class-oriented way to be social."

Ferdinand had recently learned a lesson, he said, about exclusive clubs after joining the New Orleans Athletic Club. "I waited forty-three years for this—and I find out that it's kind of funky, and now the women's locker room is bigger than the men's. I don't know how I feel about that. I think it's like a fantasy—this world you're not a part of but that they're locking you out of. But there's nothing you're locked out of that's heaven on earth." Ferdinand cited his own version of Groucho Marx's old axiom about clubs: "You're constantly pursuing this fantasy—it must be something good if I'm left out."

Those fantasies and pretensions surrounding the old clubs and krewes, suggested Ferdinand, would have lost their hold even without the ordinance. "Now these older traditions are breaking down. Comus wasn't getting the audience that they used to get, and you can't blame that on race. The emperor has no clothes. The young people in the city who are thinking out what their city is about are making changes. The older elite groups have a difficult time accepting that they are the last generation to believe in kings and queens and maids and dukes. These people live king stuff out 365 days a year—they thought it could be passed on and on and on.

"It's sad, but it's not going to be missed. Young people now in Bacchus and Endymion approach this whole thing as a lark—go to Hollywood and get a king—not that you have to be the brother of a past duke.

"I don't lament the changes. I think the Carnival clubs had to find a way to change tradition. There are ways to change without wiping everything out. For example, I would preserve the right to have an African-American marching club—but I wouldn't argue the need to keep it exclusive. I could see people of other ethnicities being part of it. On St. Patrick's Day I march with the Decatur Street Irish Club. Jim Monahan, of Houlihan's, invited me. I acknowledge it's Irish.

"If I as a male could go to a women's organization and participate without devaluing the women in the organization, it would be an opportunity for me to grow.

"If you can accept that—that there is an essence of humanity that we have in common—you can acknowledge people's real being and real nature."

The defense of Carnival by the old-line elite as an economic boon was absurd, said Ferdinand, although as a specialist in marketing, he had a few ideas for the survival of old-line Carnival. "The real value of Carnival is the music and the culture," he said. "Even the old-line krewes have something to offer. Maybe they could attract young people under the importance of tradition while not being immersed in the fantasy of elitism. They ought to fold themselves in the mantle of preservation and say, 'We're preserving the traditions of Carnival—come and see us.' "

32

Machinations

With the City Council meeting to discuss possible changes to the Carnival ordinance scheduled for February 6, there was a flurry of statements, gestures, and political maneuvers.

On January 23, Silas Lee, a sociologist at Xavier University who worked as a pollster for a local television station, published the results of a poll showing that most New Orleanians, black as well as white, regarded Mardi Gras as something of a religion and therefore not to be tampered with. According to Lee, who is black, three-quarters of whites and two-thirds of blacks who were polled said that they liked Mardi Gras the way it was. Although most black voters agreed that Carnival clubs should not discriminate, they also felt that forcing Carnival clubs to integrate was an invasion of privacy. According to Lee, the poll revealed the willingness of people in New Orleans to compromise public principles if they perceived a threat to themselves or a cherished institution, such as Carnival.

Similarly, according to a poll sponsored a week later by the *Times-Picayune*, two-thirds of the respondents said they favored repeal of the ordinance. Eighty-six percent of white voters and 51 percent of black voters declared themselves to be against the ordinance. The pollster was Ed Renwick, a professor at Loyola University, who dubbed Dorothy Mae Taylor "the grinch who stole Mardi Gras."

In response to the *Times-Picayune* poll, a group of thirty-five black ministers issued a statement, "Discrimination based on race, creed or gender is plainly and simply wrong," warning City Council members that any attempt to soften the ordinance would result in political damage. "If they reverse the vote, they'll hear from us at the polls," reported Baptist pastor Zebadee Bridges.

Two days later, the citizens' committee appointed to suggest possible modifications in the ordinance—known as the Blue Ribbon Committee—drastically moved up their schedule. Over two sessions, they agreed to recommend the modification of two of the stickier elements of the ordinance—the jail sentence for the violators and the matter of proof. The committee voted to shift the burden of proof of discrimination to the complainants. Krewes and private clubs would no longer have to prove they didn't discriminate as a condition for getting parade and liquor permits. Krewe captains and private clubs found in violation would be fined from one hundred to three hundred dollars, although they would no longer be subject to jail sentences of up to five months.

The Mediator

On the day before the council meeting, I went to see Ken Carter, the city assessor and a member of an elite black Creole Carnival club, Young Men Illinois, a group founded in 1926 as an offshoot of an older club. Carter was also a member of the Inter-Business Council, the influential breakfast club that had become perhaps the most important link between black and white leadership in New Orleans.

Carter was a tall, elegant man with a warm, gracious manner. A long-standing member of SOUL, the black Creole political organization, he was said to be on the short list of possible successors to Sidney Barthelemy as mayor. Carter, in other words, was a member of what Morris Jeff, Jr., had called the "brokerage" class—the Creoles and other elite blacks who played a mediating role in New Orleans politics. And that left him right in the middle of the Carnival issue, fraught with ambivalence.

Carter's family, he said, had always been involved in Carnival. His parents had belonged to a number of clubs, and his older sister had been a debutante. He had joined Young Men Illinois largely because of his parents. His parents' friends had always had high expectations for him, but he didn't earn his law degree until he was thirty-one. After he became a lawyer and the father of three daughters, he said, his father's friends kept telling him how important it was to join a club so that his daughters could make their debut. "They worked on my wife," he said.

In those days, he recalled of Young Men Illinois, "one or two guys ran it—it was old-line. I wasn't going to make an effort to change it. It was better to be autocratic. I thought, 'This thing works.' I never considered the social aspects from a citywide point of view." One year, one daughter was first maid, the other a princess. "My mother was ecstatic," he said, "and that made me happy. But I couldn't believe the money I spent." He felt that the experience had helped his daughters learn social graces. "But I also sensed a little exclusiveness, and I didn't like it, so we worked on that." Finally, he had concluded that "people took it too seriously, and I said, 'This is too much for me.'"

As with old-line white krewes, the old-line black Creole clubs found themselves to be an endangered species. "The old-line influence is disappearing," said Carter. "They perceive that things are not as classy as they were." He had remained a member of Young Men Illinois, although he was not eager to shout it from the rooftops. "When people mention that I'm a member, I'm not particularly proud of it," he said. "I guess I'm concerned about making a social contribution."

As for the white krewes, he commented that Dorothy Mae Taylor may have inadvertently done them a favor. "It was just a matter of time before they went under. Comus was on the way out, anyway. They couldn't have afforded to put on the parade much longer. This might be the time to integrate, for their own salvation."

His experiences with white Carnival had been mixed. "I've been to the Rex ball," he said, "and after it was over, I asked myself, 'Is that all there is?' Last year, a friend was Rex, and I was invited. I was reluctant to go, but I did. I sat there and saw this CEO, that college president—people I deal with every day—and not one black. I said, 'Where's Norman Francis, dean of Loyola Law School, or Alden McDonald, president of Liberty Bank?' If this is really a civic group, these people ought to be there. That's when it really hit home."

Last year, the wife of one of his employees had been elected queen of her all-white Carnival club. The expenses were high, and he had helped her out. She sent him an invitation to the ball and the queen's party, but had to recant when she told her captain that her husband's boss was black. "I'm secure and confident," he said, "but think what that tells people about themselves. That's what the ministers are talking about." He gathered steam. "That tells my daughter at MIT, my wife, my sister—'You're no good, you're not qualified.' That has a devastating impact to be treated like that."

There are times when being excluded, he said, could derail a life. There were deep wounds in his own psyche, he admitted, that he had to overcome to find his place in New Orleans. "I was one of the first five black undergraduates at Loyola in 1962. I had an honors scholarship, and I was a top athlete. But I was ostracized and isolated when I went out for the basketball team."

The team back then, he said, "was made up mostly of walk-ons. There were only five scholarship team members, and the rest had to go out for the team. After the tryout, it was clear I had made the team. The coach said, 'Ken, we didn't know any colored boys were coming here. I didn't know you could play. I don't have to tell you you made the team, but you can't play.' I couldn't believe what I was hearing. I asked, 'What do you mean?' The coach said, 'The Southern schools we're playing just won't play if you're on the team.' "

Carter found it difficult to go on. It was clear that the hurt was still there, that it would always be there behind the elegant, confident manner. "After that," he said, "I never could get off the ground at school. Not everybody can handle something like that. I didn't recover for nine years. But I regathered myself. I said, 'Not only am I going back to school—but I'm going to Loyola Law School.' "

As for the notion of clubs being irrelevant to one's business opportunities, he shook his head impatiently. "When you have a person walking in the Boston Club, looking around and seeing that the only black faces are the servants, and you come out and meet Ken Carter for a business meeting, how are you going to treat me fairly? You've just come out of the Boston Club, where that whole mentality is condoned. You cannot keep it behind those doors."

Nevertheless, Carter was determined not to let Carnival die. "This is on our watch. We don't want to look back and say it happened on our watch."

In his understated, diplomatic way, Carter implied that Dorothy Mae Taylor had not consulted certain circles of black leadership before forging ahead with her ordinance, and that he and other black leaders were now trying to work at damage control, to keep the fraying ties between black and white leadership in New Orleans from snapping completely.

33

A Carnival Encounter Session

As the crowd gathered for the City Council meeting on Thursday, February 6, a group of clergymen was waiting outside the cramped temporary basement chambers. A young white minister told me that they had not come to speak on the issue of Mardi Gras since, "Our folks would be divided on it." They had come, instead, to urge the City Council to focus on an issue on which they all agreed and which they felt was more crucial to the survival of the city: the drug epidemic. He said that they were not affiliated with the Interdenominational Ministers Alliance, which had thundered out in their pulpits in favor of the ordinance. "They're into election politics. We're into holding the politicians accountable."

Already in the council room was George Denegre, who observed, "As we spoke about before, time has run out. These things are anachronisms."

A City Hall operative took Denegre aside and told him that, according to his information, the council vote on the Blue Ribbon Committee's amendments to the ordinance would be four–two in favor. Ken Carter walked in, spotted Denegre, and gave him the sign for all is well—the circle with finger and thumb. Clearly, the men of the breakfast club had been working behind the scenes to ensure a harmonious compromise. I imagined George Denegre playing General Longstreet, the realist at Gettysburg, knowing a lost cause when he saw one, and Ken Carter, the diplomat, putting away for the moment his personal grievances and walking the fine line between black and white interests.

As the meeting began, it was clear that Sidney Barthelemy was

270

now speaking the language of reconciliation, and he urged the council to adopt the recommendations of the Blue Ribbon Committee.

After a series of technical questions about the amendments, the floor was open for discussion. There were a few of the same familiar faces, including Harry McCall, Jr.

One speaker, an old black man in a wheelchair, began to speak against the ordinance, but it soon became clear that he wanted to abolish Carnival altogether. "Should this ancient Babylon of evil be continued?" he asked. "Should it not be abolished and did away with?" He held out a pile of pamphlets titled *The Spirit of Mardi Gras*. "This drunkenness, nudity, homosexuality, all the pervertedness the devil can create in one day. We have allowed the gates of hell to be opened to New Orleans."

A black businessman named Campbell Gant took the microphone to address the representatives of old-line Carnival. "To those who think there is a long line of people waiting to get in your clubs," he said, "there's not. They're passé. Let's get on with the business of providing opportunity for people in the community. If we don't do something about the problems of the inner city, you can really worry about your Carnival. There is a growing discontent that can't be resolved by joining Comus. This stuff means nothing to us."

Simon Slanker, a white businessman, tried to strike a tone of moderation. "The real issue we're trying to address," he said, "is pulling the community together. The economic issue is what we're talking about. It hurts me to see our city torn apart. This is not a racial city. It's a fun city. We've got to get rid of the hate."

A young man named Brad Ott, a resident of the French Quarter who appeared a throwback to the sixties in his flak jacket and long hair, was not there for compromise. "The issue is bigotry," he said. "They can no longer hide behind their masks—having people grovel for beads."

Rodrigo Fonseca, a slender man who appeared to be in his early to mid-fifties, took the microphone. Dressed in a slightly rumpled white jacket, he could have been among the long line of bohemian writers who have found solace in New Orleans. Although he was holding a Bible, it was clear that he was there not as a preacher but as a guardian of culture.

"It has been my Mardi Gras experience to go through the streets on Mardi Gras in search of the Mardi Gras Indians," he said. "I've walked all the backstreets in Tremé and uptown, from Simon Bolivar to Washington Street. I have found groups of people pouring out of their houses to watch these small parades go by. There are dozens, hundreds, of people along these small backstreets. This has been their Mardi Gras, the only Mardi Gras that was theirs.

"We know that most of the parties, the parades—this was not their celebration. They're not free to come, and they have no interest in it. It is time for us, the few and privileged, to extend to them this invitation to be a part of this celebration."

He opened the Bible, and there were a few groans from the spectators. But there was silence as he read a passage from the Book of Psalms about what it means to be a people in exile, a people who must celebrate in an alien land, a land to which they were brought captive. "By the rivers of Babylon," he intoned quietly, "we wept when we remembered Zion. They that carried us away captive required of us song; and they that wasted us required of us mirth." He paused, and there were amens from many in the room. He continued, "How shall we sing the Lord's song in a strange land?"

By now, the meeting had become a cross between a morality play and an encounter session. Sandy Krasnoff, a former policeman, said that he had once worked fifteen to sixteen hours a day during Mardi Gras, guarding the parade routes, having to run up and down Saint Charles Avenue. "All the time, in the back of my mind," he said, "I was thinking about my father. He's eighty-three years old, the oldest musician playing the Carnival balls—he's been playing since 1940. He played for a band, the Russ Popelia Orchestra. He just played a ball last weekend."

Krasnoff described a time, shortly after the Korean War, when he had picked up his father at the back of the Auditorium following a rehearsal for a Carnival ball. "It was a blueblood organization," he said. "I was standing at the back door. My father, who came out last with the orchestra, was waiting for the captain of the Mardi Gras organization. Russ Popelia said to this gentleman, 'I need a favor. Two passes for two very important people.' This gentleman said, 'Russ, we don't allow Italians and Jews in our ball.' Russ said, 'Don't you know I'm Italian?' Russ told the gentleman he could shove the ball and the tickets up his ass. He did not play for the ball.

"Later, I said, 'Dad, you're Jewish, and you never said a word.' He told me, 'You can't win.' I've never forgotten that." At this, Krasnoff broke down in tears and sat down.

For some of those present, who were veterans of the Civil Rights movement, this was a continuation of a never-ending battle, and the speeches had a familiar ring to them. But for others, black and white, this was clearly the first time they had ever spoken in such an arena, and there was something unrehearsed and utterly sincere about them. For some, the Scripture clearly dictated the right course of action. And for others, it was a time for soul-searching.

The captain of Rex later told me that he felt the ordinance had "caused a lot of people to take inventory—whether they enjoy Mardi Gras—what it means to them. What New Orleans means to them. The bottom line is that people actively expressed what was in their hearts and minds."

For some old-line opponents of the ordinance, this feeling of standing up for a lost cause had the odor of Confederate romance about it. Conversely, the speeches from some supporters of the ordinance reeked of the politics of resentment. The sense of public-spiritedness appeared to be so desiccated in New Orleans that people were substituting the airing of private grievances for working for genuine change for the benefit of the common good. Combatants from both sides seemed to be fighting the phantoms of past battles.

For all the myopic snobbery of the old-line krewes, there was something equally dispiriting about the notion of a politically correct Carnival regulated by City Hall, a place where nothing worked, and where corruption and apathy were endemic.

The amendment, as Ken Carter had predicted, was adopted, and the ordinance softened. But as Henry Julien had predicted at the last meeting, Humpty-Dumpty could never be put back together again. As one Momus member put it, "The bubble has burst."

After the meeting, a woman I recognized as Sandy Jaffe, the

widow of Al Jaffe, a white musician who had founded Preservation Hall and played with the Olympia Brass Band, approached Harry McCall, Jr. "You could have been a great man, Mr. McCall," said Jaffe, sadly. "What happened to you?"

McCall looked at her as though she were a being of another species. "I have nothing to say to you, madam."

The Fisticuffs of Jazz

Riding my bicycle across town a few days later, I ran into George Schmidt, who was crossing Julia Street near his apartment. "I just got back from three weeks in Rome," he said. "Why wander around the labyrinth when there is a clear space of light—Italy? I found what I needed—the eating habits and customs of the ancient Romans. Ancient Carnival has to do with not eating meat. We think about the Romans eating peacock tongues and such, but they were vegetarians. The only animals they ate were sacrificed—cow, sheep, and swine."

Speaking of sacrificial animals, he said, he had just found out that two of his paintings on exhibit at a local hotel had been slashed. Curiously, the subjects had been the *boeuf gras* of Rex and a tableau of Zulu. "They should send Dorothy Mae the bill to have them repaired," said George.

George was still obsessed with the notion of Italians as the promulgators of jazz in New Orleans. The New Leviathan, he said, was dedicating their next record to Nick LaRocca, in honor of the seventy-fifth anniversary of the first jazz recording. He had listened to a tape of that original recording, he said, the whole time he was in Italy. He had just gotten a letter from a Sicilian scholar, he said, who claimed that the black contribution to early jazz had been overrated, since 30 percent of the musicians in New Orleans at the turn of the century were Italian.

George's pugnacity reminded me of a photograph I had seen at the local jazz museum of Nick LaRocca engaged in fisticuffs with Tom Brown. LaRocca had been invited to a local radio station in 1955 for a debate with Brown, one of LaRocca's contemporaries, to settle once and for all whether Brown's Band from Dixieland or LaRocca's Original Dixieland Jazz Band was the first New Orleans jazz band to go to Chicago and to have "the most authentic early jazz sound." In the photo, the two grizzled old men in double-breasted suits are going after each other like punch-happy old boxers.

VI

Parades and Pageants

34

Southern Belles

It was now less than a month before Mardi Gras day, and despite the clouds of doubt and confusion hovering over the city, the show would go on. There would be balls every night, sometimes as many as two or three scattered around the city, and parade season would begin next Saturday with the Krewe de Vieux. Tonight, I planned to join the ladies of Iris in celebrating their seventy-fifth anniversary.

To get myself into the proper Iris spirit before leaving for the Municipal Auditorium, I pulled out my sheet of rules and regulations for the ball. I was reminded that I had to remove my gloves before applauding, that I could not chew gum, that I could not drink before or during the ball, that I couldn't throw my doubloons until the finale, that I could not walk around the ballroom unescorted by a gentleman, that I could not remove my mask while on the dance floor.

Following the official Iris rules faithfully, I did not appear in the streets in my Vieux Carré artist costume, but brought it along with me to the Auditorium in a covered bag. I walked into the side entrance of the Auditorium, the mysterious door usually reserved for male maskers. The enormous dressing room had been roped off into sections for each group of float riders.

I wasn't crazy about my bright gold artist's smock, purple pants, and huge purple beret, but I felt downright lucky compared to some of the groups. Across from our section was a group of leprechauns with pink satin vests and green jackets with tails.

"You're not playing with a full deck," a woman retorted when I complimented her belly-dancer outfit consisting of orange chiffon trousers, gold bolero, and a blue fez. There were female Davy Crocketts in coonskin caps, satin-clad Indians, hillbillies in gingham, mountain climbers in orange lederhosen. "We're supposed to be apache girls, but we don't really know what that is," said a woman in a short purple satin skirt and a purple beret smaller than mine.

Later, after the introduction of the king and queen, the dukes and maids of the court, the pages, and the attendants to "their majesties," it was time to evoke memories of seventy-five years of Iris. Each group was to act out a former Iris theme, and ours was "That's What I Like About the South," so that we were to come out flirting and swishing around like Southern belles, which was somewhat difficult in our tight pants and floppy berets. A little Southern Comfort beforehand might have helped, but we'd have to wing it on adrenaline. And so when we heard our cue, the opening chords to "Are You from Dixie," we came out smiling and dancing in the best Iris tradition.

35

The Maharajah and the Sans-culottes

On Sunday, I had been invited to two pre-parade Mardi Gras parties. In the afternoon, the Krewe of Alla was gathering at Blaine Kern's Mardi Gras World, in the warehouse where the Alla floats were being stored. Late in the day, the Mistick Corpse of Comatose, the most radical subkrewe of the Krewe de Vieux, was getting together for a final planning session.

I arrived at the Alla warehouse to find Blaine Kern onstage, pacing around a platform near the entrance of the building with a microphone in his hand like a Vegas crooner. He was introducing various dignitaries, including a little girl, who he said was to be queen of Alla in the year 2002, and an elderly man named Joe Joe, "my king in 1952." Only eight kings of Alla over the last forty years had died, he said. "I guess that means being maharajah is lucky."

The kings of Alla were actually referred to as maharajahs, and they sat atop an elephant rather than a throne. This year's maharajah was to be Harry Lee, the obese Chinese-American sheriff of Jefferson Parish, who had gained national notoriety a few years ago by stopping blacks who entered the parish to inquire what their business there might be.

Meanwhile, Kern was asking the crowd, "Who is the most popular individual in the state of Louisiana?"

"David Duke," someone yelled.

Kern hardly missed a beat. "No, it's Harry Lee." And he brought the huge sheriff up onstage. "They're going to have to use the cherry picker from the power company to get him up on that float."

As Alla tradition required, Harry Lee had been weighed on a giant scale modeled after the scale once used by the Aga Khan to assess tribute from his followers. The Aga would sit on the scale, and his followers would have to balance the scale with treasure. Harry Lee had weighed in at a sybaritic 325 pounds. Only the black citizens of the area, however, could assess how fairly or unfairly he had thrown his weight around.

The Mystic Corpse

The planning party for the Krewe of the Mistick Corpse of Comatose was held at the home of Michael Nelson, an instructor at Delgado Community College, who lived near Tulane University. When I arrived, krewe members were dishing up vegetarian tacos from the kitchen. I recognized Brad Ott, the young man in the ponytail and flak jacket who had spoken in favor of the ordinance at the City Council meeting.

The krewe had adopted a name that suggested the Cadavre Exquis, the dadaist collaboration, as well as Comus, and they were known for their fearless forays into absurdity. Nevertheless, there was an air of political earnestness beneath their guise of satire.

"We're the urban rabble," said Michael Nelson, who noted that they were looking for a head on a pike. They would be carrying out a French Revolution theme, with most of them dressing as ragged sans-culottes, carrying the severed head of Momus and the corpse of Comus. "We still have a Bourbon monarchy in New Orleans," said Nelson.

In previous years, the group had satirized various groups and individuals that they regarded as particularly obnoxious or dangerous. One of their favorite targets had been the Jesus people, who tended to get particularly loud during Carnival, said Nelson. During the height of TV evangelist Jimmy Swaggart's career, before his various motel-room sins were revealed, Swaggart Ministries had sent a Soul Patrol equipped with bullhorns from their headquarters in Baton Rouge down to New Orleans.

Instead of confronting the Swaggart apostles head-on, said Nelson, they had formed their own proselytizing group, the Church of the Green Frog. "We had the evil alligator, Avarice, and we had frog songs, like 'Froggie, Froggie, Hoppaluia.'" Their mottoes, he said, had been "Frog Loves You" and "Frog Died for Your Sins." The year following Swaggart's disgrace, one of the Green Frog people had carried a banner titled THE BLEEDING PHALLUS OF JIMMY SWAGGART PLEASURE CLUB.

This year, they intended to go after what they regarded as the Jim Crow aspects of Carnival. "The Krewe of Comus was founded under slavery, and the other old-line krewes were formed under the Jim Crow era," said Nelson. "It's no wonder that their membership reflects apartheid. The most blatant aspects of the Jim Crow laws were gotten rid of during the sixties, but that system is still alive and well today."

Later, as I was describing this new incarnation of the sans-culottes and their assault on the ancien régime, a friend who was a student of political theory reminded me of Edmund Burke's comments about the fate of tradition following the French Revolution. Burke had suggested that an attack on tradition, in the name of principle, meant an invitation to tyranny of a different kind. Tradition is local, observed Burke, while principle is universal, and therefore conducive to its own kind of terrors. The ancien régime ultimately was not replaced by the radical upholders of *liberté, egalité, and fraternité,* but by the bourgeoisie.

Similarly, there was the possibility that it would not be the "rabble" that would inherit Carnival if the old-line krewes were to give up their sinecure. The real winners would most likely be the makers of "bourgeois" Carnival, like Blaine Kern and his boosters. With the old-line krewes gone from the streets, it would be nearly impossible to keep the commercial interests out of the parades. Already, in Mississippi, where casino gambling had been legalized, the casinos had organized Carnival krewes for a Gulf Coast Mardi Gras. The Casino Magic had advertised in the *Times-Picayune* for charter members for its Krewe of Camelot. And now that gambling was coming to New Orleans, it was only a matter of time before Caesar's Palace or Harrah's had a krewe to rival Rex and Zulu. A contender for the first casino license in New Orleans was already campaigning to obtain the Municipal Auditorium for a temporary casino and kick the Carnival krewes out.

36

The Escape Goat

It was Thursday, February 13, the morning of the Young Men Illinois ball, and I had driven with Henri and Paul to the Comus den, where they were putting finishing touches on some of the floats, even though there was little chance Henri's handiwork would ever roll into the streets. "I'm just putting on some more acanthus leaves," said Henri. The shells for Glaucus were half-finished. He had not yet completed the strands of beard and hair that would be streaming out from the float. "We'll have a year to do more hair, more seaweed," said Henri. "We'll just put the poppies on Morpheus," he said.

We piled into Henri's truck to drive to Jefferson Variety, a favorite source for costume materials and throws, located in Carrollton. I found the word variety to be an understatement for the bizarre array of throws and favors piled into bins and stuffed into plastic bags. There were grasshoppers and crickets, giant plastic toothbrushes, albino alligators, tiny guitars, Snoopies. Pointing out a barrel of plastic hand grenades, Henri remarked, "Those are the throws of the future."

I picked out several bags of beads and a large bag of tiny plastic poodles to throw from the Iris float, while Henri and Paul browsed through the back section, crammed with bolts of material. There were yards and yards of brocade, lamé, satin, tulle, and flocked velvet in every imaginable shade and texture. Hung on the wall, as examples of the finished product, were Carnival gowns, most of which seemed to be in jumbo sizes. Paul was looking for material to create an Escapegoat costume for Mardi Gras day. He would be the sacrificial goat who got away, he said.

We emerged from the store to find a huge hydra with nine heads wrapped in plastic, sitting in the back of a pickup truck.

"That could be used in a parade for birth control as an example of the child you should never have," said Paul.

On the way back downtown to Paul's house, where we were to have lunch, Henri and Paul pointed out several marvels of Creole architecture that had been abandoned and boarded up. "In any other city," said Henri, "each of these houses would be a jewel."

Paul had transformed his house on Clouet Street from a shrine to Mardi Gras to a mausoleum of mourning. The columns of the front porch had been draped in black bunting. Sitting on the porch was a Dorothy Mae Taylor doll in progress, a brown doll with eyeglasses.

Inside, the fireplace in the front parlor had been draped in black chiffon, and funeral urns had been placed on the mantel. A small table in the dining room, whose surface was customarily used as a kind of Mardi Gras altar, was now a memento mori. A skull was wearing a rhinestone crown, and black gloves had been placed next to a black rubber snake. Even the statue of Saint Ann had been veiled.

Even Paul's usual madcap wit couldn't dispel the air of sadness that hung over the house. Moths had assailed his Whore of Babylon costume, he said. Carnival has always been redolent with dark images of mortality, like the malevolent figure of death hovering at the edge of the crowd in the classic film *Black Orpheus*. But this year, there was an unusually dispiriting, funereal quality to all the preparations that couldn't be diffused.

Perhaps, I thought, there were mythic overtones to Paul's choice of the escapegoat as his Carnival identity. It was a slain goat, after all, that became the central image in the rites of Dionysus and the birth of tragedy. The shepherd who slays the goat dances in its skin. Girded in the goatskin, he trounces grapes into wine, in a ceremony of sacrifice and transubstantiation that turns the slain god into the means of intoxication.

Goddesses of Love

Tonight was the formal Carnival ball held by Young Men Illinois, the small club made up primarily of black Creoles. Ken Carter had decided not to attend this year, he said, because of the controversy over the Carnival ordinance, and he had not yet resolved to his satisfaction his ambivalence about the club's exclusivity.

I learned from black historian John Rousseau that the Original Illinois Club was founded in 1895 by students of a dancing teacher who had come to New Orleans the previous year. The dancing master, who was from Tennessee, rather than Illinois, noticed that there was scarce social life in New Orleans and a paucity of social graces, with dancing confined to square dances and quadrilles. He began a dancing school, Rousseau said, "for the sons and daughters of the better-class blacks, which at the time were the domestic help—the cooks and coachmen and butlers and valets."

Following a dance held at Globe Hall on Saint Peter, the students founded a club and named it after their dancing teacher, thinking he was from Illinois. In 1926, Young Men Illinois split from the Original Illinois Club. "The young turks," said Rousseau, "thought they had a better idea." Nowadays, said Rousseau, "The sons and daughters of domestic help can't get in the club," and club members now "don't want to be reminded of their origins."

Compared to other Mardi Gras clubs, Young Men Illinois is a very small club, with less than fifty members. When I picked up a program as I walked into the Municipal Auditorium, I noticed that city attorney William D. Aaron, Jr., was listed as a member, as was his father. Other members whose names I recognized included a judge and a dentist.

The social world of black Creoles is a small world, and this year's queen and first maid, Jacinta Robinet and Medria Robinet, were sisters. Their father, LaNard Robinet, was a school principal in La-Place, a small town upriver from New Orleans. Among this year's debutantes, I noticed, was Denise Julien, the daughter of Henry Julien, the lawyer who had made such a stink at the council meetings about exclusivity. Obviously, he must have shared Ken Carter's ambivalence about such things, at least when it came to his own daughter's debut. It could be argued that Young Men Illinois was as exclusive within the black community as Comus was within the white community.

The theme of this year's ball was "Hearts and Flowers," with each maid and debutante to present a vignette from the mythical history of love. Trenease Kelly Williams, a student at McDonough 35 High School, where she was a majorette in the band, represented Helen of Troy. She wore a white dress and a headdress supporting a wreath of flowers. Trenease, said the program narrator, planned to major in computer science. Denise Julien represented Narcissus, "mesmerized by the side of the pool." Denise, said the narrator, attended Brooklyn Tech High School in New York, where she was editor of the yearbook and cocaptain of the cheerleading team.

In a dramatic conclusion, Queen Jacinta emerged from a cloud of smoke, as the orchestra played "Hail to the Queen."

Following the presentation of the debutantes was a musical program by the Dillard University choir, which began with a rather mainstream version of "The Impossible Dream." The choir ended with a medley of spirituals, including "Down by the Riverside," and I glanced around at the audience, who sat rigidly in their seats. I spotted a few feet tapping discreetly, but I realized that this group of carefully screened elite families were as bound by decorum as old-line white society. It was just that they had had to work much harder, and against far greater odds, to maintain their sense of being special and set apart.

37
Body Floats

On the morning of February 15, as I was finishing up my headdress
for the Krewe de Vieux parade that night, I got a call from Mickey Gil,
the captain of Petronius. Mickey said he could take me on a tour of
krewe members getting their costumes ready for the Petronius ball on
Sunday night. Mickey, who spoke with a stagey German accent, like
the hokey bodybuilders Hans and Franz on *Saturday Night Live*, said
I could pick him up on the corner of Burgundy and Governor Nicholls Street. He'd be wearing a green silk jacket.

From his voice, I had expected someone much younger and
beefier, somehow, than the elegant, slightly built man of medium
height with the pencil mustache who was waiting for me, looking a bit
wilted in the unseasonable heat. I parked the car, and we walked up
Governor Nicholls to our first stop, the costume workshop operated
by designer Ron Aschenbach out of his apartment near the Spanish
Stables. Aschenbach specialized in theme parties and occasionally
moonlighted on debutante parties. This morning, Aschenbach was
finishing up a "body" float for a Petronius krewe member. Body
floats, an innovation of gay Mardi Gras, were actually small platforms
on wheels designed to be hitched up to the krewe member's waist and
pulled along behind him like a cart behind a horse.

The theme for this year's ball, said Mickey, was fairy tales, and
the krewe member portraying Aladdin would be pulling a genie behind him like a sort of incubus. Balanced on the platform, concocted
of copper pipe criss-crossed over a plywood base, was a huge genie,
painted purple, hunched over a magic lamp. Ron picked up a pair of
glittery diaphanous trousers to indicate the rest of the costume.

Aschenbach said he sort of invented things as he went along and haunted hardware stores for ideas. "Working with wire," he said, "is like drawing in air. You have to think in three dimensions."

Mickey had recovered some of his captainly bearing, and I gathered that the captain of Petronius was as autocratic as the captain of Rex or Comus. "The captain decides the theme," said Mickey, "and who gets to be who." This year, he said, Ron had done most of the preliminary drawings, and he had fit the different fairy-tale characters to krewe members, according to their talents and personalities.

"The thing is to avoid the Disney look," said Aschenbach, a tall man in chambray shirt and jeans, his long hair tied back in a ponytail. "Mickey was trying for a European turn-of-the-century look."

Said Mickey, "We try not to imitate the straight clubs, but to make fun of them."

Petronius, said Mickey, was trying to get away from the glitter-and-feathers look of other gay krewes. Last year's queen, said Mickey, was the Queen of Hearts, who wore no sequins or glitter. He had also been bare-assed, said Mickey, "but it was in good taste." "The queen this year does not have one rhinestone or sequin. This year, I wanted to do pyrotechnics."

As we headed up to the Garden District, Mickey explained that much of the cost of putting on the ball would be defrayed by the current production of *Vampire Lesbians of Sodom* at a local cabaret. Terry, the first lieutenant of Petronius, who planned to dress as the sorceror's apprentice at the ball, was a star of the show. He came onstage before the first act in campy drag and lip-synched "I Will Survive" while tossing Mardi Gras beads to the audience.

We stopped in front of a dove-colored cottage that had been modernized with lots of wood and glass. We walked behind the house, through a gate, into a flower-laden patio with a small pool. Richard Egyud, an interior decorator, was inside the pool house working on the most extraordinary cape I had ever seen. The lining was made of hundreds of turquoise eyes cut from peacock feathers and sewn together, so that it could have been the cloak of Argus, of the hundred eyes.

"Here you have someone who loves rhinestones," said Mickey, as Richard dotted the outside of the cape with glue and set individual rhinestones in a swirling pattern.

"I'm Scheherazade this year," said Richard. "I won't be bare-chested because I have to strap myself into this harness," he said, indicating a huge spiral headdress that would be supported from the shoulders. The dress, he said, was made of material imported from Italy.

"This is the first year I've done drag, and I've never walked in heels," said Richard. "I had to order five-inch heels from New York." The funniest thing, he said, however, was going to the Superstore to buy nylons.

As we drove farther uptown, Mickey, who had served as captain for seven years, said this would be his last year. Like Ray Kern, he was exhausted, and said he felt it was time for someone else to take over. "This is enough," he said. When he had taken over the krewe, it had been in decline. A number of the older members had died, he said, not of AIDS, but by drinking themselves to death. "That's the New Orleans disease."

Mickey said he was grooming Jamie Greenleaf, who was next on our tour, to take over as captain. And with the spectacular costumes this year, he said, he would go out with a bang. Jamie, who was already something of a legend in New Orleans, had just returned to town and wanted to make a splash.

We arrived at a large, white-columned house on Camp Street with hanging baskets of geraniums on the veranda. Two strong-looking young men were carrying a chifforobe out the front door. Inside, most of the furnishings had already been removed from the double parlor to accommodate the enormous free-standing bell skirt, a sort of white cloud covered with butterflies, that was the bottom half of the queen's dress. The young men were making more room to get the dress out the door. We stumbled over a K & B drugstore shopping cart full of tools—a costume repair kit, said Mickey, for the night of the ball.

Underneath the skirt was a wheelbase that would allow the queen to get up and down ramps gracefully. The aluminum structure covered in plywood also hid the motors and batteries that operated the chaser lights and the butterflies. Jamie, a tall, silver-haired man, said that he had done things with this costume that had never been done before. He flicked on a switch inside the skirt, and the butterflies, some large, some small, started fluttering their wings. Each butterfly was flapping at a different speed, and it was a dazzling effect.

"I've done a lot of things," said Jamie. "I've done the Miss America pageant. But this is the only place a costume like this could be called for. Except maybe Vegas or the Folies-Bergère in Paris." There were still more butterflies, he pointed out, attached to the sleeves of the bodice of the costume and to the pillow that would be used to carry out the scepter. He turned to Mickey, saying, "You wanted hocus-pocus, and you got it."

The Krewe de Vieux Rights the News

By Petronius standards, my Egyptian dancing-girl outfit for the Krewe de Vieux was tacky, tacky, tacky. And it was skimpy, skimpy, skimpy. I spent an inordinate amount of time trying to find a flesh-colored body stocking that would merely give the illusion of exposed flesh rather than the real thing.

When I arrived at Richard and Vivian Cahn's house, where Mama Roux was mustering before heading over to the starting point of the parade, the yard resembled a rehearsal for the Egyptian bondage segment of *The Ten Commandments*.

Helen Hartnell, the statuesque law school professor who was to play Dorotiti, our queen, was lying on a bed, with a high fever, while a friend applied her makeup. "The show must go on," she said with a moan. She had gotten the job as Dorotiti, she said, because they needed an imposing figure who could be pompous. She said, however, that this was going to be her farewell to New Orleans. She had just received notice that she had lost her job. It had been a comfort, she said, to tell her analyst that she was going to reign as Queen of Denial.

I got a ride over to the parade site, on Frenchmen Street, just below the Quarter, with a couple who had dressed as King Tut and Nefertiti. When we arrived, there were brass bands warming up and a walking club called the Floozies traipsing around in short satin skirts reminiscent of the Storyville Baby Dolls. A couple of Mardi Gras Indians were staring curiously at the Krewe of Lewd, who had decided to dress this year as the "Wilder Tchoupitoulas," an equal-opportunity pseudo-Indian group made up primarily of young white professionals. The "real" Indians, who were freelancing for the evening, sniffed scornfully at the last-minute assemblage of feathers and paint that passed as costumes for the krewe members. One of the "real" Indians was wearing a patch from last year's costume featuring a symbol of Desert Storm.

I walked up and down the street to get a good look at the rest of the costumes, since once the parade was under way, I'd be dancing around Dorotiti and tossing favors to the crowd.

You couldn't miss the Krewe of Underwear in their bright red long johns and fake fur hats made of foam rubber and painted with hammer-and-pickle insignia. Their minifloat carried out the Russian theme with a parody of a homeless Lenin looking for a tomb. There was a coffin with a dummy made up to look like Lenin, carrying a sign: ST. LOUIS CEMETERY OR BUST. A member of the subkrewe had donated the dummy, an inflatable doll, which turned out to be anatomically correct when they blew it up to life-size.

Krewe members planned to pass out flyers announcing a going-out-of-business sale by the Russians. Among the offerings for sale were "dozens of nuclear scientists." The ad promised, "From chemical warfare all the way up to the big one, these guys and gals can make you a world power overnight! (Will work for vodka.)" Also at a bargain price were "Statues and busts of Lenin, Stalin and other idols of the former USSR. Thousands available at take 'em away prices!" The ad offered an extra discount on items from the Chernobyl region.

The Krewe of Mystic Inane had dressed as Ku Klux Klowns in what appeared to be Klan robes and hats, red clown noses and clown makeup. Their minifloat was a giant jack-in-the-box with a Ku Klux Klown that popped out and flopped over the side.

The Krewe of the Mistick Corpse of Comatose were acting out class conflict, as they had planned. Brad Ott was dressed in drag as a bargain-basement version of an uptown debutante, in a ruffled pink ball gown and purple boa and pink bedroom slippers. "God, it's hot," he said, lifting his ratty blond wig for a moment and flinging his boa.

The Krewe of Kaos had turned their float into a moving shrine for Our Lady of Fatima. The Virgin was portrayed by Jose Perez, who hadn't bothered to shave off his mustache. One krewe member was carrying a sign announcing CIMEL PRODUCTIONS, in honor of the former New Orleans priest who was alleged to have taken pornographic movies of young male subjects. Jose would be tossing holy wafers as Mardi Gras doubloons, said one krewe member.

At the front of the parade, the mule pulling the king's minifloat was getting antsy and nudged the cop on the motorcycle who was to lead off the parade. The cop revved up his motor, and the parade started rolling, leaving Ray Kern behind, standing with his hands on his hips.

Soon, Dorotiti's barge got rolling, and we dutifully began to dance behind her, while slave masters cracked their whips at us. We crossed Esplanade, and I spotted Dalt and Josephine and a few other people I knew, but they didn't recognize me behind my mask.

We carried cloth bags filled with beads and small rubber alligators as throws. The people I passed on the street were surprisingly eager to catch something. "Anything you got, I need," said one young man. A well-dressed young woman, glancing at the gold beads I was wearing, yelled out, "I need gold." In a parade, the squeaky wheel always gets the grease, and those who were yelling the most seemed to have the most beads already.

The little kids on the route seemed frightened of the rubber alligators we tossed their way. I reached the bottom of my bag as we headed up Royal Street, and there was nothing left but a few handfuls of confetti. People were fighting even for the confetti, though, and I got a very small inkling of what it feels like to be God.

38

A New Suit

With only a few hours of work, the Krewe de Vieux had produced a funny parade, using scraps and remnants and spray paint and dime-store gewgaws. Other Carnival orphans, however, were far more extravagant in their costumes, not only in terms of expense and time, but in skill and sophistication. Unlike the regular krewes, who hired professionals like Henri Schindler or Blaine Kern to create their floats and their costumes, the orphans of Carnival took pride in producing their own. The only rivals to the gay krewes, in terms of cost and effort in proportion to income, were the Mardi Gras Indians, who put everyone else to shame.

Larry Bannock, chief of the Golden Star Hunters, one of Bo Dollis's uptown rivals, had won particular acclaim as a master crafts-man. I went to watch him in action one afternoon at a small library in Gentilly, where he had volunteered to give a sewing and folklore demonstration for a group of black children. Larry had brought along some of his beadwork "patches" and his "spy boy," Wiley.

Larry said that he lived about "as far uptown as you can get," in Girt Town. He was still working on his suit, which this year would be mostly black velvet. Parts of his suit had been sent out to allies all around the city to help him finish it, and friends in the neighborhood dropped by his house every day to help. He was still working on the patch that was to go on his apron. It was stretched out on a frame, and we could see how he applied concentric rows of beads, using different colors to create a pattern. The figure of an Indian appeared to emerge out of a kind of feathered fire, with his arms outspread and feathered like the wings of a bird.

"We let the suits tell the story," said Larry, a powerfully built man who looked younger than his fifty years, despite his graying hair. He had a kindly look about him, but I imagined that he wouldn't do much backing down in a confrontation. "These marks on my fingers say that I sewed my suit," he said, holding up his hands so that the children could see the calluses. "Every patch you see on my suit has a meaning. I love color and detail and design."

He picked up a patch, and the kids murmured in admiration at its beauty. "When the sun hits these rhinestones," he said, "it turns like a rainbow. When I'm dressed up, I get in front of a showcase window and you say, 'Whew, I'm pretty.'"

He explained, however, "You can be the prettiest but if you don't know how to move, you're nothing. Your heart and soul have to be in it."

The patches were well made, dense and tightly sewn, and Larry dropped one on the floor deliberately, with a loud thud, to show how solid it was. He explained that, from year to year, the patches were moved around from piece to piece in the costume, from apron to chestpiece. "You can stand in the rain," said Larry, "and nothing will happen to this because it's sewed so well."

Larry explained that one of the reasons the methods of making the suits have been kept secret is that "the old Indians had a superstition that someone would take it. Maybe someone from Japan would learn how to make it. We safeguarded it."

"No two suits are alike," said Larry. "There is a city ordinance you can't use the same float twice. You see a Blaine Kern dinosaur, and he'll change a color or something for next year or for another parade. With the Indians, some people wear the same patches, but they move it around. If you wear the same color more than once, they say you're a ragman." It was important, too, to sew your own suit. He looked around knowingly. "I know who's sewing and who's borrowing. Not a lot of people want to take the time."

The songs told the story, too. There was "Indian Red," for instance, which a number of tribes used to start the day. "It's like our prayer," he said.

Larry ran through a few chants like a series of commands. There was "Marti-cutie-fiyo," which meant, "Everybody come to attention," and "Jock-o-mo, hondo hondo," which could mean a number of things, depending on the mood of the chief. He smacked a tambourine with his fist, and everyone jumped.

"If you play Indian," said Larry, "there is a certain way you have to play. I walk in the door with the attitude that I'm a big chief. There are going to be people who challenge me. It's called psychological warfare. When I walk through my neighborhood and look at the old people and the young people, I'm like Rex."

Larry smiled at the kids. "Remember, no matter how old you get, men are little boys growed up." He continued, "I be almost three hundred pounds, and when I'm playing Indian, I don't feel it. But when I get downtown, at the end of the day, I holler, 'Take me home.' That's when I feel it, all those nights staying up. But I wake up Wednesday morning, and I'm ready to go again."

Endymion had offered him money to parade with them, said Larry, and he had turned them down. "This is our culture, our history." Even when Zulu had asked if his gang would parade with them, he had said no. "They have their thing, and we have ours."

The Indian tradition was unique, he said. "All of a sudden they've got experts on us. But they can't understand how a culture can come to a foreign land, survive all our lives on little or nothing.

"I'll be there as chief," said Larry, "long as I can be there. Masking Indian is about having fun and keeping our culture going.

"It's a funny thing how people can take little or nothing and make a costume or an Indian suit," said Larry, articulating one of the fundamental principles of Carnival, which applies to the oes and spangs of Comus as well as the rhinestones and flounces of Petronius and the beads and feathers of the Golden Star Hunters.

"I look at simple things and wonder how I can make them better," said Larry. "It's good that you can take little or nothing and make a masterpiece."

39

Serving Up Culture at Dooky Chase's

There is a wonderfully vivid painting by New Orleans artist Bruce Brice hanging on the wall of Dooky Chase's restaurant that portrays vignettes of black culture in New Orleans: the Olympia Brass Band, with its one conspicuously white member, Al Jaffe; a Mardi Gras Indian tribe; a jazz funeral crowded with second-liners, with a banner over the coffin reading ALL PAID UP; a Noah's Ark of a Zulu parade featuring floats laden with elephants and giraffes.

The guardians of black culture in New Orleans can look back on a brilliant panorama of music and tradition, and they might betray a certain ambivalence about "progress." The story of Dooky Chase's itself, which has been synonymous with black Carnival for half a century, reflects the history of black culture in New Orleans, just as the Chase family has reflected the changes in black society over the years.

Located on Orleans Street, across from the Lafayette Housing Project, Dooky Chase's was once a guaranteed stop not only for the Zulu parade, but for nearly every second-line parade in town. Edgar Chase's mother Leah, one of the doyennes of black society, now runs the restaurant, but Chase spent a lot of time there when he was growing up. As he described it, the restaurant started out in the 1940s as a place to serve beer and sandwiches after you played craps. His grandfather Dooky, Leah's father-in-law, was a well-known character in New Orleans. "If you've seen *Guys and Dolls*, said Chase, "he'd be the guy Sinatra played. He was a lottery vendor and gambler. He had a guy who worked for him named Big Bill, who was like Big Jule in *Guys and Dolls*. Wine, women, and song were his game.

"He liked to look neat. He wore these big-lapel suits, wing-tip shoes. He had a gold tooth and a big gold ring. He was proud, and he wanted to display a sense of having wealth. People saw that side of him. At a ballpark, he'd treat everyone to drinks. He was a true second-liner. He embodied that spirit, carefree. He'd follow the music anywhere. Whatever money he had, he didn't mind blowing it—he'd always get it back."

Edgar Chase envied his grandfather that second-line spirit, he said. "I wish I could feel as free. The other day, I saw this guy on Bourbon Street, just dancing and twirling to his own music in his mind, thanking the Lord for being alive. My grandfather was like that."

There were plenty of second-liners at the bar, too. "There would be a lot of longshoremen around. I'd only know people by their first names—like Mr. Mannie. The dock was the big mecca. We had the strongest, burliest blackest men at the bar. We didn't have Liberty Bank [the black-owned bank]. Blacks would cash their checks at the restaurant and on Fridays, the bar would be packed five rows deep— all the labor unions—carpenters, bricklayers. They would drink beer and buy po'boys and gamble in the back.

"My father used to tend bar in my grandfather's day. He had a band, and he'd keep in touch with the social whirl. They thought they were God's gift to the world in appearance. They were the Rhythm Playboys, patterned after Duke Ellington and Dizzie Gillespie.

"When the workforce changed, the restaurant changed. These blue-collar jobs have changed. We have banks we can go to now. We all use checking accounts. But before that, it generated a lot of cash. I grew up knowing people that way—seeing the men grow old and die. They have seen me as a little boy growing up and becoming a man.

"In the 1950s, my mother came aboard. The women wanted something more stable than men sitting around drinking. She gradually got things to shift to the dining room."

After Leah Chase took over, the restaurant developed a reputation for elegance as well as superb Creole cuisine. The burgundy-colored walls are hung with art by leading New Orleans black artists. Nevertheless, when sitting down to dine on stuffed eggplant with shrimp and crawfish, you can't help but think of the days when

Dooky Chase would stroll through in his finery, and burly men would be rolling dice in the back room.

Outgrowing Make-Believe

I went to Dooky Chase's one afternoon to visit Edgar's mother Leah, and I sat down at the table closest to the Bruce Brice painting. Leah, a small, gray-haired woman with a delicate, unlined face, came out in a white chef's coat and sat next to me, after ordering up glasses of ice tea. I recognized her from a photograph that was currently hanging on the wall of the New Orleans Museum of Art as part of an exhibit titled "I Dream the World," a collection of portraits of remarkable black women around the country.

Leah had come to New Orleans at age eighteen in 1942 from a small country town. When she started working in the restaurant in 1946, she said, everyone had to learn as they went along, including the customers. "Blacks had never been in a nice restaurant because there were none to go to."

When I asked Leah about the Brice painting, she pointed out that not all of her elite black Creole clientele had approved of it, particularly of the Mardi Gras Indians or the second-liners.

"This painting is typical of what we're all about," said Leah. "Some dyed-in-the-wool Creoles said it was a disgrace. But I said to them, 'This is us. If it's your culture, it's your culture, and that's it.' " She pointed to the jazz funeral in the painting. "It was our culture to dance when our ill ones died because we believed they were going to a better place. Black people don't like itty-bitty funerals. They want to be sent out big. I don't think it's so bad."

Like her son, Leah had warm feelings about Carnival in the old days, before the Interstate had turned Claiborne into an asphalt barrier. And like Ken Ferdinand and Morris Jeff, she did not feel that her experience of Mardi Gras had been second-rate because it had been mostly separate from white society.

"I live for Carnival," said Leah. "I like all the fanfare. When you outgrow make-believe, you know you're in serious trouble." When she was young, "blacks could not go all the places they go now, so we'd walk up and down Claiborne. Everybody would have open houses on Mardi Gras day. The women from the Creole community would wear their finest spring suits and hats. They'd have huge corsages with violets. You might carry a cane with a big Kewpie doll on it. The young ladies would walk up and down the street, sashaying up and down, showing their wares. I always made beautiful costumes for my children. Sometimes they were toreadors. One year they were space people in blue satin with silver cuffs. I sprayed their hair silver."

One year, when Edgar was five or six years old, he had been chosen king of his little primary school. He was stricken with asthma the night before his big day, and Leah had taken him to Charity Hospital and finished sewing up his cape there by his bedside.

On Claiborne Avenue, the Mardi Gras Indians would come bursting through the crowds, along with devils wielding pitchforks and the skeleton men. "We were scared of the skeletons," she said, "and we were not too sure of the Indians either. We always thought that people in the skeleton outfits were not considered the best sort. They would go to the butcher's and carry these bones. And then you always had the funny costumes. There were men dressed like ladies, with pillows on their rear ends. You also had the Baby Dolls. They were big fat women in little pink satin outfits."

Those were fun days, she said. "It's good to fantasize a little bit." For that reason, she was against Dorothy Mae Taylor's ordinance. "No matter how stressed out we are," she said, "we can loosen up that one day. When midnight comes, we go to praying again. That's why we're upset if anything interferes with our fun. I don't know anybody who has felt bothered by Carnival. These goings-on at City Hall haven't benefited anybody."

Leah said that one of her favorite parts of Mardi Gras had been the Comus parade. She'd sneak out of the restaurant in the early evening and head over to Rampart Street to catch some beads. Another of her favorite rituals had been watching the toasting of Rex and Comus on television. She'd finish up at the restaurant and she'd tell everyone, "I'm going home to watch Comus meet Rex." This year, however, Comus had announced it would not permit that part of its ball to be televised. "I'm so disappointed," said Leah.

40

Bearding Rex in His Den

I had been invited one afternoon to view the floats for the Rex parade by Temple Brown, a longtime krewe member who headed the club's new education program, called "Learning and Second Lining." This year's parade was titled "Voyages of Discovery," and there was to be a contest in the schools based on the theme. The winners would get a tour of the Rex den and a ride on a riverboat, and their schools would receive a donation.

I met Brown at the Rex den on Claiborne Avenue, where he spent a considerable amount of time in his role as parade lieutenant. "The den people have a camaraderie," said Brown. "The ball people have their own. We call ourselves the den rats." During the parade itself, he ordinarily brought up the foot of the parade on horseback, working as a kind of troubleshooter. There were a total of thirty-three riding lieutenants, who wore velvet-and-brocade tunics and capes and pointed hats with plumes.

Brown pointed out the standard Rex floats—the Streetcar Named Desire, which would be occupied by the George Finola band; the royal barge; the calliope; and of course, the *boeuf gras*, the fatted ox. He read about the float in the official parade description: "Surrounded by butchers and cooks, and by cornucopias of vegetables and garnishes, the Boeuf Gras' destiny is certain."

Both sides of the den were crammed with the large floats, most with towering figureheads announcing the subject of the float. There was Christopher Columbus, an obvious choice, sailing next to Cheng Ho, a less obvious figure. Ho was the fifteenth-century seafaring Chinese explorer who made voyages on behalf of the emperor to India and Africa, bringing back such exotic creatures as ostriches and giraffes. He was also a eunuch, which had earned him the nickname at the den of "Hung No Mo'."

Lewis and Clark paddled next to Jacques Cousteau, whose mascot was a hydraulic octopus. Also in close quarters were Darwin aboard the SS *Beagle*, Marco Polo in the court of Kublai Khan, Balboa on the edge of the Pacific, and Cortez plundering the Aztecs.

Temple Brown obviously enjoyed showing off the floats. On most days, he ran the family business, Brown's Velvet Ice Cream, with a factory near the Central Business District. A former college football player in the Ivy League, when he returned from service in the air force as a young man, he had joined the biracial committee of which Harry McCall and Harry Kelleher had been a part to try to defuse racial tensions in the city. His time spent in the Northeast and overseas had given him a certain perspective on New Orleans provincialism, and he had been called a "Commie pinko" by some uptown conservatives for his efforts. Now, however, he was disconcerted by the Carnival ordinance, which implied, he felt, that he and all members of Rex were racists.

"I think there's an overstated mystique with the krewes. I don't see where it's furthered anyone's economic status. I'm out in one of the toughest businesses—the food business. I don't count on Mardi Gras to contribute one darn thing to my success or failure, unless I can convince the Japanese that I'm the emperor of New Orleans."

His best Mardi Gras moment had come a few years ago, he said, when he came out onto Royal Street after a luncheon at the Royal Orleans and there was a hippie lying in the street, dressed in buckskin. "I had on my three-piece suit, looking very preppie and uptown," said Brown. "I asked him if that was his costume for Mardi Gras. He looked up at me and said, 'No, man, I think I'll go dressed like you.' "

41

The Importance of Headdresses

It was less than a week before the Zulu ball, and there was a rehearsal this morning for the ball and a "maids' extravaganza," a talent show put on by the Zulu maids, in the auditorium of the John F. Kennedy High School.

Sitting in one of the front rows of the auditorium was Morris Jeff, Sr., who was serving as protocol adviser for the proceedings. It was a role he had played, officially and unofficially, for several decades in the public school system of New Orleans. Slender and white-haired, he still had the graceful air of a dancer. I was saddened to see that he was completely blind now. "It kind of creeps up on you," he said.

When Jeff had first started out teaching physical education, there had been no equipment, so he had decided to teach everyone to dance. His students from those years learned how to waltz and fox-trot. They also learned manners. He stood up in his seat to demonstrate the bow with which they ended every waltz.

Jeff remembered when Zulu rode a barge along the canal on Mardi Gras day and landed at a wharf on Julia Street, where the train station now stands. "That was where they sold watermelons," he said. "The trucks would come in loaded with melons."

Jeff, who was now seventy-seven, had joined Zulu in 1954. The club's buffoonery had not bothered him, he said. "I thought, I'm going to go in. I don't care. Mardi Gras is make-believe. Why can't we make-believe like the other groups?" Said Jeff, "My philosophy paid off. Now we have lawyers, doctors, congressmen."

When Jeff reigned as king in 1974, however, he had made an effort to bring a bit more dignity and elegance to the role. He had influenced the design of the king's costume worn at the ball. In

303

contrast to the comical costume on Mardi Gras day, the costume for the ball now suggests more glitz than parody. "Most of the things you see now are a copy from me," said Jeff. "I changed the headpiece. I had to stoop—that's how big my headdress was. I had my robe trailing along behind me, possibly a half-block long. My costume was beaded."

Meanwhile, the emcee for the ball called for quiet. "Let's get ready for the extravaganza." The first section of the program was devoted to heroines of black history, with each maid portraying a distinguished black woman.

The maids, Jeff explained, ranged in age from high school juniors to college sophomores or juniors. First preference was given to daughters or granddaughters of members. The queen, he said, was selected by the king, subject to approval by the general membership. This year's queen was Ernestine Lillie Anderson, twenty-five, a legal clerk. Russell chose Anderson, he said, because of her impressive résumé. She had been the first black graduate of the Louise McGehee School uptown.

One of the maids announced that since they were commemorating black history, they wanted to present an award to Morris Jeff, Sr., for his contributions to the club.

Jeff accepted the plaque with panache and the welcome brevity of a professional. "I think the Zulus are the most beautiful people in the world," he said. "Now let's get on with the show."

A Crown of Feathers

I had to leave the rehearsal a little early in order to attend a jazz funeral that Larry Bannock had told me about. It was to be a grand send-off for a great Mardi Gras Indian chief, he said. By tradition, the Indians couldn't appear in their costumes, since it was not yet Mardi Gras day, but they would be out in force, Larry assured me.

The obituary for Joseph Adams, better known to his followers as Chief Joe Adams of the Seminole Hunters, had appeared that morning in the *Times-Picayune*. Adams, a construction worker, had died at the age of forty-nine from lung cancer. A navy veteran of the Vietnam

War, Joe Adams had also served as vice president of the Money Wasters Social and Pleasure Club.

At Our Lady Star of the Sea Catholic Church in the lower Ninth Ward, the crowds that had gathered were larger outside the church than inside. One woman who was waiting outside for the hearse to arrive from the Charbonnet-Labat Funeral Home said that the late chief's friends had him sitting up in his coffin at the wake the previous night.

Finally, with a police escort, sirens wailing and lights going, came a horse-drawn black carriage, followed by a caisson pulled by two gray horses.

A group of Mardi Gras Indians began chanting, "Iko, Iko," then "Hondo, hondo," followed by the prayerful "My Indian Red."

Larry Bannock, dressed in a gray suit and tie and wearing dark glasses, still managed to look fierce as he charged into the group of chanting men. "Hey pocky way," he yelled.

The Tremé brass band made their way to the bottom of the steps and began playing mournfully as a group of members from the Money Wasters formed an archway with their canes for other mourners to pass through on their way into the church.

An Indian charged up, carrying a yellow crown and a scepter with a cow skull, shouting, "It won't be long."

Another man took the crown and held it up, yelling, "Fi ya ya."

I walked inside the church, where things were more sedate. The priest was saying, "We have a home to go to when we are uprooted by death." Some of the mourners seated in the pews were holding fans with pictures of Joe Adams in a Sunday-best suit, wearing dark glasses and carrying a second-line umbrella.

The priest told the congregation, "This man is a celebrity because a soldier has gone forth to meet the Lord."

He commented acidly on the empty pews inside, with the crowd outside carrying on their own ceremony with bottles of Mad Dog or Budweiser. Said the priest, "If Joe had not lived in a certain way, what good would a jazz funeral do?"

"This is not for Joe," he said. "This is for the living. All this jumping and rocking and rolling won't get you into heaven." The

Reverend Davis than proceeded to sing "It's Over There" so power-fully that the tears inside were flowing as freely as the beer and wine outside on the sidewalks.

On the steps of the church, three little boys were trying to stare each other down, as the tambourines beat out a rhythm. They prac-ticed posing as spy boys and flag boys, their backs against each other, grimacing fiercely.

Meanwhile, a trombone slide from the Tremé brass band emerged from the church door and then the rest of the instrument and the rest of the band. They were playing "A Closer Walk with Thee," and the tuxedoed second-liners again formed an arch with their canes.

The pallbearers emerged from the church with the casket, swing-ing it to and fro, then heaved it up in the air three times. The first time was for faith, the second for hope, the third for charity. If you were a good man, Larry Bannock had told me, they'd throw it up one more time for good measure. And they did, with one last heave, before loading the coffin into the caisson.

A skinny man placed the yellow crown on the back of the coffin, and one by one, the members of the Seminole Hunters came by with bottles of beer and wine to anoint the crown. Its bright yellow feath-ers were soon soaked in alcohol.

"What a friend we have in Jesus," came the bittersweet sounds from the band in front, as the Indians in back rattled their tambou-rines.

It had begun to rain, but the second-liners, always prepared for rain or shine, sorrow or joy, raised their umbrellas and set off for the cemetery.

The Masked Ball

That night, I attended the ball sponsored by the Scuola Vecchia, a mysterious new Carnival organization that was attempting to bring elegance and whimsy back to Carnival. The ball was held in the old Quadroon Ballroom, now a part of the Bourbon Orleans Hotel, where white Creole men once picked out their mistresses from among a crowd of beautiful quadroon belles. The principal organizer of the ball, Rembert Donaldson, an architect, was wearing a velvet doublet with slashed sleeves, and many of the guests looked as though they had just stepped out of a gondola during Venetian Carnival. Dalt had gone as a sort of mad Mozart, in disheveled wig and brocade frock coat. A sorceror with a wispy beard said that he was in mourning for Mardi Gras. Henri had come as Pulcinella, and he was dancing to "Twist and Shout."

"Glamour is such a bitch," said a tall, thin man, who had removed his jewel-encrusted mask.

Frank Cole made a villainous entrance in his long black cape and declared, "You know what opera they're performing tonight at the Met in New York? "A *Masked Ball.* And the star is a Japanese tenor."

42

Rubbing the Magic Lamp

What Big Teeth

On Sunday night, I dressed in my all-purpose black lace dress for the Petronius ball, which was being held for the second year at the Municipal Auditorium. I walked down Saint Louis past Royal Street. A mad gospel singer who had appeared in the streets a few days ago was singing "Amazing Grace" with an astonishingly pure soprano. Suddenly I found myself amid a group of revelers in tuxedos with plumed masks. We passed the Bead Lady, wearing a crash helmet and a long black dress. She was muttering to herself, as usual. It suddenly occurred to me that the crash helmet might be for crashing parties. I walked past the doorway of the Wild Side bar, where our contingent picked up another cluster of tuxes and feathers.

As I arrived at the Auditorium, where a crowd of men in black tie had gathered at the entrance, I bumped into a man in full hockey garb, his face hidden behind a goalie's face mask. It was an effective disguise. I thought perhaps it might be the latest in S&M garb.

Several rows of tables and folding chairs had been laid out along the edges of the ballroom floor. In the center of the tables were setups of Coke and soda. Most guests brought their own liquor, and each table brought snacks. Mickey Gil's table was ringside. A row of blue-haired elderly women, mothers of the night's royalty, were seated across from two men in full drag.

The Duenna told me he had once attended the ball in full Carnival regalia, but that he had applied too much white powder, and his wig was crooked. He kept trying to straighten it, he said, and the hors d'oeuvres, which happened to be pigs in the blanket, had gone flying.

At each table was a naked Kewpie doll, to which wings and tiny fig leaves had been affixed, holding the table number.

The stage curtains were still closed while a young man named Chuck Davis came out on the floor to lead the group in "God Bless America."

Last year's king and queen, dressed as Oberon and Titania, came out for a bow to the wedding march from Lohengrin. Their entrance was no match for Mickey Gil, however, who emerged, with strobe lights glimmering, carrying a huge cup. He was wearing a gorgeous sorceror's robe of black and deep purple.

"Let me ask you one question," ventured Mickey, in his campy Schwarzenegger accent. "Do we believe in fairies?" The crowd roared and clapped its assent.

Mickey prepared to introduce Terry, his apprentice, saying, "Every sorceror has someone training to take his place. Often it's a big black bird that sits on his shoulder. This one, she's too big for that." Terry had fluttered out in a feathered black tunic, then spread out his wings and flapped about to the tune of "White Girl."

"Now, we have to show you something a little more innocent," said Mickey. "We have to find out who seduced who in the story of Little Red Riding Hood. And here she is, all the way from Buckingham Palace . . ."

Out from behind the curtain and down the steps came an ancient Red Riding Hood, with a red plastic rain cape serving as hood. It was John Dodt, powdered and rouged and bewigged in Little Orphan Annie curls, mincing awkwardly in red patent leather pumps, his large hands swathed in white gloves. He carried a red basket of goodies. Following him on a leash was the wolf, actually a young man who was part wolf, part hustler, in tight jeans and tank top, a fur boa, and a wolf mask. He was crawling suggestively but tamely behind John's wobbly red shoes. It was no wonder, I thought, that the story of Red Riding Hood had become such fodder for scholars of transvestism.

Next, following Rapunzel, the Fairy Godmother, and the Mad Hatter, was the Firebird, carried around to the tune of "Light My Fire" by four young men wearing nothing but flame codpieces. "Who is hotter, the bird or the young chicks?" Mickey asked rhetorically.

I could hardly recognize Richard Egyud, who made a dazzling

Scheherazade. The headpiece towered over him like a giant punctuation mark, and the myriad peacock eyes of the cape glowed in the spotlight.

Aladdin made his entrance hauling the violet genie. He stumbled, and the genie toppled over. "I guess he was rubbing the genie too much," cracked Mickey.

Another layer of the backdrop was pulled to reveal a magical woodland scene, dominated by a tree trunk that, on closer inspection, was quite obscene. The lights were lowered, and when the queen appeared in Jamie Greenleaf's glittering masterpiece, the butterfly wings flapping, and the chaser lights flickering, the audience gasped and applauded like mad. It was later agreed that this was the most spectacular costume anyone had ever seen at a Carnival ball.

At the end of the pageant, each fairy-tale subject was seated in a row alongside the stage, and I could see John Dodt sprawled in his chair, exhausted. He had removed his red pumps.

The spell was broken. At the stroke of midnight, the coach had turned into a pumpkin, the horses into mice, and Little Red Riding Hood into an elderly man.

43

Live the Life You Love

Tom Wood, sponsor of the Bourbon Street Awards, the costume contest on Mardi Gras day that actually took place on Burgundy Street, was fuming. Here it was, a week before Mardi Gras, and he had had to find a new emcee for the show at the last minute. We were having coffee at Poppy's Grill, a brand-new café Wood had just added to the list of French Quarter bars and restaurants operated by Wood Enterprises. Last year's emcee, he said, had proved too outrageous in his demands, so he had settled on a new candidate, known as Miss Scarlett. "These people that help me put on a show that I lose money on are turning into prima donnas and princesses," he said. Even the judges, he said, could get demanding. This year, his lawyer and his architect would be among the seven judges of the contest.

This was the twenty-eighth year of the contest, which was begun during the 1960s by Arthur P. Jacobs, a former policeman who ran the Clover Grill on Bourbon Street. Business had been declining, and costuming had gone downhill, so Jacobs decided to stage a contest. He closed the grill for the day, built a platform at the intersection of Bourbon and Dumaine, and strung up a public-address system. Café Lafitte in Exile, the gay bar across the street, joined the operation, contributing drinks and trophies. Since the contest was located in the heart of gay street life in New Orleans, the contest was embraced by gay contestants. The motto of the awards became "Live the Life You Love."

When Tom Wood bought Café Lafitte in Exile in 1974, he inherited the contest as well. The show became so popular that the crowds on Bourbon Street were overwhelming. I could recall going to the awards one year and being swept along in the crowd involuntarily, my arms pinned to my sides, and my feet lifted off the ground, for several yards. In 1986, Wood decided to shift the location of the contest to the Rawhide bar on the corner of Burgundy and Dumaine in order to ease the traffic congestion.

The Wheelchair Throne

There was quite a different kind of show planned later that afternoon at the Lafon Nursing Home on Cadillac Street, near the Saint Bernard housing project. Philip Frazier had told me about a function at Lafon, called "Mardi Gras and all that Jazz," at which ReBirth and a number of other musicians and celebrities would appear.

When I arrived at the home, a volunteer named Ted Jones, who had gussied up his tuxedo with a Mardi Gras tie and gold shoes, was welcoming visitors. Residents of the home had gathered in the recreation room, many of them in wheelchairs. Most of the residents were black Creoles, with an air of faded elegance about them. Many of the women were wearing lovely satin gowns, relics of past Carnival glories. Jones, who owned a clothing store, had decorated the room with silver instruments painted on a black backdrop. Musical notes hung from the ceiling.

The king and queen were waiting back in the wings, in the hallway near the kitchen. "The court had diarrhea and stomach cramps," said Jones. "They were so excited."

Jones explained that the royalty for the celebration was chosen "like a lottery. We do have to have people who are ambulatory. Everybody has a chance. Sometimes you have to go over and over with the same men, because we don't have that many."

The new king, George Montegut, was trying on his crown, a white felt band lined with feathers. He was a tiny man who looked lost in his wheelchair. "He's got a prostate condition," said the nurse, "so I don't know how comfortable he is."

Meanwhile, Dave Bartholomew, the celebrated trumpet player and bandleader, was leading off his combo in the rec room. Bartholomew had been doing a Mardi Gras show for Lafon ever since his elderly aunt had been placed in the home. Bartholomew, still an imposing figure at age seventy-two, had fronted the hottest dance band in the South during the 1950s, and he had led the shy young Fats Domino into the J & M Studio on Rampart Street to record "The Fat Man," the first of many hits for the duo.

Some of the more solitary residents who had been reluctant to join the festivities emerged from their rooms in wheelchairs or walkers and followed the sound of the music to the rec room, where a frail, light-skinned Creole woman, wearing a white satin dress and silver mask, was dancing in the middle of the floor. She was slapping her thigh and shaking her shoulders. Another woman wearing a red satin dress pushed her way up out of her chair, hobbled out to the floor, and joined her.

"Are y'all ready to do a little second-lining?" Bartholomew asked the group. Another woman wearing a bright pink chiffon dress got up and began to snake shakily across the floor, following Bartholomew, the pied piper, and a few more residents joined the line. Bartholomew's one-armed piano player, Ed Frank, who also played for the Preservation Hall Band, kept the beat bouncing.

Gary Mattingly, a local TV reporter who was acting as emcee, announced the presentation of the Lafon Carnival court. Last year's queen, Aline Verret, was led to the front of the room by Ted Jones. The queen, who was deaf, nevertheless smiled brilliantly as she took tiny, halting steps to the folding chair that would serve as her throne.

"For those who can stand," said Mattingly, "let's welcome our queen, Helen Wells, who will be escorted by Mr. Buford Jones of the New Orleans Saints." Helen Wells wore a white lace dress and walked gracefully, braced by the strong arm of the Saints football star. The queen, said Mattingly, had been a nurse at Lafon for thirty-six years before becoming a resident.

The king, George Montegut, was pushed into the room by the Saintsations, the cheerleaders for the New Orleans Saints dressed in scanty two-piece gold outfits. "Just think," said Mattingly: "Out of the wheelchair into the arms of the Saintsations."

As the staff poured champagne for the court, Mattingly introduced another guest dignitary. Jim Russell, king Zulu, had arrived to distribute beads to the group. Said Mattingly, "Some seventy-six years ago, Zulu started out with a garbage wagon pulled by mules. And now it's my pleasure to introduce to you the greatest king of Carnival, who has been a member of Zulu for fifty-nine years."

Russell told the group, 'I felt lonesome reminiscing about Zulu way back then till I saw Dave Bartholomew, and I realized I had company." He gave the ladies a wink. "All right, shake out the cobwebs. It's party time."

Dave Bartholomew introduced "the greatest jump band in the land," and ReBirth entered with the first notes of "Eh Làbas," which were like the call to post for a second-liner. *Bomp-bomp-bomp!* The cafeteria workers, still in their aprons and hair nets, joined in the second line.

Meanwhile, yet another performer had arrived. Kevin Austin, a young blind man who appeared even younger because of his short stature, took the microphone for a soulful version of "Georgia." Austin then launched into a rousing version of "What'd I Say," another Ray Charles classic.

An old woman in the front row slapped her thighs in glee and mouthed the words. A woman in a janitor's uniform who worked at the school across the street took the floor for a solo second-line. The late afternoon sun illumined the floor at a slant, almost like a spotlight, as she danced, lending her a shadow as a partner. I heard Gary Buford tell someone, "This is the best therapy in the world."

The ancient king was smiling, the blind boy was singing, the one-armed piano player was rocking, the janitor was dancing, the old women were jumping in their chairs, all moved by joy. A cafeteria worker told the janitor, shaking her head, "They're not going to believe this when I tell 'em about it at home."

I felt as though I had been present as a lucky bystander at the miracle of the loaves and the fishes, when a small repast for a few was multiplied to feed all who were present.

44

The Artistic Voodoo Heart

"Fragments . . . shored against my ruins." I thought often of that line from T. S. Eliot's *The Waste Land* when I was in New Orleans, and it seemed particularly appropriate as my friend Bob Tannen and I dined in a small café that had opened up in the former bar of the now-defunct Marti's restaurant. The rest of the building was boarded up, but the new café, with its appealing pastoral fresco of old New Orleans, had become a popular outpost on the ruins of Rampart Street.

Tannen had come to New Orleans from New York as a city planner, engaged to work on building a second bridge across the Mississippi from New Orleans to the West Bank. He was also an artist of considerable whimsy, whose work tended toward visual jokes and puns. One of my favorite Tannen creations featured a bust of Lyndon Johnson with a rearview mirror wired to his head. A nerve disease had begun to impair Tannen's movement, but he continued his work apace, transforming the rambling old house on Esplanade he shared with his longtime girlfriend, Jeanne Nathan, and her mother into an oddball showplace.

"I've lived in New Orleans for twenty-two years," Tannen was saying, "and I still don't understand it. You can't deal with the city in a rational way. This city functions out of and plays out a lot of unconscious behavior. It's a very Jungian place.

"An economist I know who studies the movement of cargoes says that if the food in a city is good, if the architecture is good, chances are the economy is in trouble. Cities in the world that have the great architecture are not the modern with-it places, like Hong Kong. New Orleans has inertia—it resists success."

It was that resistance to success, however, that was also its salva-

315

tion, said Tannen. "The city will survive, and it will survive the attempts to improve it. There are the conventional things like improving the tax base and the schools. But what's really going to help the city survive is its artistic voodoo heart."

We had finished our coffee and adjourned to the house on Esplanade to finish the conversation. The yard, guarded by Catahoula hounds named Baroness Pontalba and Princess Elizabeth, was filled with giant silver Monopoly houses, "archisculptures" titled *Stacked Shotgun Houses*, products of Tannen's imagination, and a very real 1955 Cadillac Spratling in fading silver.

"Every morning I hear the school kids out on the street," said Tannen, "practicing their horns on the way to school. You don't hear that in other cities. These kids are more serious about the city than their parents. They're interested in where the city came from."

And then Tannen said something astonishing. "I feel more hopeful about the city now than I did in 1972, when I first got here. We lived here like tourists—wrapped up in a romantic idea of New Orleans—the nineteenth century, the old culture. That's gone."

Most of the old French families who once inhabited the grand old houses on Esplanade had already gone. Gradually, most of the yuppies and urban pioneers who had moved to Esplanade also moved out, and black families had moved in.

"We thought when we moved here that if it changed, it was all over," said Tannen. "A lot of people thought if the city got any blacker, there would be trouble. But in some ways, the city's African heritage has more vitality than its French heritage. It's evolving in subtle ways that are not immediately recognizable. The mixture of Catholicism and Afro-Caribbean culture makes for a wild product.

"People who are bailing out of New Orleans are looking for a typical American situation. But that typical American situation may not be happening anywhere."

Tannen himself had no plans to leave. "I could stay here on Esplanade for the rest of my life," he said.

45

Unexpected Gifts

New Orleans did have a way of surprising you when you least expected it, of giving even when it seemed to be taking away. Henri called, his voice sounding considerably cheerier than it had in several weeks. "I'm in such a good mood," he said. "I got a letter today." The letter had not been delivered by the postman, however, but by children who lived in the neighborhood. The kids had clamored at the gate, shouting "Mr. Henry," then run away, leaving behind a missive. It was addressed to "Mr. Henry," and the sender had even drawn a stamp on the envelope with crayons, complete with cancellation and perforations. Henri had opened it up to find a portrait of himself, labeled "Mr. Henry."

Henri described the drawing. "I have blond hair, pink skin, blue-and-white pinstripe hot pants, and polka-dot shoes." Below the picture was a message: "Where we used to stay, white people never used to talk to us." On the back were four smiling faces of black children, labeled: Ashley, Curtis, Marlon, and me (Kurtisha). There was a postscript: "And Happy Mardi Gras too."

"I'm delirious," said Henri with obvious delight. Kurtisha and her siblings, he explained, used to live in the house next door. Once, one of the children had warned him when a would-be thief was trying to beat down his back door. The family had recently moved a few doors down, but they still stayed in touch. "I get 'em some goodies once in a while," said Henri. "I gave them a bag of cookies the other day."

Said Henri, "I've been kind of flipped out about this. It's the first feel-good thing I've had since this ordinance business began."

46

Goddesses of the Rainbow

It was the Saturday before Mardi Gras, and you'd think the sun had risen just to shine on Miss Irma's parade. The costumed legions of Iris had gathered in a ballroom in the Hilton Hotel to await word from our captain and captain emeritus to board the buses for the trip uptown to the mustering point of the parade.

Joy Oswald, dressed in an off-the-shoulder silver gown, made a dramatic entrance to the tune of "Hello, Dolly." "It's Mardi Gras, ladies," she trilled. "We always ride in the sunshine." She was joined by Miss Irma, who was wearing a white silk suit with green flames shooting up one shoulder.

Joy and Miss Irma and the Iris court would be heading for the viewing stand in front of Gallier Hall, where they would be joined by the mayor to watch the parade. The rest of us were to load up the buses and don our masks. One of my float-mates, however, had discovered that she couldn't fit into her purple pants, and I offered to exchange mine, which were far too roomy for me.

The yellow school bus was packed with my fellow purple-and-gold-clad Vieux Carré artists and a bevy of Southern belles in starchy skirts and flower-bedecked bonnets. Among them was Adelaide Wisdom Benjamin, a niece of Judge Minor Wisdom. Adelaide had ruled as queen of Carnival during the 1950s and was working now as a partner in one of the top law firms in town. Also on the bus, according to my seat-mate, were a flight attendant, a convention planner, a caterer, and a few models.

We could see a small crowd already lining up on Saint Charles, just for us. Most of them were old hands at snagging throws, and they had concocted their own portable viewing stands and bead-catchers.

We turned up Claiborne Avenue, and someone began singing the old Mardi Gras Indian anthem, "Hey Pocky Way." It was "Hey Pocky Way" past Mason's Motel, a popular black nightclub, "Hey Pocky Way" past the Crescent Gun Repair, "Hey Pocky Way" past Henry's Soul Food, "Hey Pocky Way" past the Rex den until we reached our floats at the corner of Claiborne and Napoleon.

I located Float 15, which featured an artist at work painted on the side. The artist was leering at a vampy model and painting her portrait, his oils dripping from vials that resembled pill bottles. We were to be followed in the parade by a small military band from the University of Alabama at Tuscaloosa and then by Float 16, "The Universal Language of Music," which featured a giant beer stein as a figurehead. The riders were dressed in lederhosen and alpine hats.

Finding my spot on the top tier of Float 15, I hung up my meager supply of beads on hooks, stacked my Iris cups, and prepared my plastic poodles for easy flinging. I felt like a miser compared to Mignon Faget, the jewelry designer, who was riding next to me. Mignon unloaded a treasure trove of throws, including dozens and dozens of the long strings of fake pearls so prized by the crowds.

Mignon had designed this year's Rex proclamation, as well as the king's favors, and she told me, in confidence, that Temple Brown was going to be this year's Rex.

Mignon said that her design for the Rex proclamation had been inspired by the quincentenary of the discovery of the New World by the Europeans and by a related exhibit at the Smithsonian called "Seeds of Change." The theme was cultural and botanical exchange between the two continents, and the primary images were corn, sugarcane, the potato, the horse, and disease. She might have included Carnival itself, another European legacy to the New World, which had evolved curiously in its new environment.

Behind us, a woman named Shirley, a former nursing-school dean, was unloading a cache of throws that included plastic backscratchers and giant toothbrushes. Shirley told the driver of the tractor pulling our float to slow down at the Baptist Hospital, where her friends would be lined up.

The float sergeant gave the signal, and we hooked the safety belts looped around our waists to the side of the float. The driver turned on his ignition, and we were on our way with a lurch. When we reached the corner of Saint Charles and Claiborne, the crowd, five or six deep, was standing on tiptoe with their arms reaching up prayerfully like the congregation of a charismatic church. We started flinging madly, and there was bedlam on either side of us. I spied a tall, sullen-looking young man wearing a T-shirt with a picture of Malcolm X and the slogan: BY ANY MEANS NECESSARY. I threw him an anniversary Iris cup, and he reached out for it instinctively.

Fathers had lifted kids to their shoulders, and eager bead-hunters were holding up fishing nets, basketball hoops, and fried-chicken buckets on sticks as targets.

I practiced the whimsies of a fickle deity, withholding my bounty from those who wanted it most, choosing those who least expected it.

Suddenly there was a loud thump from the front of the float. A rider named Rose, a frail older woman, had fallen, but her safety belt had kept her anchored inside the float. The float stopped, and two policemen who had been holding back the crowds rushed on board. Someone in the crowd had thrown an object at Rose, hitting her in the chest, and she had collapsed, nearly passing out. She was diabetic, she said, and someone gave her a drink of orange juice. The policemen offered to escort her from the float to the hospital, but she insisted on finishing the parade.

At the corner of Saint Charles and Constantinople, I realized half my bead supply was gone, although I still had plenty of poodles. A young man on a ladder held up a sign, IRIS IS A BABE FEST, and he was showered with goodies.

I hurled a string of purple beads at a persnickety young man, who threw them back at me, yelling, "Take this sucker back." At Lee Circle, I saw Dalt and a friend, and after taking careful aim, I hit Dalt in the head with a poodle.

The crowd got thicker and thicker as we neared Gallier Hall, and on the mayor's viewing platform, I could see Miss Irma, cheering us on. I threw her an Iris cup, and she caught it easily, like an old baseball veteran shagging a fly.

Finally, we turned the corner from Saint Charles to Canal Street, and there it was, the roaring panorama of packed humanity that has become the most famous image of Carnival. I could feel a surge of adrenaline, and I began to throw feverishly. Earlier, I had been aiming for individual faces in the crowd that struck my fancy, but now, I was hurling indiscriminately, and the crowd still wanted more. When we finally reached the Hilton Hotel, my arm was exhausted, and I could feel the phantom ache of an old softball injury.

The ride down Canal Street had been exhilarating, and I now understood why my float-mates spent more than they should on silly trinkets. In the matter of beads, it was indeed better to give than to receive. And I could also understand, I think, why the old-line parades had survived so long. It was an unexpectedly heady feeling to be able to please so many people with so little.

Mimicking Ancient Court Life

Later that day, as the crowds from Canal Street descended on the French Quarter, I ventured over to Bourbon Street, whose upper blocks, laden with strip joints and peep shows, I usually avoided. I got caught up in a group of black evangelists from the Apostolic Outreach Center, dressed in white cassocks, who were carrying a large wooden cross and passing out leaflets. The group's leader, who identified himself as the Reverend Bobby, said that he used to hang out on Bourbon Street in a different guise, smoking and drinking. The previous year, he said, the group had prayed in front of a "homosexual establishment," and it had burned down.

I passed Club Second Line, the Old Absinthe House, the Desire Oyster Bar, the Sho-Bar, and Papa Joe's Female Impersonators, which once featured strippers swinging on a trapeze bar through an open picture window onto the street. At She, Inc., an emporium of risqué goods, a tourist inquired of her group, "Anyone need to grow a pecker?" She pointed out an ad for a small sponge that inflated, when immersed in water, into a giant-sized appendage.

As I passed the Bourbon Burlesque Club, a young woman wearing a seemingly modest black top and pants appeared at the door and began to bump and grind and pull a string of beads from her crotch.

Although I was dressed in a long, drab black coat and a baseball cap, I was continually propositioned by men of all ages and of various geographical origins.

*　　*　　*

This scene reminded me that I had never enjoyed Carnival nearly as much as most of the men I knew, straight or gay. Although various theories of Carnival (particularly of Brazilian Carnival), promulgated by various academics, focus on images of feminine sensuality, the famed licentiousness and sensuality of Carnival are designed particularly for the gratification of men. Rio, wrote one anthropologist, "worships Aphrodite on the half-shell." Carnival, I reflected, is not "naturally subversive," nor is it particularly liberating, as some of its theorists have claimed.

The participation of women in Carnival as float riders rather than dancers or strippers was something of an anomaly. And it also seemed to me that for all of Miss Irma's verve, the Iris revels were disappointingly tame. Rather than following the bawdy female traditions of Scarlet Carnival, which would have risked krewe members being branded as floozies, or creating some sort of feminist rites involving goddess worship or powerful mythic female roles, Miss Irma had opted to create a ladylike imitation of male krewes.

Female bonding, in any case, doesn't usually require the sort of mumbo jumbo that men indulge in when they get together in groups. Most women just don't get the same charge as men do from bonding together in secretive clubs, wearing funny costumes, and observing arbitrary rules. Nor do women find it nearly as much fun as men to caper around wearing a mask—perhaps because men tend to hide or repress so much more of themselves on a daily basis.

I was not surprised that the penalty for discriminating against women in Carnival was finally omitted from Dorothy Mae Taylor's ordinance. When the new ordinance, with all its amendments and conditions, was finally entered into the city's legal code, the section explaining why it was legal for male krewes to continue their all-male exclusivity was a wonder of double-talk, with rationales involving dramatic license, preservationism, and that old chestnut, separate-but-equal opportunity. The council found that:

1. Carnival organizations have traditionally engaged in parades, processions, tableaux, and other activities that have, in large part, a dramatic theatrical character, involving elaborate costumed role-

playing by participants who frequently imitate or portray the behavior of ancient or medieval court life;

2. Although such traditional carnival activities most often involve participation by both women and men, the participants traditionally engage in courtly roles defined and differentiated according to the sex of the participants, as was the case in ancient and medieval court life;

3. The preservation of the traditional mimicry of court life is worthy of preservation as a significant aspect of the common cultural heritage of all the people of New Orleans;

4. Most women and men in the city who wish to find ways of participating in carnival organizations can do so . . . therefore, the Council finds that the traditional organizations, by restricting their membership to one sex, do not significantly impair the ability of women or men to make business contacts, secure professional advancement, or otherwise participate in trade, commerce, the professions, or public life in general.

47

The God of Wine

Tonight was the last rehearsal for the Wild Magnolias before Mardi Gras day, and although I planned to attend the Bacchus ball later, I didn't want to miss the scene at the H & R. I put my evening clothes in the trunk of my car and wore a less conspicuous outfit to the bar.

My friend and I arrived a little early at the H & R, and the crowd was sparse. We sat down at a table with a man named Marcel and an older couple, who were drinking glasses of Thunderbird. An entire bottle, we discovered, cost less than three dollars. Marcel, who was a Vietnam vet, knew how to sew, but he preferred to help other members of the tribe finish their costumes rather than sew for himself. "I sew the patches," he said. "I'll help anybody who's not ready."

He said the tribe used to sew tiny mirrors on the costumes "to catch the eye," but the mirrors reflected too much light and spoiled the photos.

"Some Indians use glue, but that's tacky. We have to run behind with a needle and thread. People are taking pictures, and they don't want to see you looking tacky. The chief takes the crown off at a stop. I'll check it out and see if it's looking raggedy."

Harold pointed out a new banner hanging on the back wall. It read: HEADQUARTERS OF THE MARDI GRAS INDIANS. There was a caricature of Bo Dollis standing on a carpet, holding a spear and an ax.

I asked what to expect on Mardi Gras day, and he said that Bo would come first to the H & R to get dressed and then go down the street, to the Watering Hole bar at Third and Dryades, for a toast, before setting out downtown, with the tribe following closely. "You got to get behind him, serving him up." First, however, the gang

324

would have to find out if there was another tribe out in the street that might cause friction. "That's why they have the spy boy. He's like the front man in Vietnam. But he's got to be dressed pretty too. He open up his costume to let the guys see he's prettier than them. And he show 'em wild animals on his suit that are going to attack. Like the cougar. That's something to see. That's the challenge. There's more excitement with us than Zulu, with all the challenging." Unlike Zulu, however, they would keep to the backstreets on their way downtown, he said. "They don't want us on Saint Charles Avenue. We're too rowdy.

"It's more civilized now. They used to use real hatchets. As a child, it was traumatic, a guy putting a hatchet in some guy's forehead. It was playing it out like it was real, tribe meeting tribe."

Marcel described the chants that they practiced in rehearsals. "For us, it's like natives in Africa, coming from the heart. We don't read no music. In here, you're beating like you feel, everything you have. It lets out your frustrations, beating and slapping that drum or that chair. Anything that sound comes out of—a bucket, bottle, tambourine, cowbells. It's something to identify yourself—something to show, 'I'm Marcel.'

"It gets hot in here. We're generating heat in the corner and drinking firewater—that's what we call it."

We were joined by a tall, slender man named Henry Singleton that Marcel introduced as the "bongo man." Henry's uncle was Jim Singleton, the city councilman. Henry, like Marcel, was a Vietnam vet. "I went to 'Nam in '67," said Henry, "and even then I was thinking about practicing all the time. The Wild Magnolias are my life. It's so hard to put into words—once you become a Wild Magnolia, it's part of you. All of a sudden you have a rhythm in your head. It's like a train the way it moves.

"To us, it comes natural because we came up through this tradition. Grandfather to father to son. It's like the military. You have to pay your dues. You got to work your way up. We have codes and respect and honor.

"We're very strong. The Wild Magnolias have been holding their ground for years. Bo is one of a kind, and we like to stick with our chief.

"We're going to do it tonight. My drums are ready. I put 'em in the oven to bake for a little while. I like to swell the heads."

A tour guide I recognized from the French Quarter came in, still wearing her red blazer with her official name tag, leading three young white men in T-shirts and jeans. They walked up to the bar and looked around, trying to appear insouciant.

On the large TV above the bar, there were scenes of the Bacchus parade that had just begun to roll downtown. Masked men were frantically throwing beads, left and right, from the double tiers of the huge green Bacchasaurus. I noticed that a young woman standing at the bar was actually wearing a purple Bacchus sweatshirt.

Fast Dancing in the Slow Lane

Later, when we arrived at the Convention Center for the Bacchus ball, the floats had already entered the side door of the huge arena and circled around like wagons in a wagon train, with krewe members tossing beads like crazy. The tables around the hall were laden with booty. Gerald McRaney, otherwise known as TV's Major Dad, who was reigning as Bacchus XXIV, had left his throne and was making the rounds of VIPs in the crowd in the company of his wife Delta Burke, the actress recently fired from the Southern-belle sitcom *Designing Women*.

Soul singer Irma Thomas was onstage singing an Indian song, "Iko, Iko," the same song we had heard on the jukebox at the H & R.

I thought about how black culture permeated life in New Orleans, and yet you could sit down to dinner in your Saint Charles mansion, just a block or two away from the H & R, and remain oblivious to the drums of the Mardi Gras Indians. For some upper-class New Orleanians, it was like living in a colonial culture, keeping the cricket fields green and trim while the natives were doing war dances in their villages.

For many of us, though, the music that had flowed outward from black culture had permeated our lives, threading its way through our memories.

New Orleans was one of the few places in the country with

genuine local heroes. The movie stars who came to Bacchus were so irrelevant to life in New Orleans, they might as well have come from outer space.

Bacchus, with its imported celebrities, was more attuned to mass culture, to Disneyland, than the old-line krewes. It didn't even pretend to ritual. It was just entertainment. And in fact, it was a great deal more fun than the old-line parades or balls.

Yet this was New Orleans, and there were moments of fine madness amid the glitz. I looked out on the dance floor during Irma Thomas's rendition of "Shake a Tail Feather" and saw two frail-looking elderly women, their dowager's humps apparent even in their satin finery. One was wearing a bright green dress, the other bright pink, and they were whirling madly to the music, locked together in a tight embrace, their faces set with determination. They could have been figures atop a surreal music box. They continued whirling together, faster and faster, until the music stopped.

48

Farewell to the Flesh

I woke up just before dawn on Mardi Gras day, and I could hear the action on the street already. There was a forecast for morning fog, and as I opened the French shutters of the studio, I could feel a cool breeze coming from the river. I put on my Egyptian dancing girl outfit and headed over to the Moonwalk, the boardwalk named for Moon Landrieu, opposite Jackson Square, to search for the apocryphal Krewe of Stella. I had heard about a group of college men—frat rats with a literary bent—who tried to emulate Marlon Brando's torn-T-shirt charisma as Stanley Kowalski in *A Streetcar Named Desire*. I wasn't sure the krewe actually existed, since no one I knew had ever managed to get up early enough to see them.

I intended to start the day with this fraternal homage to Tennessee Williams, then scurry down the Moonwalk to catch the departure of the boat carrying King Zulu up to Canal Street. I planned to get around the rest of the day by bicycle, since so many streets would be blocked off, and I would be able to weave my way through the crowds.

Stel-la-a-a!

When I arrived at the Moonwalk, a small crowd had already gathered. They were peering out at the river. A man wearing a feathered headdress and ill-fitting tuxedo suddenly yelled and pointed upriver at an object bobbing along on the current. "There they are!" It was a small rowboat painted green and purple, with a tattered banner attached to a stick, slowly heading toward the bank. The name *Stella* was painted crudely on the stern. There were two people aboard, along with a big yellow beer keg. As the boat washed ashore, a young man wearing a sheer white nightgown disembarked first, followed by a young man wearing an admiral's jacket, plumed hat, and plaid Bermuda shorts. He was bare-chested underneath the jacket. The two men hauled the boat out of the water, revealing its amphibious equipment. There were wheels attached to the boat, and on land, it became a keg-hauling minifloat.

The young man in the admiral's hat threw out his chest and squinched up his face, Brando style, yelling, in glorious agony, "Stel-la-a-a!"

A young man wearing a headband over his long hair teetered a bit on his feet as he watched. "He's living it," said the young man in an awed tone. "He's living the dream."

The crowd started moving across Decatur Street to Jackson Square, two of them dragging the boat, and by the time they reached the Pontalba building, they were running, all of them yelling, "Stel-la-a-a," dozens of Brandos searching for solace, a horde of the lusty vulgarians Williams had envisioned as both the last hope and the destroyers of a refined and inbred culture. It was the end of Belle Reve and the debased dreams of Blanche DuBois and the last gasp of method acting.

As spectators rushed out to their balconies, the running Brandos turned the corner and headed up Chartres Street, still yelling, on their way to Saint Peter Street, where Tennessee Williams had lived for a time. Since the real streetcar named Desire was now an outdoor exhibit near the French Market, they would have to find a less symbolic means of transportation home.

I stopped by the Café du Monde to grab a cup of coffee and a bag of beignets, and as I glanced through the takeout window into the kitchen, I noticed that the flour for the beignets came in big sacks marked BIG CHIEF H & R FLOUR, and I considered that the influence of Bo Dollis might reach further downtown than I thought.

I walked down to the Toulouse Street dock where the SS *John James Audubon*, a small paddle-wheel riverboat, was anchored, adjacent to a barge laden with RVs with license plates from Ohio. I had to dodge a group of male joggers wearing red shorts and feathered masks who zipped by in runners' oblivion. The *Audubon* ordinarily cruises the Mississippi several times a day, churning up to the Audubon zoo and back, but this morning, it had been chartered to take King Zulu and his followers up to their floats at the Canal Street pier.

There were a number of families waiting on the dock. The children resembled bumblebees, zipping around in their black-and-gold Zulu T-shirts. Even though King Zulu and his entourage had not yet arrived, we were allowed to board. With excited anticipation, we gathered on the top deck, where a breakfast buffet was being served.

An older woman wearing a beautiful African-style beadwork hat said that her mother used to ride the Zulu boat on the morning of Carnival in the days when it was a barge coming down the old canal, and she would have to wrap up in blankets to keep warm.

A fleet of white limos arrived at the dock, carrying the Zulu royalty and attendants. It was hard to recognize the men in their blackface makeup. They looked as though they had been hired to play the natives in an old Marx Brothers movie about Africa. Nick Harris, the club's public-relations director, was wearing a grass skirt and a white-and-turquoise tunic. Neither Joe Falls nor the club president, however, who were dressed in black tie and tails, was wearing blackface.

Behind the limos was a busload of men wearing black bodysuits and leopard-skin tunics. They clambered out, carrying spears and shields adorned with a big Z. These were the "Soulful Warriors," the king's personal guards. They lined up in two rows and crossed their spears to create an archway. The queen emerged from a limo and proceeded under the spears, followed by Jim Russell, who looked dignified and conspicuous in royal purple robes.

Russell proceeded into the wheelhouse to hold court. He sat next to the ship's wheel, ready to pose for pictures with the families already lining up.

Before the boat left the dock, I ran down the plank. Unlocking my bicycle, I sped down Poydras Street toward the junction of Earhart Boulevard and South Claiborne, which formed a kind of lost square beneath the Interstate. It was here that the Zulu parade was to line up. I was peddling so fast, I actually passed the Zulu floats, which had been loaded up with riders at the Hilton. The float riders, already dancing and waving beads at curious onlookers, were clearly feeling no pain. One of them was holding up a sign, HONK IF YOU WANT TO SEE ME RIDE IN REX NEXT YEAR! On one of the floats, the riders were unfurling a long banner that declared COMUS AND MOMUS QUIT, BUT WE'RE TOO LEGIT TO QUIT!

Milling around at various junctures along Claiborne Avenue were the marching clubs, school bands, and equestrian clubs that would squeeze into the parade between floats. The powerhouse high school bands, Saint Aug, McDonough 35, and JFK, had unloaded from buses.

The Saint Aug drum major was striding around, getting things in order, his hair circled by a sweat band, which would steady his tall plumed hat. You could tell the tuba and the bass drum players from the rest of the musicians by their sturdy physiques. They were putting on their purple-plumed gold helmets, which resembled the headgear worn by jousting knights in royal tournaments.

Ronald Castenell, wearing a sweatshirt that identified him as band chaperon and vice president of the band booster club, said the band members were in good shape. Their drills, which began two weeks before parade season, had gradually been increasing, and on Sunday, they had managed two parades on the same day. He had advised them to eat a healthy breakfast this morning, he said.

I spotted band leader Edwin Hampton, wearing a purple T-shirt and dark pants. He looked vigorous and athletic, despite a generous waistline and a distinguished gray beard. He planned to walk with the band, he said, all the way downtown to the Municipal Auditorium. "We'll pace ourselves," he said. "It'll be hot." The band had memorized a repertory of thirty-five songs that they would play in sets. "We'll get a little bit more roxy today than we would for Rex," he said. "All the parades have different timbres. Today, anything goes. We'll do a little bit more Mardi Gras music today. We'll play Top 20, some Earth, Wind and Fire. Second-line tunes go well in a thing like this."

The JFK band was warming up with a fanfare down the street, and I spotted Philip Frazier and the other ReBirth musicians waiting on the pavement under the expressway columns. Philip was carrying a shiny new tuba, just a week old. They played on a float last year, said Philip, but this year, they'd have to march the whole way.

Saint Aug had lined up next to the corrugated-tin headquarters of IMI—Industrial Machines, Inc. After a few moments of scattered tuning, the Purple Knights started warming up, and everyone for blocks around paid attention. It was like hearing a slumbering giant wake up and roar. The drums laid down a mesmerizing beat, a solid foundation you could build a house on. Then came the trumpet players, who flipped their instruments up smartly, followed by the trombone players. They progressed slowly up and down the scale. A Zulu hotshot came along, smoking a big cigar, to listen and nod approvingly. The single-note scale spread into a series of chords, up and down, major to minor. The volume had been steadily increasing, and I was getting goose bumps. Now the band was a jumbo jet revving up its motors before taking off.

Almost imperceptibly, the tubas segued into the dramatic opening chord from Strauss's "Thus Spake Zarathustra." With each successive chord, another section of instruments joined in. The cumulative power was so great, you could understand how Joshua and his trumpet blew down the walls of Jericho.

They were magnificent, these unlikely knights in purple and gold, and as they stepped out, brandishing their instruments, I felt as though they were marching out to battle. They were setting out on a crusade to conquer despair and indifference, to redeem the city with music, the only weapon at hand.

The Zulu float maker was the firm of M. J. Cantrell and Son, the same outfit that made the floats for the Iris parade, and the floats looked familiar, with a single large figure in front and various figures and scenes painted on the side. The king's float, with two leopards on the prow, was first in line, although it was currently occupied by a stand-in, sitting on the throne beneath a white cupola, holding up the king's enormous headdress, waiting for Jim Russell to arrive.

Two krewe members wearing zebra-striped pajamas strolled by. They were both in blackface, but as I looked closer, I realized one was white, and the other black. From a distance, they could have been brothers.

Finally, at 9:10 A.M., Jim Russell and the driver of the king's float were rounded up, and the parade began. The JFK school band, dressed in royal blue, set out first. The Zulu officers stood at attention by the king's float, waiting for Jim Russell to climb aboard. Then came McDonough 35, the pride of Esplanade Avenue, in forest green, the pom-pom girls wearing gold tiaras. As they passed by, Kermit Ruffins raised his trumpet and played along with them. Philip blared his tuba under the underpass, the *oompahs* echoing. The Zulu maids hung on to their headdresses as their float moved out with a jolt. A wagon pulled by the Coors Belgians was followed by a small pooper-scooper wagon. Then came the Algiers Brass Band and the Gold Trumpets Social and Pleasure Club in bright blue.

The O'Jays rode their own float, followed by Mr. Big Shot, Harold Gross, who was wearing a huge homburg hat. The character of the big shot had been created in the 1930s as a rival to the king. He was said to represent the wealth of Africa. His followers were wearing pink satin outfits and cards stuck in hatbands. Poker chips had been painted on the side of the float.

Next came the witch doctor, with a big skull grinning on the front of the float. Lionel Daggs was wearing a headpiece with bullhorns poking out from either side and brandishing a big bone. He waved when he saw me. The float riders, who included a number of women, were wearing bones in their hair and leopard-skin tunics.

An equestrian group dressed in blue suits folded in between the witch doctor and the Zulu ambassador, whose followers were wearing clown suits.

A number of the floats had actually been recycled from the Iris parade, with just a slight change here and there, which usually meant painting the figurehead brown. The mayor's float featured a de-mented-looking black leprechaun on the front, and the riders were Irishmen in blackface, with shamrocks on their costumes and hats topped with pots of gold.

The blackface riders gave a sort of surreal twist to the float themes, so that almost everything appeared to be a double parody. The figurehead on the province prince's float, a butterfly with a woman's face, had blond hair, but her face had been painted brown. The snake-charmer's float had a Santa Claus on the front, with rein-deer painted on the side. I particularly enjoyed the float loaded with black hillbillies in straw hats.

I was startled to see that Float 11, the civil judge's float, was the same float I had ridden during the Iris parade. The big artist in front had been painted brown, but otherwise the float was the same. The costumes were similar, too, with gold berets and smocks.

Darwin on Saint Charles Avenue

By now, the Rex parade was on its way out of the den, and I peddled up Claiborne Avenue as fast as I could. The parade lieutenants were circling on their horses on the neutral ground across from the den as the floats emerged from the den, to be hitched up to their tractors. Blaine Kern was out in the middle of the street with a bullhorn, directing traffic. "Have a good ride," he told each float team. Float 13, dedicated to Charles Darwin, was the next to emerge from the den. Behind the giant figure of Darwin was a big ape, holding a skull.

The king's float was already well on its way down Jackson Avenue toward Saint Charles Avenue. Temple Brown had risen at five-thirty and had a bowl of cereal with the security guard assigned to every Rex. He had gone out shortly after dawn to launch a road race before coming to the den, where he was toasted in his dressing room by a contingent of former Rexes dressed in morning coats. "Hail, Rex!" He had donned his fake beard and crown and mounted the throne, where he was strapped in. He had turned down the advice of some krewe members to wear a bulletproof vest. "Black people are not assassins," he said later. "Why would anyone shoot you if you're doing something good?"

As the Rex float reached Saint Charles, Temple Brown looked over on his left and waved at a group of children from the Special Olympics. He turned to his right and was startled to see a broken-down Zulu float. It was Float 19, the emperor's float, whose theme was "Fiesta Mexico," and it was filled with sombrero-wearing caballeros in blackface, one of whom yelled up at Rex, "Hey, how about a ride?" Rex replied, "Sure, just don't step on the mantle," then said, "That'll wow them at City Hall."

Rex didn't realize that the Zulu float captain, Owens Haynes, was a fellow monarch; he had ruled as King Zulu in 1989. Later, as the truck floats following the Rex parade passed the disabled float, they showered the Zulu riders with beads and cold drinks and even pieces of fried chicken.

Meanwhile, the front of the Zulu parade had stalled on Saint Charles, near Moon Landrieu's viewing stand, and the JFK band was standing at attention. As time passed, the crowd began to get impatient. People were shouting, "Play!" The band had just marched more than two miles in the sun, in their hot uniforms. Almost imperceptibly at first, the drum major began to dance in response to the chants. The crowd continued to chant and clap, and the musicians began to improvise, and the young man's dance got wilder and wilder. It was as though he were dancing the wild bamboula, possessed by spirits called up from old Congo Square, except that this was his own dance, distilled from a multitude of sources and influences into this brief command performance.

Big Chief at the H & R

I was running late, and I peddled back uptown, passing a plump young man scampering down Dryades Street wearing only a large diaper and carrying a balloon. I arrived at the H & R bar, to find a few second-liners waiting outside for Bo Dollis's arrival. Inside the H & R, the separate pieces of Bo's outfit were set out on a table like a buffet beneath the new Wild Magnolias banner. The basic color was a Day-Glo chartreuse, so bright the costume seemed to vibrate. The crown was adorned with large pink diamond-shaped rhinestones. There was a beaded buffalo dancer with bright red skin on the patch adorning the apron, and another patch with an Indian on a white horse on the inside layer of one of the "wings" that would hang down from Bo's arms.

There was a sudden influx of second-liners into the bar, preceding Bo, who strode inside, wearing a basic body suit of chartreuse, a shirt and pants, and beaded chartreuse moccasins. He pulled the apron from the table and placed it around his waist experimentally. He looked in the mirror on the side of the bar and yelled approvingly, "Yeah!"

He tried on a pair of beaded chartreuse gloves, and then placed a beaded band, with long braids attached at the sides, over his hair. He tried on the crown, but it was a bit loose, and someone brought out a staple gun to fix it. Bo's young son, Lil Bo, wearing a chartreuse shirt, brought in more pieces of the costume and placed them on the table. Two little boys were dancing with lances, while a third played the tambourine.

Bo's Spy Boy Alfred Womble opened his arms like bright yellow wings to reveal beaded scenes of Indians hunting buffalo. On the outside panels were fierce-looking cougars.

Bo was now slipping on his chest piece, with a geometric diamond design, and a ruffled vest with a patch showing a cougar attacking an Indian mounted on a horse. Marcel had arrived, and helped Bo with his arm patches. He said he had helped Bo finish three of the new patches. More men came in, shouting in awe, "Big Chief!" Almost instantly, the bar was packed, and everyone raised their arms in tribute. "Big Chief!" Someone brought in Bo's feathered staff, and Bo began dancing with his Spy Boy. "Hey pocky way!"

Bo went to the door to look out. The street outside was jammed with admirers. He came back inside and began to sing, "Big Chief got plenty of firewater," the traditional song that served as a request along the march for free drinks.

Bo and his Spy Boy ventured out into the light of day in all their splendor. Bo's crown began to slip, however, and he checked himself out in the side mirror of an old Cadillac on the street and grimaced. "Bo knows aggravation," said a wiseass observer. Bo looked fierce, and he had already accepted a number of tributes of firewater. "Let's go get 'em," chanted the second-liners, who were ready to go. And they were off, the Spy Boy leading the way.

Bo's second chief, Thomas Landry, had just emerged from his house on Simon Bolivar Street, and he would meet Bo on the corner. Chief Landry was dressed in a suit of brilliant burnt orange.

I left the entourage reluctantly and rode downtown, passing by the Young Warriors, a tribe headed uptown. I hoped for their sake that they didn't intend to tangle with Bo and his gang.

Upstaging Rex

Meanwhile, King Zulu was on his way down Canal Street, and Rex was being toasted at Gallier Hall by the mayor. There were some observers who said that the mayor's toast to Zulu was more exuberant than his salute to Rex. The mayor had hailed Zulu as a "true leader," an epithet he had omitted from his toast to Rex. Rex himself had been somewhat subdued, though properly respectful, in his own salute to the mayor. Temple Brown said later, "I didn't want to be glowing in praise for leadership that had not been evident. I had no intention of being hypocritical and saying something totally flowery that I didn't mean."

I parked my bicycle and ventured into the Quarter, heading for the Bourbon Street awards pageant. On my way down Burgundy Street, I saw a set of walking crayons in various hues. The sidewalk was crowded with urbane cowboys and Indians, who looked ordinary from the front, but who seemed to have forgotten the back halves of their costumes. One wrangler was wearing his chaps without much of anything underneath.

There was a jostling mob surrounding the stage set up in front of the Rawhide bar, but it was possible to get in close with a certain persistence and a tolerance for exotic aftershaves. Emcee Miss Scarlett had just finished introducing the judges, who included police captain George Bourgeois, head of the precinct that encompassed the French Quarter. There were six categories in the contest—Male, Tits, Group, Leather, Fantasy, and Female. For a number of the contestants, who overlapped various boundaries, deciding which category to enter was almost as difficult as putting together a costume. The judges would hold up numbers for each contestant, from one to five, indicating their approval rating, and someone would collate the scores.

Murderous cannibal Jeffrey Dahmer turned out to be a favorite subject for parody. Already onstage was a man pretending to be Dahmer, dragging a victim by a pair of handcuffs. The victim's body was outlined in black, with edible parts labeled, like a beef chart: liver, sirloin, chops.

The next contestant was a fireman/flasher. "Show us your hose," said Miss Scarlett, suggestively.

The next contestant was a drag queen in a red rhinestone-trimmed dress and red boa. The crowd was not merely under-whelmed, but hostile. "A walking cliché!" shouted one observer. The judges didn't even bother to hold up numbers.

Things began to pick up with the "group" category entries, many of which involved elaborate pantomimes. In one scenario, a tubby man in a leather-bar outfit ran across the stage, chased by a group of men wearing police uniforms, some from the California Highway Patrol, others from the city of Atlanta mounted police. The fake highway patrolmen handcuffed the leather fugitive and pretended to beat him senseless with clubs.

Next, the Maids of Comus arrived to clean the stage. Wearing kerchiefs over fright wigs, they pulled on rubber Playtex gloves and got busy, spraying air freshener all over the place, dusting the rails, and tossing clothespins into the crowd. They got fives from most of the judges.

The next notable group was Phone Sex. They wore large pay telephones made of cardboard fitted over their torsos, with holes for arms and legs. The phones were embellished with cone-shaped paper breasts and fake penises spilling out of the coin-return slot.

The next group, the Slut Machines, had a similar idea. They wore cardboard slot machines, but when they pulled their levers, tiny pictures of blond bimbos spun around instead of the standard slot-machine fruit symbols.

A Vanna White impersonator was next, pulling her own *Wheel of Fortune* minifloat. The wheel, however, was labeled with various categories of sex and abstinence, including "Your turn," "My turn," and "PMS."

Comic relief came in the form of a circus fat lady—in drag, of course—carrying an enormous can of Diet Coke. "She's wearing maximum-strength panty hose," said Scarlett.

The next group theme was "Pretty Babies," with seven elderly men dressed in green diapers and bonnets and carrying huge baby bottles. They had brought along what appeared to be large high chairs, and after sitting in them briefly, they stood up, turned away, and mooned the crowd. One of the elderly babies, I suddenly realized, was John Dodt.

The geriatric babies were soon upstaged by Barbara Bush and the Washington Redskinettes. A Barbara Bush impersonator laden with pearls came out simpering, along with a group of cheerleaders in drag doing a Rockettes number. The enthusiastic judges gave them all fives.

There hadn't been much beefcake, so far, except for a good-looking cowboy named Tex who did some suggestive things with a lariat. The drought was soon ended by a young man who carried out the theme of "Fried Green Tomatoes" by wearing nothing but a frying pan lined with tomato slices over his crotch and carrying a bottle of ketchup. Some wondered how he kept the tomatoes in the frying pan, while others wondered how he kept the frying pan anchored in its strategic spot.

As the show wound down, it was time to announce the prizes. The Maids of Comus won the best of show, while the Washington Redskinettes won the prize for the best group. Vanna White was the best "female" entrant, with a Bead Lady impersonator coming in a close second. Tex was the best "male," followed by Mr. Fried Green Tomatoes. Ebony Ross, a black female impersonator, won the fantasy category for his Diana Ross impression.

The Bourbon Street contestants strolled through the Quarter, outclassing most of the other costumes, although there were a few good ones, including a Marge Simpson impersonator, wearing a blue wig several feet tall. There was a whole family wearing large papier-mâché breasts outside their clothing—mom, dad, and eight-year-old son.

A group of Texans had come as waiters and waitresses for the Road Kill Café. On a tray, a waitress carried appetizers of Possum pâté and Nutria nachos. One waiter carried a sign, CROSS THE LINE TO THE WILD SIDE. TRY ONE STILL IN THE HIDE.

Still more grisly was another Jeffrey Dahmer impersonator who was pushing a deli cart offering human delicacies. On one end, a baby doll was simmering on a grill. Handpainted signs advertised such offerings as kidney pies and fried fingers.

On Royal Street, a marching group appeared called the Ducks of Dixieland, acting out their theme of "People Who Forgot to Duck." All were dressed as duck-billed versions of historical characters who had either been assassinated, executed, or murdered. As they walked beneath a balcony on Bourbon Street, they looked up to see Governor Edwin Edwards tossing beads gleefully from a balcony, accepting the adulation of the crowd. The fickle crowd soon moved farther down the street, however, when a woman leaning over a balcony railing removed her top.

Rex's Palace

Later, on our way to the Rex ball at the Municipal Auditorium, my companion and I walked down Saint Louis Street, stepping over garbage bags lining the streets. The gutters were full of plastic go-cups. We passed a young man sprawled in a doorway who was using a trash bag for a pillow. There was a small fracas near Bourbon Street, as police searched the pockets of a young black man. We walked past the open doorway of a bar on Rampart Street. We could see two naked white men dancing on tables inside.

Lafcadio Hearn had written differently about an early evening on Mardi Gras day, when the idea of attending a Rex ball was like a fantasy come true: "And the glorious Night is approaching—the quaint, old-time night, star-jeweled, fantastically robed; and the blue river is bearing us fleets of white boats thronged with strangers who doubtless are dreaming of lights and music, the tepid, perfumed air of Rex's Palace, and the motley rout of merry ghosts, droll goblines, and sweet fairies, who will dance the dance of the Carnival until blue day puts out at once the trembling tapers of the stars and the lights of the great ball."

We took our seats in the large side of the auditorium beside a black couple who seemed rather ill at ease.

Gold velvet drapes opened onstage to reveal the royal setting. Water fountains surrounded by yellow mums had been placed on either side of the long garden bench that was to serve as a throne. Suspended above the throne was a large hand-carved golden crown, symbol of Rex.

Everyone in the audience stood at the arrival of the Fourth Marine Aircraft Wing Band, which played the national anthem and then the "Marine Corps Hymn," followed by a medley that included "Shenandoah." Vice Admiral John H. Fetterman, Jr., U.S. Navy, chief of naval education training, and other military guests stood to be acknowledged.

Following the departure of the band, the captain of Rex, dressed in a tuxedo, sounded a whistle, and the orchestra began a drum roll, as Rex lieutenants, costumed like stage courtiers in purple, gold, and green velvet, strode into the room, followed by buglers who announced the arrival of the Rex court.

Elizabeth Kelleher, Queen of Carnival, looked properly regal in a dropped-waistline gown of metallic gold lace over silk organza. The traditional Medici collar, anchored invisibly by a shoulder harness, framed her face and upswept blond hair.

Even though he was wearing a fake mustache and beard rather than a mask, I would never have recognized Temple Brown as Rex in his blond pageboy wig and bejeweled gold tunic, white leggings, and gold boots.

Following the introduction of the debutantes, there was general dancing. It was a remarkably sedate scene, and the black couple next to us was having a difficult time keeping their eyes open. We adjourned to the Comus ballroom next door, where the ceremony was just getting under way.

Return of the Cowbellions

In lieu of their parade, which would have taken up most of the early evening, the Krewe of Comus had decided to hold a dinner at the Red Room, also known as the Annex, of Antoine's restaurant on Saint Louis Street. Returning to their Cowbellion roots, they had brought along rakes and cowbells, a milk bucket, and even a papier-mâché cow. "The room echoed with the ringing of cowbells and tomfoolery," one observer said later.

Following their celebratory dinner, the men had walked over to the Auditorium, tossing doubloons to bystanders along the way and ringing their cowbells.

They had not relinquished the bells even after changing into their costumes. When we entered the Auditorium, the krewe was gathered at the left side of the room, wearing the cowbells around their necks. They were an eerie sight, dressed in bright satin costumes that resembled pajamas and funny hats with plumes. Their full-face masks looked like death masks, pale and expressionless.

After the royal procession introducing the masked king and his queen, Rosemary McIlhenny, an heiress to the Tabasco fortune, the krewe members capered onto the dance floor, wildly ringing their bells and ululating like Hollywood Indians. The king was an elderly man in his seventies, as revealed by his spindly legs, although the Comus mask, with its insipid frozen smile, revealed little about his identity.

We returned to the Rex ballroom to find that much of the audience had drifted away. Some had joined the Comus crowd, as we had, and some had left for the evening.

At 10:50 P.M., as tradition required, the masked captain of Comus, dressed in white satin, accompanied by his lieutenants, arrived to present Rex with an invitation to visit Comus. Rex and his queen disappeared and reemerged in the Comus ballroom, where they made their way in a royal procession to the stage, where Comus was holding his silver cup. Comus offered his magic cup to Rex, while the other three monarchs waved their scepters. The monarchs then circled the auditorium in a final farewell, and the evening was over.

On our way back to the studio, the crowds had thinned out into a few stumbling individuals or laughing knots of revelers. We passed the Rawhide, to find that all the fantasy and frills had vanished, leaving only a minimal leather scene. Farther down the street, at about the stroke of midnight, a man wearing a pair of bright red frilly panties that could be clearly seen through a gauzy dress, stopped to remove the panties, only to reveal a pair of plain BVDs underneath. The magic spell had been broken.

EPILOGUE

Ash Wednesday and After

On the morning of Ash Wednesday, which began the forty-day season of Lent, the streets had been swept, but the gutters were still full of garbage. The Duenna stumbled over an abandoned Slut Machine as he crossed Elysian Fields on his way home. At Jackson Square, the outside walls of Saint Louis Cathedral were still reeking with the urine of incontinent revelers. The bells of the cathedral, as Blanche DuBois had once declared, were "the only clean thing in the Quarter."

Inside the cathedral, the pews were filled with penitents who were there to receive the symbolic smear of ashes on their foreheads. Hardly anyone was contrite enough, however, to vow that they would never again indulge in Carnival. It was a ritual, after all, destined to be repeated again and again.

Carnival, said a friend, is lust to lust, ashes to ashes. On Mardi Gras day, Henri and Paul had carried even more bags of ashes than usual to the river, where the remains of their friends, mixed with bright confetti, were scattered with prayers and remembrance. This ritual, too, would undoubtedly be repeated again and again. The words of a poster on the wall of Josephine's studio, advertising one of her shows, were taken from the poet Rilke: "So we live here forever taking leave."

Kurtisha, Henri's young black friend, had left another note at his gate. He had been so touched by her Mardi Gras greeting that he had bought her a set of colored pencils, and she had sent her thanks on a piece of folded notebook paper. On the front of the paper was the carefully printed statement: "An unfinished picture is an incomplete sorrow." He opened it and found a face, looking sadly out into a void.

*   *   *

A few evenings after Mardi Gras, I was typing away in the studio on Saint Louis, when I heard a band coming down Chartres Street. I knew immediately it was the Purple Knights of Saint Aug. I ran out to the balcony, and I could see the glint of the streetlights flashing off the brass instruments. I could see marchers fanning out and contracting through the streets, like a river moving within its banks. They turned left down Saint Louis, and I ran out on the street to follow them, as they turned up Royal Street. The color guard were bringing up their knees so smartly, the cymbal players dipping and bobbing, their heads down, while the trumpets and trombones were swinging left and right.

They began playing a song that sounded familiar, and I realized it was "Tears from Heaven," the poignant song Eric Clapton wrote about the death of his young son. People began running out of doorways along Royal to watch. I recognized a dignitary from Young Men Illinois coming out of Mr. B's restaurant. As the band moved onto Canal Street, a group of young black kids who were standing in their path, just hanging out, were pulled along in their wake, turning into a spontaneous second line, mingling with the tourists and conventioneers who were parading along with self-conscious funkiness.

The bittersweet comic joy of the scene reminded me of the drum major who had started dancing when the Zulu parade stalled in front of Gallier Hall on Mardi Gras day. Bob Tannen, who had been sitting there in the viewing stand, later described that moment in wonder. "This was a perfect model of what can happen in this city under the present demography," he said. "All this talk about kids being undisciplined—here they were, wiped out, and yet in response to the crowd, they were able to come up with a very creative, avant-garde response. They started out very disciplined socially, standing at attention, and then they broke out musically into something original and powerful—and generous."

Such moments, said Tannen, verified his faith in New Orleans. "These kids are a clue to the future. The fact that we can have so many kids in a school system that's otherwise falling apart who can play an instrument so well—they're not gone. They're not a disposable generation, a lost generation. If you touch the right nerve, you find a lot going on to give you hope.''

There had been many such moments during the time I spent in New Orleans. There were many such scenes in which New Orleanians seemed to be saying, as Edgar Chase put it, ''Nothing you can do will defeat my spirit.''

I thought about how many times, during the years I had spent in New Orleans, this irresistible force had taken over the streets, this current of pure celebration sweeping along everything in its path.

This was the spirit of the second line, a tradition that had arisen from the black community, but which had come to include all who wanted to join in. I had found such parades, which often took place in the context of funerals or other solemn occasions, to be a kind of sacrament peculiar to New Orleans, celebrating the full cycle of human life, affirming the sacred worth of each and every soul.

These were communal experiences, something like what went on inside church, but without an authority figure or external order or structure. Music and dancing in the face of death and sorrow broke down barriers of reserve and isolation and created a kind of transcendence that I found hard to define.

It was one of my students at Tulane who had taught me the most memorable lesson about the power of the second line and about the inexplicable joy that attends even the saddest of jazz funerals.

Dorris Bagur, a retired social worker in her fifties, had been the star of the fall writing workshop I taught in a continuing education program. She disappeared in early October, however, and returned a month later with a new batch of poems. She had written them in New England, where she had gone to see the autumn leaves. And to learn how to die. Dorris had been diagnosed with inoperable cancer, she confided, and she was determined to go out in a burst of glory. With their last, glorious blaze of color before winter, the trees, she said, were throwing themselves a jazz funeral.

Dorris knew what all poets of autumn know—that the images of incipient decay and death can be as compelling as those of first bloom, and that there can be joy even amid loss.

Dorris died a few months later, and as she had requested, her family and friends attended a jazz funeral in her honor, like the ones that had sent the great musicians of Bourbon Street to their rest. That day, the Olympic Brass Band led the second line, and the music and dancing were so infectious that strangers swelled our numbers.

Such moments, I think, are akin to the state of being that anthropologist Victor Turner once called *communitas*. This form of spontaneous community, as Turner described it, creates bonds between people that are "undifferentiated, egalitarian, direct, extant, nonrational, existential, I-Thou, spontaneous, immediate, concrete." *Communitas*, he said, "is not shaped by norms, it is not institutionalized, it is not abstract." It differs from the camaraderie found in everyday life because it "tends to ignore, reverse, cut across, or occur outside of structural relationships."

The second line defies—or deconstructs—the strict lines of the military marching band, just as it cuts through the boundaries between life and death, joy and sorrow, friend and stranger.

If structure—or all the things that hold people apart, define their differences, and constrain their actions—is one pole in a charged field, the opposite is *communitas*, which, as Turner explained, "represents the desire for a total, unmediated relationship between person and person, a relationship which nevertheless does not submerge one in the other but safeguards their uniqueness in the very act of realizing their commonness."

When Carnival partakes of the spirit of the second line—of *communitas*—rather than following the constraints of class or racial boundaries, it, too, becomes inclusive rather than exclusive.

Carnival krewes, however, like most clubs, tend toward exclusiveness. The true principle of New Orleans Carnival, I discovered, is not subversion, as some scholars have suggested, but affirmation. There are no real surprises behind the mask. For Comus, that affirmation has meant exclusion of others in order to celebrate their rapidly declining hold on the city of their ancestors. For Petronius, it has meant drawing the line at hustlers and dwarfs, in order to keep up certain standards. For the Mardi Gras Indians, it has meant holding their ground, like giant birds, by means of voice and signals and a display of feathers. For Iris, it has meant remaining resolutely feminine in order to hold on to a small corner of Carnival.

It is in the entire array of Carnival that the real inclusiveness lies: the span from rich to poor, the spectrum of skin colors and sexual identities, the panorama of jostling differences from uptown to downtown.

The healing power that Walker Percy and Tennessee Williams and so many others have perceived in New Orleans lies in the unwillingness of so many of its citizens to observe the usual boundaries. It lies in a reluctance to settle for either/or, to choose black or white, to label gay or straight, to separate reality from dreams.

I thought about all of those I have known in New Orleans who have tried to live in the realm of magic and celebration. It was like a kaleidoscope, a parade of memories and impressions: Henri and Paul, who love Carnival so much they have wept at its finale; Dooky Chase, so nattily dressed, dropping everything to follow the music in the street; the young black men dancing in the cemeteries; Duncan Strachan shooting off his musket at the Half Moon Bar; George Schmidt and his Storyville dreams; Henry Singleton warming his bongo drums in the oven; the school janitor second-lining in the rec room of the Lafon Nursing Home; the Mardi Gras Indians pouring their offerings of Mad Dog and Budweiser over Chief Joe Adams's golden crown.

No city has ever been loved more passionately or celebrated by such a strange assortment of people—white Creoles, black Creoles, descendants of slaves, descendants of plantation owners, playwrights, transvestites, novelists, Carnival captains, chefs, piano professors, dance teachers, bankers, lawyers, black Indian chiefs. Many of the celebrants have come to realize that it is the whole gumbo of the place that they love, not just their own "bouillon cubes of social distillation," as George Schmidt put it. It is those who love New Orleans most dearly who have experienced the greatest despair but who have found the most hope for its future.

Carnival, despite the Carnival wars, has carried on, although in 1993, three old-line krewes declined to parade: Comus, Proteus, and

Momus. It was sad to think of those beautiful Comus floats stuck in their den, immobile, like Blaine Kern's Wonder Wall, still unfinished in their metamorphoses, frozen forever in incomplete transition: Glaucus forever swimming toward his love, Merlin forever locked in enchantment stronger than his own, Arachne trapped in her web. The butterfly of winter lay still in its cocoon. Comus was locked in the past, immobilized by fear.

As Victor Turner once observed, rites, as well as communities, must be dynamic and fluid in order to last. To become static, or rigid, impervious to change, is to risk obsolescence or overthrow. Who, then, would break the spell and bring Comus back to life again? An unfinished parade is an incomplete sorrow.

Many wounds remained unhealed, and New Orleans, too, was still incomplete in its metamorphosis. There were still other battles to succeed the Carnival wars and still other bubbles to distract citizens from the problems of living in a declining city.

Fresh from its assault on Carnival, the City Council took on the elite men's clubs that had so far remained immune from change. New Orleans seemed embarked on a series of symbolic skirmishes. Liberty Monument, which commemorated the 1874 uprising by the White League, again came under fire. Restored briefly to an inconspicuous spot near the French Quarter, it was moved yet again, this time banished forever from the streets of New Orleans by the City Council. Attorney Henry Julien, who had been so influential in the Carnival wars, had also led the fight against the monument. Uptown New Orleanians, whose ancestors had fought in the uprising, remained detached from the battle this time, leaving the defense of the monument to the defanged followers of David Duke, most of whom had fled Orleans Parish for the safer environs of Jefferson Parish.

A new inscription at the base of the monument, intended to defuse its racially charged symbolism, could serve as a motto for the Carnival wars as well: "A conflict of the past that should teach us lessons for the future."

After a mysterious vote by the state legislature to establish a casino in New Orleans, the rush to the city by various gambling interests resembled John Law's Mississippi Bubble. As various factions feuded over the right to build the world's biggest casino on Canal Street, a temporary casino was proposed for the Municipal Auditorium, which would drive the Carnival krewes out for good.

There were signs, however, of healing in New Orleans. There were plans to transform Armstrong Park, which had become run-down and crime-ridden, into a theme park of jazz. Rex opened up its doors and invited three black members to join, and they accepted. The club also asked Henri Schindler to work with Blaine Kern in putting together their parade.

Kern, meanwhile, had other fish to fry. Although he was busy creating a miniature temple of Luxor for a new Las Vegas casino, he found time to announce plans to put together a new krewe to take the place of Proteus on the Monday night before Mardi Gras. This krewe, said Kern, which he was forming with crooner and native son Harry Connick, Jr., would have ten celebrities riding floats rather than just one.

The other Kern, Ray "Plain" Kern, who had sworn that he would never again serve as captain of the Krewe de Vieux, was enlisted again. Henri was chosen king of the 1993 parade, and he reigned as King Sarcophagus I, riding the most funereal float ever seen in Carnival. There was a big tombstone borrowed from a movie set, lots of urns, and purple and black bunting. There was even a wicker casket, in which Paul Poché rode, lying in a dark shroud.

Carnival would go on, but whether it would continue as an unfinished sorrow or an unfinished joy, remained for the citizens of New Orleans to decide.